Bateman Thomas

Ten Years' Diggings in Celtic and Saxon Grave Hills,

in the Counties of Derby, Stafford and York, from 1848 to 1858; with Notices of

Some Former Discoveries, Hitherto Unpublished, and Remarks on the Crania and

Pottery from the Mounds

Bateman Thomas

Ten Years' Diggings in Celtic and Saxon Grave Hills,
in the Counties of Derby, Stafford and York, from 1848 to 1858; with Notices of Some Former Discoveries, Hitherto Unpublished, and Remarks on the Crania and Pottery from the Mounds

ISBN/EAN: 9783337297091

Printed in Europe, USA, Canada, Australia, Japan

Cover: Foto ©ninafisch / pixelio.de

More available books at **www.hansebooks.com**

TEN YEARS' DIGGINGS

IN

CELTIC AND SAXON GRAVE HILLS,

IN THE COUNTIES OF

DERBY, STAFFORD, AND YORK,

FROM 1848 TO 1858;

WITH

NOTICES OF SOME FORMER DISCOVERIES, HITHERTO UNPUBLISHED,

AND

REMARKS ON THE CRANIA AND POTTERY FROM THE MOUNDS.

BY

THOMAS BATEMAN,
LOCAL SECRETARY FOR DERBYSHIRE, OF THE SOCIETY OF ANTIQUARIES;
FELLOW OF THE ETHNOLOGICAL SOCIETY, ETC.

LONDON: J. R. SMITH, 36, SOHO SQUARE.
DERBY: W. BEMROSE & SONS, IRONGATE.
1861.

TO

LADY ADELIZA ELIZABETH GERTRUDE NORMAN,

WHOSE LIBERAL AND ENLIGHTENED ASSISTANCE

HAS ENCOURAGED OUR RESEARCHES,

THIS VOLUME

IS GRATEFULLY AND RESPECTFULLY INSCRIBED BY

THE AUTHOR.

PREFACE.

THE time has fortunately passed away in which it would have been needful to introduce a book like the present by an apology for Antiquarian researches; their importance as bearing on the ethnology and unwritten history of the human race is now fully admitted by all who are competent to give an opinion on the subject; it therefore remains only to assign as our reason for publishing the ensuing narrative, that it will be found to contain (when taken in connection with the "VESTIGES OF THE ANTIQUITIES OF DERBYSHIRE," published in 1848) a greater amount of information respecting the primæval sepulchres of Britain, derived from actual excavations than has ever appeared in a single work, except, perhaps, in the costly folios of Sir Richard Hoare's "ANCIENT WILTSHIRE," which are in a great measure useless to the scientific student, from the absence of any Craniological Notices or Measurements. The List of Skulls, and the Remarks on the Pottery of the Mounds, at the end of this Volume, are, we think, of considerable value, and are likely to remain permanent standards of comparison in their respective classes, from the extreme improbability of any future writer having the opportunity of examining so large a collection of ancient Celtic crania and vases, arising from the rapid disappearance and exhaustion of the sources of discovery, from causes constantly in operation, among which we include agricultural improvements, and the ill-conducted pillage of idle curiosity. That this is no unfounded claim, will appear from a comparison of the number of Skulls in our list, with those of similar date in the catalogues of all the most extensive and famed ethnological Museums, both in Europe and America; whilst it has rarely fallen to the lot of any one to record the systematic opening of more than 400 tumuli; this has, however, been accomplished by the co-operation of zealous and intelligent fellow-labourers, whose minute and carefully-written observations have been amplified, where requisite, by descriptions of the objects discovered, and by occasional remarks in illustration of any interesting feature. These Gentlemen were, Mr. SAMUEL CARRINGTON, of Wetton, Staffordshire, who has conducted most of the diggings in that County with extraordinary care and perseverance; and Mr. JAMES RUDDOCK, of Pickering, Yorkshire, to whose labours I am indebted for the Yorkshire portion of the volume.[*]

I will only add, that theory, the bane of nearly all the older Antiquarian books, has been avoided, and that the very few deductions I have ventured to make from recorded facts are either demonstrable, or such as may be fairly inferred. There will, however, be found an accumulation of suggestive facts, sufficient to enable the student to elaborate his own theory with regard to the origin, affinities, belief, customs,

---

[*] When completing the text of this book, I received intelligence of the death of Mr. Ruddock; he was for many years, and even during his last illness, singularly imbued with an enthusiasm for Antiquarian pursuits. In his case the ruling passion (and it was no loss) was strong in death.

personal appearance, and civilization of the ancient inhabitants of the country of the Cornavii and Parisii.

Lastly, I tender my thanks to T. J. PETTIGREW, Esq., and the Council of the BRITISH ARCHÆOLOGICAL ASSOCIATION, and to J. B. DAVIS, Esq., the learned Author of the "CRANIA BRITANNICA," for the use of some wood engravings, which have been lent for the book.

THOMAS BATEMAN.

YOULGRAVE, 1861.

CONTENTS.

	PAGE
Tumuli excavated by THOMAS BATEMAN, from January 1848 to September 1860	17-111
Barrows opened in Staffordshire, by SAMUEL CARRINGTON, from May 1848 to May 1858	111-192
Notice of desultory excavations on the site of a Romano-British village, near Wetton, Staffordshire, by SAMUEL CARRINGTON	193-203
Notice of Barrows in the North Riding of Yorkshire, opened by JAMES RUDDOCK, from February 1849 to 1858	204-241

APPENDIX.

Miscellaneous Discoveries, 1847—1859	243-246
"A Collection of Memorandums relating to Antiquity," by JOHN WILSON, Esq., of Broomhall, near Penistone, Yorkshire (born 1719, died 1783). *(Now first printed from the Original Manuscript)*	246-256
Descriptive List of Skeletons and Crania exhumed from the Tumuli	257-278
Observations on Celtic Pottery	229-287
List of Barrows in the Counties of Derby and Stafford, distinguished by the word "Low," or otherwise indicated	289-296
Patronymical Names of Places in Derbyshire	296-297
Animal Remains found in the Tumuli, associated with works of Human Art	298-299
Vegetable Substances, Traces of which have been found in Tumuli	300
Minerals and Rocks used by the Occupants of Tumuli	301-302

ILLUSTRATIONS.

	PAGE
Section, Gib Hill Tumulus	18
Cist, Gib Hill Tumulus	19
Section, Parcelly Hay Barrow	23
Necklace, Middleton Moor	25
Interment, Middleton Moor	25
Saxon Drinking Cup, Benty Grange	29
Saxon Enamels, Benty Grange	30
Saxon Helmet and details, Benty Grange	31
Detail of Chainwork, Benty Grange	32
Bronze Dagger, End Low	39
Ground Plan of grave, Blake Low	42
Necklace, Grindlow	47
Saxon Box for Thread, "Top of the Hurst"	53
Iron Implements, "Top of the Hurst"	53
Cinerary Urn, Ballidon Moor	59
Section of Barrow, Ballidon Moor	60
Plan of Flax Dale Barrow	63
Section, Flax Dale Barrow	63
Iron Sword, Javelins, &c., Brushfield	69
Plan of Interments, Bee Low	73
Plan of Barrow, Monsall Dale	76
Plan of Barrow near Monsall Dale	78
Plan of Cists, Minning Low	82
Hob Hursts House, Baslow Moor	87
Cist, Hob Hursts House	88
Plan of Ringham Low	94
Cists, Ringham Low	94
Rock Grave, Smerrill Moor	103
Plan of Interments, Top Low, Swinscoe	107
Vase, Wetton-near-Hill	139
Cist, Long Low, Wetton	145
Kumbe-Kephalic Skull, Long Low	146
Bone Tweezers, Bailey Hill	170
Stone Vessel, Wetton	173
Bronze Vessel, Wetton	173
Bone Draught-Men, New Inns	180
Glass Cup, Cow Low	188
Romano-British Fork, Wetton	198
Romano-British Knife, Wetton	199
Celtic Drinking Cup, with Handle, Pickering	209
Celtic Incense Cup with Feet, Pickering	238
Urn and Incense Cup, Matlock	244
Urn, Eyam Moor	247
Circles and Tumuli, Eyam Moor	248
Jet Pendant, Eyam Moor	249
Stone Figure, Brough	252
Urn, Woodlands	253
Urn, Winhill	255
Celtic Sword, Lancashire	255
Circle, Leam Moor	255
Skull, Long Low	268
Urn, Flax Dale Barrow	280
Urn and Incense Cup, Stanton Moor	281
Incense Cup, Baslow Moor	283
Vases, Arbor Low	283
Plan of Cists, Arbor Low	284
Vase, Cross Low	284
Drinking Cup, Green Low	286
Drinking Cup, Flints, &c., Liffs Low, Biggin	286

INTRODUCTION.

"Now since these dead bones have already out-lasted the living ones of Methusaleh, and in a yard under ground, and thin walls of clay, out-worn all the strong and spacious buildings above it, and quietly rested under the drums and tramplings of three conquests; what prince can promise such diuturnity unto his reliques? Time which antiquates antiquities, and hath an art to make dust of all things, hath yet spared these minor monuments."—*Hydriotaphia, Urn-Burial, or a Discourse of the Sepulchral Urns lately found in Norfolk, by Thomas Browne, Doctor of Physick,* 1669.

THUS wrote with suggestive eloquence, Sir Thomas Browne, one of the master-minds of his age; concerning the accidental discovery of a number of incinerated deposits, which, although actually of somewhat more modern date than was then supposed, have become classical in giving origin to the strangely fascinating book from which the extract is taken.

It is indeed impossible not to coincide with the spirit of his observations whilst contemplating the bony relics of men who passed the life of simple hunters, or existed in a scarcely more advanced pastoral state at the earliest time of which we have evidence of our country being inhabited; a period only to be realized by a setting up of mental landmarks in the long waste of unrecorded ages intervening between those primeval days and the commencement of modern history, but we here experience a difficulty in finding any point of contact between the state of Britain and the chronologies of more well-known nations of antiquity, as the earliest notices of the former in the Greek writers would indicate a more advanced state of civilization than is compatible with discoveries in the older sepulchres. It therefore can only be said that centuries, perhaps tens of centuries, before the lust of conquest tempted the Roman Legions across the Channel—at a period, it may be, coeval with that in which the Egyptians toiled to accumulate those imperishable stone barrows, the Pyramids, while Abraham yet assembled his herds on the Mesopotamian pastures; and the cities of the Plain (soon to be overthrown), were yet accessible to the traveller; there existed in Britain a population, possibly pre-Celtic, at all events having habits corresponding with those which were universally disseminated by the primitive races in their radiations from the trans-Himalayan cradle of the species.

That the perishable remains of these patriarchs themselves should yet remain for us to handle and to descant upon, that we can still study and measure the bones, and in a great degree reproduce the outward presentment of the individual, throws an air of romance over the researches of the antiquary little suspected by many, which is by no means diminished by the glimpses of mental and moral feeling traceable in the make of the accompanying ornament or weapon, and in the motive which prompted its burial with the owner. The innate conviction of a future life offering to man in the first ages nothing more than a repetition of the occupations and joys of the present, and devoid of the terrors implied by the subsequent establishment of ritualism, has occasioned the preservation of nearly everything from which conclusions may safely be drawn respecting the primitive condition of man. All written or traditionary literature except the Hebrew Scriptures and the oldest portion of the Vedas, being either so late as to possess little authority, or so much overlaid with myth and fable as to be inextricably confused and contradictory, so that we gladly recur to the buried treasures, and as the geologist re-peoples our planet from fossil remnants of the fauna and flora of its successive strata, each group presenting characters by which it may be distinguished from all others, so we exhume materials for the reconstruction, or rather for the elucidation of the history of mankind, a theme of all purely scientific subjects the most interesting, and only of late arrived at the importance it deserves.

Indeed the study of ethnology as allied with archæology and other cognate branches of research, is as yet of too recent establishment to have solved many problems connected with this history, but we look forward with confidence to the time when it will do so, and when the immense mass of invaluable facts and observations already accumulated, compared and generalized, and subjected to a process of induction, shall yield conclusions on questions that have hitherto been merely subjects of hopeless speculation. Such facts are obviously afforded by well authenticated and carefully described discoveries of remains existing in the tumuli or other burial places of an ancient people, and it is fortunate for enquirers of the present day, that one strong feeling has pervaded almost all tribes of men living in an uncivilized or semi-barbarous state, arising from a simple view of the requirements of the future existence and manifesting itself in the respect, and in many instances in the splendour with which the dead were committed to the grave, not less than in the self-denying affection which suggested the interment of articles valued by the deceased, along with his corpse. Though it may well be surmised that such articles, consisting as they did chiefly of Arms and personal Ornaments, would have been of great use to the surviving friends. From this similarity of sentiment and from the universal prevalence of tumular interment throughout the globe at a remote date; had we no other authority for saying it, we think there is sufficient evidence to shew that on this point, at least, "all men are brethren," or in other words, that the human family, however varied, sprang originally from one stock, and that in its world-wide dispersion, the members long retained, and in some places do yet retain their primitive usages almost unchanged, or simply modified by accidental position.* These observations are peculiarly applicable to Barrow burial, which we find has been practised from the most remote antiquity to our own day, in some part of the world, for instance amongst the Esquimaux as related by Captain Parry, in his second voyage. Amongst the Israelites we find that Achan and his family being immolated by Joshua, and afterwards burned, were burried under a Barrow of stones in the Valley of Achor; and the King of Ai, was likewise interred in the same manner. The practice of burying weapons with the dead is also referred to by Ezekiel. "They shall not lie with the mighty that are fallen of the uncircumcised, who are gone down to hell † with their weapons of war, and have laid their swords under their heads."‡ Diodorus informs us that Semiramis, wife of Ninus, the founder of the Assyrian Empire, (whom some of the learned have confounded with Nimrod) buried her husband in the Palace, and raised over him a great mound of earth, which remained after the destruction of the city. Indeed, it appears from a passage in Mr. Layard's work upon Nineveh and its remains, that there is at least a possibility of this tumulus being yet in existence. The tombs explored by that gentleman, in Assyria, although now undistinguished by any mounds, present the same features as most others with regard to the interment of vases and ornaments along with the corpses of the owners : it is also remarkable that these articles partake of the Egyptian style of manufacture, than which, none is more easily identified.

---

* I am well aware of the difficulties connected with either view of the question of unity of the human species, and confess myself totally unable to account satisfactorily to my own mind, for the existing variations having become permanent, even with the assistance of an unlimited chronology; but from a rather extensive course of reading on the subject, and from a careful consideration of anatomical and psychological analogies, I have been led to adopt the opinion expressed in the text, as presenting, on the whole, the fewest difficulties.

† Sheol, or Hades, the grave—the place of Spirits. Not our Anglo-Saxon hell, which conveys a distinctly different idea.

‡ 32nd chapter, 27th verse.

The Egyptians themselves had their Pyramids, huge barrows of masonry, enclosing chambers in which they deposited the bodies of their kings after embalment. Herodotus has left a highly interesting account of the various modes in which this process was effected, and modern research has fully established his veracity in this particular.

The embalmed body was generally enclosed in a decorated wooden coffin, fitting to the shape, upon which were painted certain invocations, and figures of Deities: this was sometimes protected by a second wooden case, before being deposited in the stone chest, or sarcophagus; the latter are mostly of intractible granite, yet are sculptured in such an extraordinary manner, that on some, years of labour must have been expended.

Of course the mass of the people were placed in the tomb without such costly obsequies, although the same solicitude for the preservation of the embalmed remains of their friends was a distinguishing feature of the whole of the dwellers in the Nilotic valley. The Greeks had large Barrows both of earth and stone, surrounded at the base with walls built of immense blocks of stone, and often enclosing dome-shaped chambers, constructed of overlapping courses as the Treasury of Atræus still remaining. These barrows were ancient in Homer's day, to whose mythic Heroes some of them are attributed. Pausanias mentions the monument of Laius, the father of Oedipus, where he and his servants were buried; "collected stones" being thrown over them.

Tydeus, killed in the Theban war, was buried beneath an earthen barrow; as was also Lycus near Sicyon. Hector's barrow was of stones and earth. Achilles erected a tumulus upwards of an hundred feet in diameter, over the remains of his friend Patroclus. The mound supposed by Xenophon, to contain the remains of Alyattes, father of Crœsus, King of Lydia, was of stone and earth, and more than a quarter of a league in circumference.

In later times, Alexander the Great, caused a tumulus to be heaped over his friend Hephestion, at the cost of twelve hundred talents, no mean sum even for a conqueror like Alexander, it being £232,500 Sterling. It thus seems that both the Greeks and the Trojans, practised this rite at an age anterior to the historic period, and that it was continued down to an era of which many authentic records still exist: modern investigations have furnished corroborative proofs of the high antiquity of some of the Grecian tumuli, in the Archaic style of ornament on the vases accompanying the calcined bones of their occupants.

Travelling towards the west, innumerable traces of the custom are to be observed in most countries. Dercennus, an ancient King of Latium, was buried under an earthen mound, at least, so Virgil says, and it is sufficient for the purpose to prove the existence of the custom, without entering into any question regarding the particular individuality of the person so said to have been entombed. The Etruscans, who where a civilized people, skilful metallurgists, potters, and otherwise excelling in the Fine Arts, and inhabiting Italy previous to to the foundation of the Roman Empire, which took place near eight hundred years before the Christian era, were great Barrow Architects, who spared no expense either in the construction of their tumuli, or in furnishing the precious objects they buried within them. the sides of the chambers, enclosed within the mounds, or excavated in other tombs, were frequently painted with figures in various attitudes, or engaged in different occupations such as feasts or processions, mostly having reference to the funereal rites or subsequent judgment; in other instances they were hung round with vases of bronze or painted earthenware of surpassing beauty, both as regards shape and ornament, in the manufacture of which the

Etruscans particularly excelled; sometimes the walls were decorated with votive shields of embossed silver, or bronze. The bodies were sometimes burnt, but generally interred in the natural state; being in either case frequently enclosed in chests of terra-cotta, or baked clay: on the covers of some of these were the figures of the deceased modelled in clay, so as to represent the individual in a reclining position. In these sarcophagi have been found bodies of warriors clothed in bronze armour, enriched with golden ornaments of the finest and most elegant workmanship. Also of ladies who had been buried, wearing their choicest robes, and jewelry, and accompanied by mirrors of polished metal, now defaced by rust, but still exhibiting traces of high finish. Not only did the more civilized nations of Antiquity use this mode of sepulture, the Barbarians, as they were then called by the more polite Greeks, practised it almost universally; it will therefore be necessary to give a very brief outline of their proceedings, commencing with the widely spreading Scythian Tribes, now better known as the Tartars, who then, as now, extending from the frontiers of China to the Caspian Sea, were profuse of the riches they entombed in their barrows.

The description of their funeral rites as given by Herodotus, the Greek traveller, who wrote upwards of four hundred years before Christ, has been proved to be substantially correct in its details, the main features of it are, that upon the burial of one of the Khans or Chiefs, the mourners were in the habit of barbarously sacrificing, under the idea of their accompanying him into a future state of existence, one of his wives, some subordinate attendants, and his horse. He was also supplied with weapons, apparel, and ornaments, together with many vessels of gold. In an early volume of the Archæologia, is an account of the opening of one of these large barrows in Russian Tartary, undertaken by order of the Russian Government, when the various skeletons of the individuals interred precisely as decribed by Herodotus were discovered, together with sheets, and vessels of pure gold to a very large amount. Another, opened about the year 1841, in the neighbourhood of Asterabad, and by Baron de Bode communicated to the Society of Antiquaries, contained articles of immense value and interest. Large numbers of these tumuli have been plundered of their contents from time immemorial, and numbers still remain intact, from the Crimea on the one hand to the remote regions of Mongolia and Chinese Tartary on the other. In India the tumuli which abound indicate a similar feeling on the subject of interment; they have been observed more particularly in the North of India, and Afghanistan, where they surround those remarkable Buddhist temples called Topes, or Stupas, themselves depositories of human relics, which were noticed by two Chinese Pilgrims, who travelled in Hindostan, the one in the year 400 A.D., the other about two centuries later. In this case the tumuli probably contain the remains of Priests or Devotees, attracted by the sanctity of the Topes. In Mexico and South America, like habits prevailed at a later, but still ancient period. Antiquities brought from the sepulchres of the New World cannot fail to interest from their close similarity to, and in some cases their identity with, many articles observed in our own Celtic Barrows. A most complete and interesting series of these remains is deposited in the Ethnological room at the British Museum; the articles were principally obtained from excavations undertaken by Captain Evan-Nepean, in the Island of Sacrificios, on the coast of Vera Cruz. For the following notice of the Sepulchres of the North American mound builders, I am indebted to the authors of the "Ancient Monuments of the Mississippi Valley, New York, 1848," a book replete with information most important to the Ethnological Student.

The tumuli therein described are principally situated in the State of Ohio; they are mostly composed of solid earth, and vary from six to eighty feet in height, they enclose skeletons deposited within rectangular cells, constructed of the trunks of trees, or of stone, the former were most frequently used owing to the scarcity of stone in the alluvial plains, and although the timber has of course ceased to exist, the casts, or impressions of the trees remain visible upon the earth that has been in contact with the rude sarcophagus; around the skeletons are traces of bark, or matting, in which it is presumed the bodies were enveloped, they are likewise accompanied by great quantities of personal ornaments, such as beads of bone, shell, or metal; bracelets and other ornaments of copper, and plates of mica. Weapons are not so frequently discovered with the bodies, such as have been, are analogous to those of the Celts, which are distinguished further on.

Urn burial does not seem to have prevailed in the same district, but in the mounds on the Wateree river, South Carolina, many urns have been found, containing human remains, in some cases calcined, but in others packed within the vessels in their natural state, after the flesh was removed. As an instance of the prevalence of barrow burial in modern times, it may be well to state, that the Indians have for ages interred in these mounds, although they were originally erected by a more ancient people, no other traces of whom are supposed to exist, if we except the earthworks in connection with the mounds. With some of these later interments articles of European manufacture have been found, including swords and small silver crosses, probably introduced amongst the Indians by the French. But to return to the old world, the Teutonic, or German tribes are described by Tacitus, as in his time interring the remains of their dead in barrows, after the bodies had undergone the process of cremation. And innumerable urns containing such remains have been found in various parts of Germany to attest the accuracy of the historian, and are described in a late volume of the Archæologia, by Mr. Kemble. The Scandinavians, or Northmen, also buried in grave-hills for many ages, and the contents of such of the earlier of these tumuli as have been opened, resemble in most particulars, antiquities discovered under like circumstances in this country; but there was one description of interment that was practised in Denmark and Norway by the later Pagan inhabitants, widely differing from what has been observed in other regions, yet highly characteristic of the people, who were at that time a nation of maritime adventurers, sailing under the flags of their Sea Kings, in frequent expeditions to wherever plunder was to be obtained, or danger encountered. Sometimes the bodies were placed in the small ships or boats of the period, which were dragged on shore and then buried under a barrow within view of the ocean. It is with interments of this late and peculiar description, that the greatest variety of curious and rare objects is found, consisting of arms, personal ornaments, and various useful articles, such as combs, knives, tweezers, &c. Further details may be found by consulting Lord Ellesmere's Guide to Northern Archæology, "London and Copenhagen, 1848," to which I am indebted for the particulars just mentioned. The Gaulish tumuli seem to be identical with those of the Ancient Britons, which are next to engage our attention, so that to enter into an account of the former would cause mere repetition.

However, before describing the contents of tumuli in this Kingdom, it may be as well to remark that the fundamental design of them, with the exception of the very few chambered or galleried mounds in Berkshire, Wiltshire, and Ireland, &c., as New Grange, Wayland Smith's Cave, Uleybury, and others, and those of the incalculably later Saxon period, is pretty much the same in most places: the leading feature of these sepulchral mounds, is, that they enclose either an artless stone vault, or chamber, or a stone chest, otherwise called a Kistvaen, built with more or less care, and in other cases a grave cut out more or less below the natural surface, and lined, if need be, with stone slabs, in which the body was placed in a perfect state, or reduced to ashes by fire; when the latter method has been adopted, the fragments of bone have been carefully collected, and, in many instances, placed in an earthenware vessel which was then deposited within the vault. These stone chambers vary in their dimensions from the size of a small room, to that of a receptacle suited only to contain a few calcined bones. They are constructed in many ways, sometimes by walling, but more frequently by four or more large stones being placed on an end, and covered in with a fifth stone of greater size; when vaults constructed in this manner are denuded of the earth which in most cases originally covered them, they are very conspicuous objects, and as such used formerly to be considered Druidical Altars; but researches commenced by Borlase, the historian of Cornwall, upwards of a century ago, have almost invariably developed their sepulchral character. Sometimes galleries or passages built on the same plan lead to the principal chambers, as at the large barrows at New Grange, in Ireland, Gavr'Innis in Brittany, and Five Wells, near Taddington, in Derbyshire. We at length come to the description of the contents of barrows in this kingdom, the works of its Celtic inhabitants, and the Saxons, very few being attributable to the Romans, who, indeed, seldom buried in this manner during their stay in Britain. The barrows at Thornborough, in Buckinghamshire, and the Bartlow hills, in Essex, are however, exceptions, as the relics therein discovered are doubtless of Roman manufacture, being vases and lamps in bronze; also glass and pottery of the most elegant and classical description, one of the vases is most beautifully enamelled, an art, however, in which some of the Gaulish tribes are said to have excelled the Romans; others are enriched with chasing, the effect of which is heightened by the introduction of silver or niello in some of the designs; but as this discovery has been several times published, it may be as well to allude no farther to it, excepting to surmise that after all it might pertain to some British dignitary in the Roman service. We will, then, advance, or rather recede to the purely Celtic period, the remains of which in the shape of barrows and stone circles, are to be seen on most of the elevated lands in Derbyshire and the North of Staffordshire; many of the former have been explored by various antiquaries, the first of whom was the Rev. Samuel Pegge, Vicar of Whittington, who died towards the end of the last century, a man of great research and profound learning, which he brought to bear on many subjects connected with Archæology. In these tumuli have been found many varieties of urns of imperfectly baked clay, some containing calcined bones, these are called funeral or sepulchral urns; others placed with skeletons exhibit evidences of having been filled with animal matter, probably deposited as an offering or viaticum for the deceased; of the same nature are the drinking cups which are of a more elegant shape, and are covered with indented and scored designs; some, again, of very small size, have been found within the funereal urns amongst the burnt bones, the use of which is not evident, though Sir Richard Hoare, the celebrated Wiltshire Antiquary, and others, have supposed them to be for the purpose of holding unguents or incense at the burning, and have thence called them incense cups, by which name they are now generally known. An example of this mode of interment was found in the beginning of the year 1848, in cutting the line of Railway near Matlock-Bridge, and numerous instances of their discovery will be found in the Yorkshire portion of this volume. Besides these vases there are found weapons of flint, stone, bone, and bronze, consisting, for the most part, of arrow heads, daggers, hammers, and celts or adzes, sometimes in company with horns of the red deer, and tusks of the wild boar, indicating the resting place of the successful hunter of the indigenous game. At other times occur complex ornaments and beads of bone, amber, jet, and Kimmeridge coal, a species of bituminous shale that takes a high polish; such things as these were, in all probability, the personal decorations of women, whose form and comeliness, frequently of no mean order, has long since faded into dust. In barrows of the Romano-British, and Saxon periods, the construction approaches more nearly to that now in use, namely, a small mound raised over a grave of some depth beneath the surface, so that they are, strictly speaking, grave hills; there are certainly some large barrows of this era, but they are exceptions, indeed in many localities the elevation is so slight as to be scarcely perceptible, as in the case of the very curious Saxon cemetry at Cotgrave, Nottinghamshire, described by me in the journal of the British Archæological Association for the year 1848. In North Derbyshire the Saxons have generally taken advantage of the Celtic tumuli, and have interred their dead at an inconsiderable depth in them, in the same manner as the North American Indians have done in the ancient mounds in their country. The contents of these Saxon graves are extremely varied, almost every article of personal use or ornament then known, has been found in the graves appropriated to females: beads of amethyst, amber, variegated glass and porcelain, formerly thought to be Celtic, brooches of gold or copper ornamented with filigree work, and enriched with settings of garnets and coloured glass, pins of gold or bronze, silver needles, glass tumblers, ivory combs, small bronze thread boxes, and iron knives form a small part of the catalogue; whilst with the men are found, straight swords, seaxes, spears, knives, and the centres of shields, always of iron, in one case even the remains of a superb helmet surmounted by a crest; occasionally are found buckles of silver, brass, or iron, rare specimens of which are sometimes ornamented in the same style as the brooches of the females; also peculiar enamelled ornaments of intricate design have several times been found with bodies of males. These are the most modern barrows in this country, as in the sixth century of the Christian era, not very long after the settlement of the Saxons in England, they embraced Christianity and consequently soon discontinued their Pagan rites, amongst which barrow burial held a prominent position, and which they were unwillingly induced finally to abandon.

THOMAS BATEMAN.

May, 1860.

TUMULI

EXCAVATED BY THOMAS BATEMAN, IN 1848.

The large barrow upon Middleton Moor, called Gib Hill, situated about 350 yards west from the circular temple of Arborlow, and connected with it by a serpentine ridge of earth, had been previously examined by the late Mr. William Bateman, in 1824, without much success. From the analogy borne by Arborlow and its satellite, Gib Hill, to the plan of Abury with its avenue of stones terminating in a lesser circle on the Hak Pen range of hills, no less than by the remarkable similarity of the names, I had ever reckoned this tumulus to be of more than common importance, under the supposition that a successful excavation of it might yield some approximate data respecting the obscure period of the foundation of the neighbouring circle.

Owing to the large size of the mound, our operations extended over several days, the result of each being noticed diary-wise as at once the most simple and intelligible arrangement.

January 10th was occupied in removing the upper part of the hill, the trench being commenced about half-way up its side, pretty much in the line of the former opening. A few splinters of animal bone and a flake of calcined flint, only, were the product of the day.

January 11th.—The cutting was carried forwards to the intended limit beyond the centre of the barrow, yielding in its progress more animal bones, a dog's tooth, numerous calcined flakes of flint, and a neatly formed arrow head of the same substance.

January 12th.—The trench being widened at each side, a space nearly, but not exactly, in the centre of the barrow, was found to consist of loose stones, whilst the outer part of the mound exposed to view by the section, was composed of tempered earth approaching the consistence of hard clay. In the course of this day a small piece of the border of an ornamented urn, a circular instrument, an arrow point, and many chippings of flint were found.

January 13th was passed in deepening the trench, principally through the before-named clay, varied by layers of decomposed wood and charcoal. From the appearance of the bark still remaining on some of these fragments, they were decided to be hazel. Amongst them were found animal bones and flints as before, one of the latter being a fine instrument of semicircular shape.

January 14th.—Our excavation was continued until the undisturbed surface of the earth was reached and laid bare for the space of 25 feet by 18, without disclosing any interment whatever; the appearance presented by the section of the barrow, here about 15 feet high, was as shewn in the diagram,

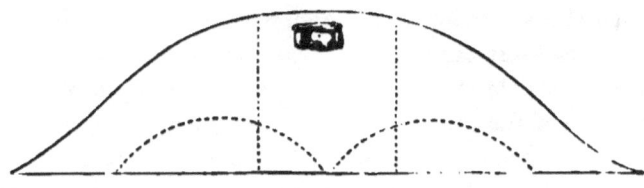

Section of Gib Hill Tumulus.

thus making it evident that the tumulus had been originally raised over four smaller mounds, each consisting of indurated clay intermixed with wood and charcoal, the superimposed materials being of a looser description. On the natural soil beneath the little mounds were flints as usual, one of them a round instrument, and large disconnected bones of oxen very much decayed.

January 15th.—A tunnel was driven from the west side of the trench at right angles, in the hope of finding an interment, but after carrying it three or four yards it was deemed unsafe to continue it; and the supporting timbers being knocked away previous to abandoning the work, the whole superstructure fell in, and, much to our surprise, revealed the interment near the top of the mound, which we had been so laboriously seeking at its base. This consisted of a rectangular cist, measuring inside 2 feet 6 inches by 2 feet, composed of four massive blocks of limestone, covered in by a fifth of irregular form, averaging 4 feet square by 10 inches thick. The cap-stone was not more than eighteen inches beneath the turf clothing the summit of the barrow; in fact the men had been working directly under the cist for some time. By the sudden fall of two of the sides and the adjacent earth, a very pretty vase of small size was crushed to pieces, the fragments mingling with the burnt human bones in company with which it had for ages occupied the sepulchral chamber. The urn measuring 4¼ inches in height, has since been restored almost to its original perfection; it is of that class of vessels indifferently deposited with human remains, burnt or unburnt, and which may probably have contained food or drink, but never the remains, as is the case with cinerary urns. A review of these facts leads to the conclusion that Gib Hill was not in the first instance a sepulchral mound, so large a portion of the interior having been removed down to the natural rock without any deposit of human remains being found, it appears impossible for any interment to have escaped observation at the base of the tumulus, where it would naturally have been placed at the time of its formation, had any such existed.

January 17th.—A molar tooth from the lower jaw of a horse, and a piece of white flint, were found in the rubbish that had fallen out of the cist the day before. The cist itself was removed and re-erected in conformity with its original plan, in the garden at Lomberdale House, where it now remains.

Cist of Gib Hill Tumulus.

The articles found in Gib Hill in 1824, comprise a battered celt of basaltic stone, a dart or javelin point of flint, and a small iron fibula which has been enriched with a setting of some precious stone now absent: the last was found in the upper part of the mound, and might have been deposited with a late interment which was destroyed about the year 1812, or earlier, in an abortive attempt to open the barrow. (See Vestiges of the Antiquities of Derbyshire, page 31.)

KENSLOW BARROW MIDDLETON-BY-YOULGRAVE.

February 1st we commenced re-opening the barrow upon Kenslow Knoll, which was formerly investigated by Mr. William Bateman, in 1821, when it appears that the primary interment was discovered, and besides it, some other relics which indicated that there might still remain additional deposits in that part of the barrow that was not then disturbed. By taking a wide trench through the middle of the barrow from the outer edge, it became apparent that its convexity had chiefly been preserved by a border of large limestones placed with great regularity on the surface of the natural soil. On clearing the area within them, many pieces of calcined flint and animal bones were picked up; also a splinter from a stone celt, a round piece of slaty sandstone which had been burnt, and a crescent-shaped ornament of bone having two perforations: the latter is precisely like one found at the prior opening, and gives the idea of a large canine tooth of a wolf split down the middle, being convex on one surface and level on the other, although in reality it is cut out of solid bone, and has been carefully polished all over.

February 2nd.—The trenching of the barrow was continued, disclosing, near the centre, a depression below the natural level, which had contained the deposits formerly exhumed. In the course of the day pieces of three different urns were observed, one of coarse material and workmanship, another having been a neatly ornamented drinking cup, and lastly of a kiln-baked vessel of brick-red colour that had been made upon the wheel, and which must be therefore much more modern than the two former. There were also found three more of the bone crescents, part of a large ring of inferior jet or Kimmeridge coal, a small spatula of bone, probably used in the fabrication of pottery; a few instruments of flint, human and animal bones, both burnt and unburnt, and a tine from a stag's horn which has been roughly cut round, most probably with a flint saw.

February 3rd.—The excavation of the grave cut in the rock, which contained the previously discovered interments, was commenced: the rubbish being cleared out, we found some portions of the skeleton which had evidently lain undisturbed; with them was a small and neat bronze dagger, 3 inches long, with the three rivets by which the handle was attached, remaining. A little above these we found an iron knife of the shape and size usually deposited with Anglo-Saxon interments, which had most likely been thrown in unobserved when the grave was refilled in 1821. About the same place was a bone pin with a perforated head. By digging in the outer parts of the barrow, another bone crescent and several good instruments of flint were found.

February 4th.—The grave was very carefully cleared out, but yielded nothing further except a few burnt bones. In other parts of the mound we met with a seventh bone crescent, a bone javelin point, and some more flints. A comparison of the various relics found in this barrow in 1821 and 1848, with others brought to light in the course of these researches, demonstrates not only their varied antiquity, but also the order in which the successive interments had occupied the central grave. The first would be by cremation, the incinerated bones being placed in a coarse sepulchral urn, the fragments of which are before alluded to. The second would evidently consist of an unburnt skeleton, accompanied by a highly ornamented drinking cup, a decoration formed by a combination of the bone crescents, the bone lance heads, and the most carefully wrought instruments of flint; some of the latter would, however, be equally likely to pertain to the oldest interment.

The next occupants of the grave had not been disturbed until the former opening of the barrow in 1821, they were then described as being two in number, though sufficient care was not taken to discriminate the relics found with each: it is quite clear that the lowest (some of whose bones we found unremoved) had possessed the stone axe and the polished stone implement found in 1821, in addition to the bronze dagger found in 1848.

The other which lay higher up in the grave was of much later date, being the owner of the kiln-baked vessel, the iron knife, and the small copper fibula or ring-pin, found in 1821. The vessel appears, from the fragments remaining, to have had a narrow neck, and to have resembled that found at Brun-Cliff, in 1847, (see Vestiges, page 101) in form, colour, and paste. It is the skull of this latest, and perhaps Romano-British skeleton, that is described in the former work.

CROSS FLATTS MIDDLETON-BY-YOULGRAVE.

February 10th.—A small barrow in the Cross Flatts' plantation was re-opened. Its sepulchral character was first ascertained in 1827, by a labourer engaged in making holes for planting, who found the skeleton of a young person, accompanied by an iron knife. On the present occasion no more interments were found, but in turning over the earth, the following articles were met with:— part of a large stag's horn, a celt of basaltic stone, some pieces of hand-mills, flints, and fragments of red pottery. On looking over the bones of the skeleton before disinterred, it was found that two of the lumbar vertebræ were attached together by an abnormal growth of osseous substance.

PARCELLY HAY NEAR HARTINGTON.

March 6th was passed in opening a cairn or tumulus of stone in a plantation near the Parcelly Hay wharf of the Cromford and High Peak Railway. We found the primary interment beneath the middle of the barrow, in a small oval excavation in the rock below the natural surface of the land, about three feet in depth, and not exceeding the same in its greatest diameter, consequently the body had been placed upright in a sitting or crouching posture, as was abundantly evident from the order in which the bones were found. The grave was roughly covered in with large flat slabs of limestone, which had prevented the materials of the tumulus from quite filling it up; a good deal of earth had, however, been washed in, which had the effect of preserving the bones in unusual perfection. The remains accompanying the body were of the poorest description, consisting merely of three pieces of chipped flint, some shreds from a drinking cup, and various animal bones and teeth, some of which were calcined. The fine skull from this interment has been engraved in the magnificent work by Messrs. Davis and Thurnam, entitled "Crania Britannica," where its internal capacity is given at 72½ ounces; length of the femur, 18·3 inches. The high antiquity of this interment may be inferred

Section of Parcelly Hay Barrow.

when we take into consideration the fact, that upon the covering stones there lay another skeleton, quite unprotected from the loose stone of the barrow, and accompanied by weapons indicating that the owner lived at a very remote period. This body was badly preserved, owing to the percolation of water through the over lying stones, but it appeared to have been laid as usual upon the left side, with the knees slightly advanced; near the upper part of the person were placed a very elegantly formed axe head of granite, with a hole for the shaft, and a very fine bronze dagger of the earliest or archaic bronze period, with three studs for fastening the handle. The engraving gives an accurate section of this remarkable barrow.

BARROWS NEAR ARBORLOW.

On the 15th of March, we re-opened a barrow near the boundary of Middleton Moor, in the direction of Parcelly Hay, which was unsuccessfully opened by Mr. W. Bateman on the 28th of July, 1824; nor did our researches lead to a more satisfactory result, as the entire mound seemed to have been turned over by deep ploughing by which the interments, consisting of two skeletons and a deposit of burnt bones, had been so dragged about as to present no characteristic worthy of observation. A neat whetstone was picked up amongst these ruins, and a carefully chipped leaf-shaped arrow-point of flint has since been found by ploughing across the barrow. About fifty yards South-east of the last, is another barrow of very small size, both as to diameter and height; so inconsiderable indeed are its dimensions, that it was quite overlooked in 1824. Fortunately the contents, with the exception of one skeleton that lay near the surface, had been enclosed in a cist, sunk a few inches beneath the level of the soil. As in the companion barrow, the skeleton near the top was dismembered by the plough, so that it afforded nothing worthy of notice—the original interment, however, which lay rather deeper, in a kind of rude cist or enclosure, formed by ten shapeless masses of limestone, amply repaid our labour. The persons thus interred consisted of a female in the prime of life, and a child of about four years of age; the former had been placed on the floor of the grave on her left side, with the knees drawn up; the child was placed above her, and rather behind her shoulders: they were surrounded and covered with innumerable bones of the water-vole, or rat, and near the woman was a cow's tooth, an article uniformly found with the more ancient interments. Round her neck was a necklace of variously

Beads and Interment on Middleton Moor.

shaped beads and other trinkets of jet and bone, curiously ornamented, upon the whole resembling those found at Cow Low in 1846, (Vestiges p. 92,) but differing from them in many details. The various pieces of this compound ornament are 420 in number, which unusual quantity is accounted for by the fact of 348 of the beads being thin laminæ only; 54 are of cylindrical form, and the 18 remaining pieces are conical studs and perforated plates, the latter in some cases ornamented with punctured patterns. Altogether, the necklace is the most elaborate production of the pre-metallic period that I have seen. The skull, in perfect preservation, is beautiful in its proportions, and has been selected to appear in the Crania Britannica, as the type of the ancient British female. The femur measures 15¼ inches. The engraving represents the arrangement of the cist.

SHARP LOWE NEAR TISSINGTON.

On the 27th of March, was opened a low flat barrow, called Sharp Low, situated on the summit of a hill to the left of the road to Dovedale, from the New Inns toll-bar. In no part did the elevation exceed 18 inches. In the first place, an excavation was made from the south side to the centre; it was then continued at right angles to the west; in each of these cuttings was found a skeleton; and in the middle of the barrow was a stone, beneath which lay the horn of a bull, accompanied by another bone. The body in the south trench, first discovered, was apparently that of a young person, and was laid upon its right side in a contracted position, without the least protection or accompaniment by cist or weapon. The other in the western cutting was equally unprotected, but was accompanied by an iron knife of the usual form, which lay at the left side of the skeleton, which, from the impression retained by the rust on the knife, must have been swathed in fine woollen cloth. It is worthy of remark that this body, although evidently interred at a comparatively late epoch, was laid on the left side in the contracted posture so uniformly observed by the earlier Celtic population. In illustration of this remark, it may be stated, that we do not remember having previously met with an instance of an interment of the iron period, otherwise than at full length; nor, on the other hand, have we seen any skeleton accompanied by relics of the earlier ages, fully extended. In the vicinity of the latter skeleton were a few animal bones, and two pieces of well baked earthenware; but the usual layer of rats' bones was absent.

March 30th.—Another barrow about a mile from the preceding, and very much resembling it in every respect but the height, was opened : it was about four feet in elevation at the thickest part, and appeared perfect and undisturbed ; yet by digging it proved the contrary, as the bones of two skeletons were found in a heap upon the level of the ground, lower than which no one had penetrated since the mound was formed. Around the bones were many fragments of iron which had been broken and left as worthless by former excavators, they appear to have been principally nails or rivets, and buckles; one piece of larger size is evidently part of a flat ring or disk, which has been riveted upon wood, the grain being very visible on one side.—These have probably been the metal fittings of a shield.

About the centre of the barrow were two large limestones, covering an oval cist, sunk down about three feet through the easily removed upper beds of the limestone rock ; in which depository were calcined bones, forming the original interment ; with them was a very neatly ornamented food vase, which, owing to the grave being full of large stones, had long been crushed—it is now repaired, all the pieces having been carefully gathered up—there was also a piece of stag's horn inside the grave, but no implements or weapons whatever.

BARROW NEAR DOVEDALE.

On the 3rd of April, a most beautiful and genial day, was

opened a barrow of apparently large size, situate in a clump of trees crowning an eminence on the Derbyshire side of the Dove, near Thorpe Cloud. The depth of factitious material in this mound was inconsiderable, a natural elevation having been chosen for its site; nevertheless, about the middle was a rock grave which increased the depth to about two feet. In this was the skeleton of a man, lying in the usual flexed position, on the left side, amidst myriads of water rats' bones, but destitute of either instruments or pottery: slightly higher were the bones of another skeleton which had been partially disturbed, most likely when the trees were planted. With the latter remains were found some neatly ornamented pieces of a vase of thin Celtic ware.

BENTY GRANGE NEAR MONYASH.

May 3rd.—It was our good fortune to open a barrow which afforded a more instructive collection of relics than has ever been discovered in the county, and which are not surpassed in interest by any remains hitherto recovered from any Anglo-Saxon burying place in the kingdom.

The barrow, which is on a farm called Benty Grange, a high and bleak situation to the right of the road from Ashbourn to Buxton, near the eighth milestone from the latter place, is of inconsiderable elevation, perhaps not more than two feet at the highest point, but is spread over a pretty large area, and is surrounded by a small fosse or trench. About the centre and upon the natural soil, had been laid the only body the barrow ever contained, of which not a vestige besides the hair could be distinguished. Near the place which, from the presence of hair, was judged to have been the situation of the head, was a curious assemblage of ornaments, which, from the peculiarly indurated nature of the earth, it was impossible to remove with any degree of success. The most remarkable are the silver edging and ornaments of a leathern cup, about three inches diameter at the mouth, which was decorated by four wheel-shaped ornaments and two crosses of thin silver, affixed by pins of the same metal, clenched inside.

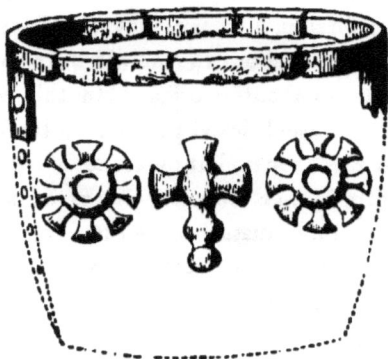

Saxon Drinking Cup of Leather.

The other articles found in the same situation consist of personal ornaments, the chief of which are two circular enamels upon copper 1¾ diameter, in narrow silver frames, and a third, which was so far decomposed as to be irrecoverable; they are enamelled with a yellow interlaced dracontine pattern, intermingled with that peculiar scroll design, visible on the same class of ornaments figured in Vestiges p. 25, and used in several manuscripts of the VIIth Century, for the purpose of decorating the initial letters. The principle of this design consists of three spiral lines springing from a common centre, and each involution forming an additional centre for an extension of the pattern, which may be adapted to fill spaces of almost any form. Mr. Westwood has shown in a most able paper in the 40th No. of the Journal of the Archæological Institute, that this style of ornamentation is peculiar to the Anglo-Saxon and Irish Artists of the period before stated. The pattern was first cut in the metal, threads of it being left to show the design, by which means cells were formed, in which the enamel was placed before fusion, the whole being then polished became what is known as Champ-levé enamel. There was also with these enamels a knot of very fine wire, and a quantity of thin bone variously ornamented with lozenges &c, which was mostly too much decayed to bear removal; it appeared to have been attached to some garment of silk, as the glossy fibre of such a fabric was very perceptible when they were first uncovered, though it shortly vanished when exposed to the air. Proceeding westward from the head for about six feet, we arrived at a large mass of oxidyzed iron, which, being removed with the utmost care, and having been since repaired, were unavoidably broken,

Saxon Enamels.

now presents a mass of chainwork, and the frame of a helmet. The latter consists of a skeleton formed of iron bands, radiating from the crown of the head, and riveted to a circle of the same metal which encompassed the brow: from the impression on the metal it is evident that the outside was covered with plates of horn disposed diagonally so as to produce a herring-bone pattern, the ends of these plates were secured beneath with strips of horn corresponding with the iron framework, and attached to it by ornamental rivets of silver at intervals of about an inch and a half from each other; on the bottom of the front rib, which projects so as to form a nasal, is a small silver cross slightly ornamented round the edges by a beaded moulding; and on the crown of the helmet is an elliptical bronze plate supporting the figure of an animal carved in iron, with bronze eyes, now much corroded, but perfectly distinct as there presentation of a hog. There are too,

Saxon Helmet and Details.

many fragments, some more or less ornamented with silver, which have been riveted to some part of the helmet in a manner not to be explained or even understood, there are also some small buckles of iron which probably served to fasten it upon the head. Amongst the chainwork is a very curious six-pronged instrument of iron, in shape much like an ordinary hay-fork, with the difference of the tang, which in the latter is driven into the shaft, being in this instrument flattened and doubled over so as to form a small loop apparently convenient for suspension; whether it belonged to the helmet or the corselet, next to be described, is uncertain. The iron chainwork already named, consists of a large number of links of two kinds, attached to each other by small rings half an inch diameter; one kind are flat and lozenge, shaped, about an inch and a half long; the others are all of one kind but of different lengths, varying from 4 to 10 inches. They are simply lengths of square rod iron with perforated ends, through which pass the rings connecting them with the diamond shaped links; they all show the impression of cloth over a considerable

Detail of Chainwork.

part of the surface, and it is therefore no improbable conjecture that they would originally constitute a kind of quilted cuirass, by being sewn up within, or upon a doublet of strong cloth. The peculiarly indurated and corrosive nature of the soil in this barrow is a point of some interest, and it will not be out of place to state that such has generally been the case in tumuli in Derbyshire, where the more important Saxon burials have taken place, whilst the more ancient Celtic interments are generally found in good condition owing to there having been no special preparation of the earth, which in these cases has undergone a mixing or tempering with some corrosive liquid; the result of which is the presence of thin ochrey veins in the earth, and the decomposition of nearly the whole of the human remains. The following extract from Professor Worsaae's Antiquities of Denmark, illustrates the helmet which is the only example of the kind hitherto discovered either in this country or on the Continent.

"The helmets (of the ancient Scandinavians) which were furnished with crests, usually in the form of animals, were probably in most cases only the skins of the heads of animals, drawn over a framework of wood or leather, as the coat of mail was usually of strong quilted linen or thick woven cloth."

To this the translator of the English edition appends the important information, that "the animal generally represented was the boar; and it is to this custom that reference is made in

Beowulf where the poet speaks of the boar of gold, the boar hard as iron."

"Swyn eal—gylden
Eofer Iren—heard."

Nor are allusions to this custom of wearing the figure of a boar—not in honour of the animal, but of Freya, to whom it was sacred—confined to Beowulf, they are to be found in the Edda and in the Sagas; while Tacitus in his work, De Moribus Germanorum, distinctly refers to the same usage and its religious intention, as propitiating the protection of their Goddess in battle. As a further illustration, not only of the helmet, but also of the chainwork, the following extracts from Beowulf are transcribed from Mr. C. R. Smith's Collectanea Antiqua, vol. II, p. 240.

"eofer-líc sciónon
ofer-hleor beran;
ge-hroden golde
fah and fyr-heard,
ferh-wearde heóld.

They seemed a boar's form
to bear over their cheeks;
twisted with gold,
variegated and hardened in the fire,
this kept the guard of life:
I. 604.

Be-fongen freá-wrásnum,
swa hine fyrn-dagum
worhte wœpna smith,
wundrum teóde,
be-sette swín-lícum,
that hine sythan nó
brond né beado-mecas
bitan ne meahton:

Surrounded with lordly chains,
even as in days of yore
the weapon smith had wrought it,
had wondrously furnished it, [swine,
had set it round with the shapes of
that never afterwards
brand or war-knife
might have power to bite it;
I. 2901.

Æt thœm áde wœs
eth-ge-syne
swát-fáh-syrce
swyn eal-gylden,
eofer íren heard:

At the pile was
easy to be seen
the mail shirt covered with gore,
the hog of gold,
the boar hard as iron:
I. 2213.

Hét thá in-beran
eafor heáfod-segn,
heago-steápne helm,
[se] are-byrnan,
guth-sweord geáto-líc:"

Then commanded he to bring in
the boar, an ornament to the head,
the helmet lofty in wars,
the grey mail coat,
the ready battle sword.
I. 4299.

BARROW NEAR ECTON, STAFFORDSHIRE.

On the 6th of May was opened a small barrow at the summit of a rocky-hill, near Ecton mine, called by the natives "The Comp." One side of the mound was formed by a natural elevation of rock, the other consisted of large stones piled up against it in such a manner as to leave a hollow place in the centre, which served as a cist for the original interments which had never been disturbed. These comprised the calcined remains of an adult, accompanied by a perforated bone pin and spearhead of flint, which had both passed the fire; and secondly, the unburnt skeleton of a very young child, which lay at the bottom of a cavity immediately beneath the ashes of its parent, as we may reasonably suppose them to be.

SHUTTLESTONE NEAR PARWICH.

On the 3rd of June we examined a mutilated barrow in a plantation upon Parwich Moor, called Shuttlestone, which had originally been about four feet in height; it consisted of a compact mass of tempered earth down to the natural surface of the land, below which point, in the centre of the barrow there appeared a large collection of immense limestones, the two uppermost being placed on edge and all below being laid flat, though without any other order or design than was sufficient to prevent the lowest course resting upon the floor of the grave, inside which they were piled up, and which was cut out to the depth of at least eight feet below the natural surface; thus rendering the total depth from the top of the mound to the floor of the grave not less than twelve feet. Underneath the large stones lay the the skeleton of a man in the prime of life and of fine proportions, apparently the sole occupant of the mound, who had been interred whilst enveloped in a skin, of dark red colour, the hairy surface of which had left many traces both upon the surrounding earth and upon the verdigris or patina coating a bronze axe-shaped celt and dagger, deposited with the skeleton. On the former weapon there are also beautifully distinct impressions of fern leaves, handsful of which, in a compressed and half-decayed state, surrounded the bones from head to foot. From these leaves being discernible on one side of the celt only, whilst the other side presents traces of leather alone, it is certain that the leaves were placed first as a couch for the reception of the corpse with its accompaniments, and after these had been deposited, were then further added in quantity sufficient to protect the body from the earth. The position of the weapons with respect to the body was well ascertained ; and is further evidenced by the bronze having imparted a vivid tinge of green to the bones where in contact with them. Close to the head were one small black bead of jet and a circular flint; in contact with the left upper arm lay a bronze dagger with a very sharp edge, having two rivets for the attachment of the handle, which was of horn, the impression of the grain of that substance being quite distinct around the studs. About the middle of the left thigh bone was placed the bronze celt, which is of the plainest axe-shaped type. The cutting edge was turned towards the upper part of the person, and the instrument itself has been inserted *vertically* into a wooden handle by being driven in for about two inches at the narrow end—at least the grain of the wood runs in the same direction as the longest dimension of the celt, a fact not unworthy of the notice of any inclined to explain the precise manner of mounting these curious implements. The skull, which is decayed on the left side, from the body having lain with that side down, is of the platy-cephalic form, with prominent parietal tubers—the femur measures $18\frac{1}{4}$ inches.

BOOTH LOW, NEAR LONGNOR, STAFFORDSHIRE.

June the 9th we opened the second of three large barrows at Booth Low, the first of which had been excavated not long before by a resident in the neighbourhood, who discovered a deposit of calcined human bones near the centre of the tumulus, unaccompanied by any urn or instrument. Each of the barrows is about forty yards in circumference, and eight feet high: that under consideration is nearest the village of Longnor. One successful section through the middle shewed that the funeral rites had been performed upon the spot, the body having been reduced to ashes on the natural level of the ground, the remains were then gathered into a heap and covered with a layer of clay, above which a large fire of oak timber was made, the remains of which, in the shape of large pieces of charcoal, perfectly exhibiting the characteristic grain of oak, were then covered up with successive layers of tempered earth, mixed with a few stones, by which means the mound was formed. A few chippings of flint and a small piece of stag's horn were noticed in the course of the excavation.

On the 23rd of June we made an unsuccessful examination of the third barrow at Booth Low, situated near the last. With the exception of a few pieces of charcoal, there were no indications of interment observed during the progress of a very large cutting through the centre, which was extended to a slight depression below the natural surface, making the entire depth from the top of the mound rather more than eight feet.

LOW BENT.

On the same day was opened a smaller barrow at Low Bent, situated on low ground about half-a-mile from the last. Near the centre was a deposit of calcined human bones, placed on the level of the natural soil, and surrounded by an irregular circle of sandstone boulders; accompanied by a piece of stag's horn worked into an oval shape, three good spear points, and two rather indefinite instruments of flint, all which had been submitted to intense heat, probably from having accompanied the remains of their owner on the funeral pile. The flints have acquired a glazed appearance from the fusion of their surfaces. At a short distance from this interment the ground appearing to have been cut out and refilled with stones, we removed them to the depth of 18 inches, when we found a second deposit of burnt human bones placed amongst the stones, without any article or weapon whatever. The ground still shewing proofs of its having been disturbed, the work was resumed, until about two feet more of stone and earth being thrown out, we had the satisfaction of arriving at the solid floor of the grave, on which lay another heap of calcined bones, with one solitary bead of jet amongst them, of very primitive form, being only a rough piece perforated. The entire depth, from the apex of the mound to the bottom of the grave, was about five feet, three feet being below the natural surface.

ROUND LOW, HARBOROUGH.

On the 5th July, a barrow called Round Low, near Harborough Rocks, on Hopton Moor, was opened; but, owing to the labours of former excavators, we met with but little success, all the middle of the barrow having been removed. Yet sufficient traces of the original interment remained to determine its character. The deposit appears to have consisted of calcined bones, accompanied by a few inferior flints, enclosed within a coarse urn.

CRAKE LOW, TISSINGTON.

On the 6th of July the remainder of a mutilated barrow near Tissington, called Crake Low, were explored, attention having been directed towards it by human bones being dug up by persons destroying the mound for the sake of the limestone to be found in it. Upon making a section across the presumed centre of the barrow, which had long since been levelled with the ground, we met with two interments which had escaped the general ruin; but which, owing to their nearness to the surface, were in an advanced state of decay. They consisted of the skeleton of a young person, accompanied by two calcined flints; and a deposit of burnt human bones, with one burnt flint, both placed within a rough cist formed of limestones set on edge; between the two was a small vase of coarse clay, $5\frac{1}{2}$ inches high, perfectly devoid of ornament.

A further discovery of two skeletons and a very small plain vase, which was placed at the head of one of them, was made by some labourers opening a stone quarry near the edge of the mound in December, 1850. The vase and part of the skulls are preserved at Lomberdale.

DOWEL OR DOWER.

July 10th we opened a small mound on the summit of a hill called Brownedge, near Church Sterndale; it was raised about two feet above the natural level, and covered a grave three feet deep cut in the sandstone rock. The grave was filled, and the barrow was entirely constructed with stones mostly of grit, but with the addition of a few pieces of limestone, which must have been carried a mile or two to the place. Having removed these materials to within six inches of the bottom of the grave, without meeting with anything more important than rats' bones, we were much annoyed by the appearance of a considerable quantity of water, which effectually prevented any view of the floor of the grave, or the objects there deposited, and rendered it necessary for us to fish for the expected treasure. The interment had been by inhumation, and, owing to the wet, very few traces of the skeleton remained, and these were in great decay. The body was accompanied by a small and elegantly ornamented drinking cup, 6¾ inches high, which from the circumstance above named was recovered in a very dilapidated condition; a conical stud of jet with the usual double perforation, and two flints, one of them an arrow point.

END LOW NEAR HARTINGTON.

On the 13th of July we re-opened the large barrow at End Low, which was first attempted in 1843, without our finding the primary interment. Our researches this time resulted in the discovery of the remains of the original occupant, which were, after the expenditure of much labour, found in a cist cut down in the rock to the depth of six feet beneath the natural surface, and upwards of ten feet from the top of the barrow. The skeleton was that of a finely proportioned man, rather above the middle size, and was in good preservation, with the exception of the head, which was decayed at the left side, from contact with the floor of the grave. The bones lay apparently without much regularity, which was attributable to the settling down of the stones upon the body during the process of decay. At a small distance from them was a bronze dagger and spear head of flint, of a grey colour. The grave was

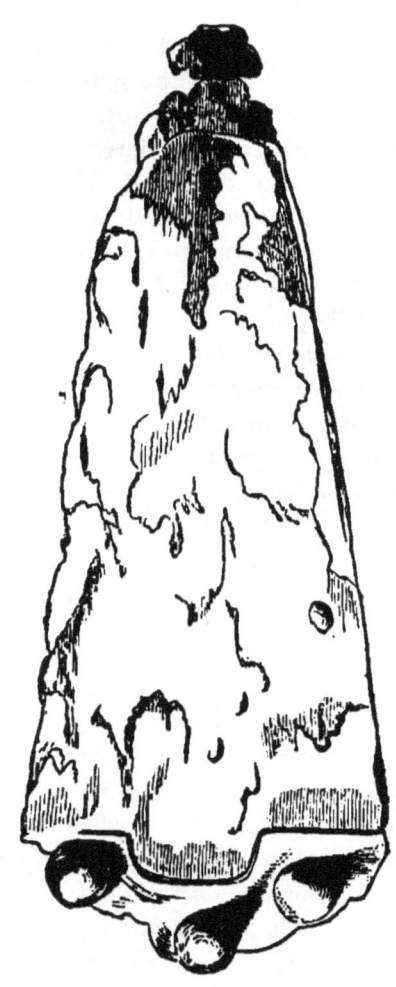

Dagger from End Low.

bounded on three sides by rock, and the remaining one was walled up to a level with them with loose limestones. The skull is engraved in the Crania Britannica, and is described by the learned writer as "a well-formed head, presenting very clearly the conformation of the true ancient British cranium, of which it may be regarded as belonging to the typical series." The femur measures 18·8 inches.

MONEYSTONES.

There are two barrows in the valley adjoining a hill near Hartington called Casking Low, which are commonly called Moneystones. The largest has been nearly removed, for the sake of the limestone it contained, and has been further rifled by treasure-seekers allured by the attractive name. On this account our researches on the 15th of July proved unavailing, as we found nothing but fragments of human skeletons and bits of flint. The smaller barrow is in the same field, about one hundred yards from the other, measures about six yards across, and is surrounded by a circle of large limestones, whose grey and lichen-covered surfaces, rising above the turf, present a venerable and old-world appearance. Near the surface, about the centre, we found a skeleton having no implements. Somewhat lower down the earth at first sight appeared to be quite undisturbed; but on closer examination we detected particles of charcoal, and consequently proceeded till, at the depth of about a yard, we discovered two more skeletons, lying in the usual contracted posture upon the top of the natural rock. They were both much decayed, and had each but one spear head of flint, though they were surrounded by a slight sprinkling of chippings of the same material.

LONGSTONE EDGE.

On the 17th of July we broke ground in a fresh district, by opening a barrow near Longstone called Blake Low, which had been a good deal mutilated by the removal of stone. Nevertheless we found the interment in the centre to be quite undisturbed, though the remains of about six individuals in a rude cist close by were in a state of the utmost disorder. These were accompanied by four neat instruments of flint, and the remains of a curiously-decorated urn. The preservation of the central deposit was owing to the body having been laid in a grave cut in the rock to the depth of two feet. The skeleton was that of a very young woman, or rather of a girl, and lay on the left side, with the knees drawn up. At the head was a drinking cup, rather more globular in form than usual, $7\frac{1}{2}$ inches high, the upper part ornamented by parallel grooves; and along with the skeleton were the bones of an infant, with the tine of a stag's antler. The grave was filled up to the level of the natural soil with limestone, amongst which was as large an accumulation of the bones of the water-vole as we have seen in any barrow.

On the 25th of July we opened another barrow, at no great distance from the last, situated on a more elevated point of the "Edge." Its mutilated appearance gave rise to no very sanguine expectations of success, and we were, therefore, neither surprised nor disappointed by finding, on examination, that the mound had been thoroughly rifled. There were some very large limestones placed on edge for a considerable length in the centre of the barrow, but whether they had been portions of cists that had been removed by former excavators, or not, is uncertain. In all parts of our diggings we observed scattered pieces of bone pertaining to skeletons, both human and animal; amongst the latter were those of the horse, ox, hog, dog, water rat, and a few specimens of the beaks of birds. The only manufactured remains were two small pieces of a drinking cup, and a circular flint which has been calcined.

On the 29th of August we opened another barrow, near the last, situated on a part of the hill still more elevated. Externally it has the appearance of a cairn or tumulus solely composed of stone, which in fact it was, so far as artificial means had been employed, but in the middle the rock rose above the natural level, and caused the tumulus to appear of greater extent than it really was.

In the centre was an irregularly shaped rock grave, about three feet deep, lined with flat stones placed edge-way, and covered with four or five large slabs laid over it without much regularity. It contained a deposit of calcined bones, evidently of an adult, with bits of stags' horn intermixed, laid in a heap near the middle of the grave, which was the chief interment; in one corner was the decayed skeleton of a child of tender age, around which were numerous rats' bones; and in the opposite corner were two vases of different shapes, something like those found at Arborlow, (Vestiges, p. 65,) which yet stood upright in their original position, and contained nothing but fine mould; casually were found some cows' teeth, two hoofs of deer, and a bit of flint. Having cleared out the grave, a triangular hole, measuring about a foot each way, was found to have been sunk at one side to the

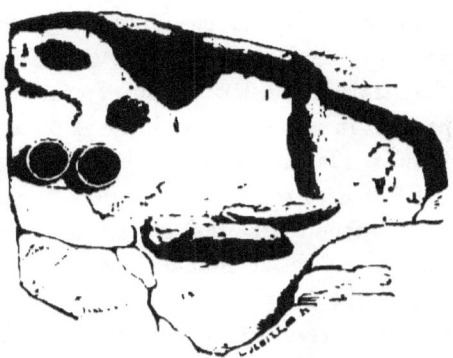

Ground plan of Grave at Blake Low.

depth of 18 inches. As we found nothing in it but a few fragments of bone, it is possible that it was originally made to receive the vases, and was abandoned because too small to hold them conveniently; or it might have had some connection with a prior interment, as we found a portion of the cranium of another subject just outside the lining stones of the grave.

The analogy between the Arborlow deposit and the present is very remarkable, the interment in each being by cremation, each accompanied by two vessels, and the vessels in each case being of relatively distinct forms, that is to say, a highly ornamented one, with an opening wide in proportion to the height, and a plainer one in which this peculiarity is not seen.

MIDDLETON-BY-YOULGRAVE.

On the 10th of November we commenced excavating a barrow in a plantation near Kenslow Wood, called Rusden Low, where a skeleton was found by the planters in May 1828. Being situated on a natural rising of the land it had been quite overlooked till the previous day, when it was noticed whilst shooting. The first step was to cut as near the centre as possible, and the result was the discovery of a skeleton, lying on its left side, with the knees drawn up, in a slight depression in the rock which was very near the surface. The lower extremities were quite undisturbed, although the upper part of the body had been much injured at a former period, perhaps by the planters. In the course of the day we found the relics described below, none of which occupied any well-defined position in connection with the skeleton, though they were not far from it. It will be seen that they are of various ages, commencing with a neat spear point of flint burnt white, and a tine of stag's horn, found near the feet of the body; and a flint arrow near where the head should have been. Outside the depression in which the body lay was part of a very neatly made comb, composed of several pieces of bone rivetted between two strong ribs of the same with iron pins: it had been furnished with teeth on both sides, which were nearly all broken away. The blade of a clasp knife of iron, apparently very ancient, as it is completely oxydized through the substance of the metal; and a small brass coin of Constantius Chlorus, reverse Victoriae Lactae Princ. Perp.; teeth of animals, and pieces of Romano-British pottery were found throughout the cutting, which, with the comb, knife, and coin have probably been deposited with a much later interment than that which we found.

November 11th we continued the examination without success until near dark, when we found a long grave in the rock parallel with the depression occupied by the former skeleton, and not more than a yard from it. It was eighteen inches deep, and covered with large stones; in it lay the skeleton of a young female, as usual on the left side, in a contracted posture. Before the face were indications of the skeleton of a very young child, and a highly-ornamented drinking cup of red clay, which lay crushed upon its side with the mouth towards the feet of the skeleton: it contained one broken instrument of flint. It was evident that the grave had been occupied by a previous tenant, whose bones, together with the remains of another drinking cup beautifully decorated, and a bit of stag's horn, had been collected and placed under one of the large stones that covered the grave. This had clearly been done at the time when the female was buried. Owing to the lateness of the hour at which this interment was found, we were obliged to clear out the grave by candlelight, and thinking that something further might be discovered by day, we resumed the search on the 13th of November, but found only one rude flint arrow point in the grave; and a piece of a sandstone quern in refilling the excavation. There were many rats' bones in some parts of the mound, but not in the profusion sometimes met with.

YOULGRAVE.

On the 16th of November we opened a small barrow in a field on Meadow-place Farm, called Greenstor Meadow, close to the Conksbury road-side. The land having long been under tillage may account for the flatness of the barrow, and for the little success that attended our researches, which were rewarded by a few scattered articles only, there being no perfect interment found, although we detected remains of two human bodies, one of them calcined. There were also bones of rats, the tibia of a cow, a few instruments of flint, and a good specimen of a spear of the most primitive description, made from a large splinter of dense animal bone, nicely ground or rubbed to a point. It measures seven inches in length, and illustrates the account of Tacitus wherein he describes the more barbarous German hordes as using bone points to their weapons, owing to their ignorance of metal.

BARROWS OPENED BY THOMAS BATEMAN, IN 1849.

MIDDLETON.

On the 5th of February we re-opened the barrow at Borthor Low, first examined in September, 1843, (Vestiges, p. 48.,) when no central interment was found, although it appears that the cutting on that occasion was carried to within six inches of a skeleton, which lay on its left side in a very contracted posture, and which appears to have been the interment over which the tumulus was originally raised. The only relic found in close proximity to the body, was a rudely formed arrow head of burnt flint, but in the earth not far distant were two more pieces of flint and a chip from a stone celt. In the course of the excavation we noticed rats' bones in profusion, and near the surface some small pieces of earthenware.

NEWHAVEN.

On the 27th of April we opened a mutilated mound of earth in a field near Newhaven House, called the Low, two-thirds of which had been removed, and the remainder more or less disturbed. So that nothing was found in its original state; which is much to be regretted, as the contents appear to be late in date, and different in character from anything we have before found in tumuli. The mound itself, being constructed of tempered earth, bore some analogy to the grave hill of the Saxon Thegn opened at Benty Grange about a year before; and like it was without human remains, if we except a few fragments of calcined bone, which are too minute to be certainly assigned either to a human or animal subject. The articles found comprise many small pieces of thin iron straps or bands, more or less overlaid with bronze, which are by no means unlike the framework of the helmet found at Benty Grange. There is also a boss of thin bronze, 3 inches diameter, pierced with three holes for attachment to the dress (?) and divided by raised concentric circles, between which the metal is ornamented with a dotted chevron pattern, in the angles of which are small roses punched by a die. Another object in bronze is a small round vessel or box of thick cast metal, surrounded by six vertical ribs, and having two perforated ears, serving probably better to secure the lid and suspend the box. Although it measures less than an inch in height, and less than 2 in diameter, it weighs full $3\frac{1}{2}$ ounces. A similar box, with the lid, on which is a cross formed of annulets, found with Roman remains at Lincoln, is engraved at page 30 of the Lincoln Book of the Archæological Institute, where it is called a pyx. Two others, discovered at Lewes, are engraved in the Archæologia, Vol. XXXI., page 437, one of which has the lid bearing a cross precisely similar to the Lincoln example, whence it is certain that they must be assigned to a Christian period, probably not long previous to the extinction of the Saxon monarchy. The last object there is occasion to describe is an iron ferrule or hoop, $1\frac{1}{2}$ inch diameter, one edge of which is turned inwards so as to prevent its slipping up the shaft on which it has been fixed. We also found some shapeless pieces of melted glass, which from their variegated appearance might be the product of fused beads; and observed many pieces of charred wood throughout the mound, which may possibly not have been of a sepulchral character.

A laughable circumstance occurred in connection with one article found here, which is really too good to be lost. I sent a sketch of the bronze box to a metropolitan archæologist in order to ascertain its use. It was submitted to a well known collector, since deceased, who sent word that it was a Chinese weight! which he had recently seen knocked down at Stevens' saleroom!!

OVER HADDON.

On the 30th of April a barrow near Over Haddon, in land called Grindlow, was examined as completely as the meeting of three walls on its summit would allow. It had been much mutilated; but fortunately the primitive interments lay too deep to receive injury from the labours of those in search of stone, by whom an important interment of secondary date had been destroyed. The original deposit had been made on the rock a little below the natural surface, and about 5 feet from the top of the mound; it comprised three skeletons, laid in the usual contracted position, two of which were females; with them were one or two rude instruments of flint, and a fine collection of jet orna-

Beads from Grindlow.

ments, 73 in number, which form a very handsome necklace. Of these 26 are cylindrical beads, 39 are conical studs, pierced at the back by two holes meeting at an angle in the centre; and the remaining 8 are flat dividing plates, ornamented in the front with a punctured chevron pattern, superficially drilled in the jet; 7 of them are laterally perforated with three holes, to admit of their being connected by a triple row of the cylindrical beads, whilst the 8th, which is of bone, ornamented in the same style, has nine holes at one side, which diminish to three on the other by being bored obliquely. Above these bodies, which were covered with stone, the mound was of unmixed earth, very compact and clayey, and between the stone and earth were many pieces of calcined bone, and numerous splinters of the leg bones of large animals, some of which are likely to have been used as points for weapons. In the earth near the summit of the barrow were some relics of a later interment, probably of a distinguished Saxon, with whom had been deposited a circular enamel, of which only the silver plated frame remained, the latter is engrailed on the front, and engraved with a lozengy pattern round the edge; and a bowl of thin bronze, very neatly made, with a simple hollow moulding round the edge, which when complete was 7 inches diameter, and appears to have had two handles soldered or cemented to the sides. The bowl was broken when found, and no handles were discovered; but it is probable that both they and some other ornaments, as well as another of the bone plates with 9 perforations, which is wanting to complete the necklace, would have been found if the triple wall could have been removed, as the point of junction was directly over the place where the interments lay, which were exhumed by a dangerous undercutting.

May 4th we partially excavated the remains of Grindlow proper, originally a large cairn 25 yards across, wholly composed of stones of all sizes, but now almost demolished: we were therefore unsuccessful in our search for interments, but found broken human bones, accompanied by those of the rat, in every direction. We also met with a broken lance head of flint, and part of the tusk of a wild boar.

PARWICH.

Next day we were engaged in opening barrows upon Low Moor near Parwich. The first was, to all appearance, a large and perfect tumulus, but we were disappointed by finding the remains of a lime-kiln in the middle, which had been constructed above a large grave in the rock, the covering slabs of which had been converted into the roof of the draught hole of the kiln. After this discovery we abandoned the search, having found no human remains. The other barrow was much smaller, the central elevation being only a foot, it was, nevertheless, found to cover a grave sunk through the natural soil into the rock, to the further depth of six feet. About two feet from the surface we met with fragments of pottery, pieces of human bone, burnt and unburnt, and traces of decomposed wood which lay in a regular stratum amongst the stones by which the grave was filled. After much labour we succeeded in emptying the grave, which did not exhibit any marks of former opening, until about the end of our operations, when such became too evident on the discovery of the skeleton of an infant and some pieces of a roughly ornamented vase, carelessly thrown together in a corner; while, to make assurance doubly sure, at the other end of the grave was a piece of rusty iron, bearing a suspicious resemblance to the end of a pick, by no means primitive in form. The former opening must have taken place at an ancient, perhaps medieval, period, as the stones filling the grave were all of one colour from having lain in the damp so long, and were quite free from earth which might have fallen from the surface, so that we had no idea of its having been disturbed till we reached the bottom.

VINCENT KNOLL.

May 24th.—We explored the remnant of a large barrow in a field near Parcelly Hay, called Vincent Knoll. The portion remaining had been the central part of the mound, and had been recently disturbed down to the natural surface of the field, fortunately without injury to the interments, which lay about two feet deeper in an irregularly shaped grave cut in the rock for their reception. To make the description intelligible we will call the grave an elongated oval, though it was not strictly so, the rock having been removed in accordance with the natural angular and irregular joints. At one side of the grave was a skeleton, lying on its left side with the legs gathered up, accompanied only by the core of a cow's horn which lay upon the ribs. This skeleton, which was that of a male, exhibited a singular malformation of the upper part of each femur; close to its feet, and near one end of the oval, was a second skeleton of slender make which had been buried in a slovenly manner, it had with it a very large tooth of some animal, which, as well as both skeletons, was much decayed: they were surrounded by rats' bones, and a few inches above them was a thin layer of black earth, running through the small stones that filled this part of the grave. On the opposite side lay a third skeleton which faced the first, and was deposited in the same position on its left side, the head being, of necessity, in the contrary direction: near the pelvis was a very neat circular ended instrument of white flint, and about a foot from the legs was a small iron spear with an open socket much corroded, which, however, did not appear to belong to the interment. This body in better condition than the others, was not surrounded by so many rats' bones, and was covered by larger stones. Following the side of the grave to the end of the oval, opposite to that occupied by the second skeleton, was found, about two feet from the last, the upper part of a fourth, to which, it is probable, the iron spear belonged: the bones were in good condition, but lay huddled together as if the body had been hastily buried. Careful observation at the time led to the conclusion that the two first bodies were interred at the same time, that the third deposit took place at a subsequent, but very early period, and that the fourth was of comparatively modern introduction, not dating earlier than the Pagan-Saxon age.

CHELMORTON.

On the 20th of June we examined two barrows on a tract of high land, called Great Low, between Hurdlow and Chelmorton:

the first had been removed almost to the surface of the land, so that nothing was found but a small piece of Romano-British pottery. The other, called Nether Low, originally a large barrow, but mutilated by stone getters, still covers an area 25 yards across, and is 4 feet high: it is composed exclusively of stone. Although we failed on this occasion to discover the primary interment, we found remains of two individuals, one of whom had undergone cremation; and myriads of rats' bones, which were most abundant near some very large stones on the natural surface, about the centre of the mound.

23rd of June we opened a small low barrow in the neighbourhood of the last, which covered a rock grave three feet deep, the irregular shape of which was corrected by an interior lining of stone slabs. It was chiefly filled with stones, but had a layer of tempered earth above and below them: the latter had the nature of exceedingly tenacious clay, and in it was imbedded the skeleton of a tall man of middle age, who lay extended on his back, with the head raised and pointing to the west; the hands, with the fingers extended, were placed on the thighs; an iron knife much corroded lay in an oblique direction across the left side of the pelvis, and was itself crossed by the bones of the wrist. The right femur had been fractured about 6 inches below the neck, but had firmly reunited, apparently with the effect of shortening the limb, Parallel with the right side of the body, for its whole length, was a ridge of dark-coloured earth so remarkably dense that we could not detect the substances of which it was composed in any part excepting between the right humerus and the ribs, where it contained remains of wood and of animal's skin, the earth separating with ease where the latter had been folded, and exhibiting a hairy surface almost as perfect as would be shown by a recent hide under the same circumstances of damp and pressure, colour alone excepted. Although there was a hard mass of tempered earth above the grave, a few water rats had left their bones near those of this Saxon.

On the 5th of July we resumed the examination of the barrow at Nether Low, and found at the west side about five yards from the centre, four interments, three of which were placed in angles of a shallow depression in the rock, of irregular form. The most important of these was the skeleton of a middle aged man, lying contracted in the western angle, having beneath the head, and in contact with the skull, a beautiful leaf-shaped dagger of white flint, 4¼ inches long, with the narrower half curiously serrated. A few inches from this unique weapon, was a plain but neat spear head of white flint. In a joint of the rock at a right angle with this interment, was a slender skeleton, probably of a female in the prime of life, accompanied by a prism-shaped piece of white flint, a piece of hematite, a boar's tusk, and a large globular bead of jet; the last found close to the neck.

The third skeleton was that of a much younger subject, and lay on the rock a little nearer the centre; it was not provided with implements, but between it and the others was a single piece of a calcined human skull. They were all about 4 feet from the top of the barrow.

Another skeleton was discovered about two feet from the surface, in a cist covered by a large flat stone and constructed across the joint of rock occupied by the female skeleton; it was accompanied by stags' horns of large size, and an arrow point of grey flint; and appeared to be the body of a person 17 or 18 years old.

In another cutting, near the outside, we found the remains of an infant, and a very neat instrument of white flint of uncertain use.

HURDLOW.

On the 7th of July we opened the first of a line of three small tumuli, occupying the summits of hills between the Buxton and Ashbourne road and the village of Church Sterndale. The field in which it is placed is called "Top of the Hurst." The mound, about 12 yards across, and not more than a foot high, consisted of earth, tempered in that part immediately above the grave, which was so far sunk into the rock as to render its floor rather more than two feet below the turf. It was cut nearly from east to west, and contained a skeleton extended at length, with the head to the latter point; the lower bones were fairly preserved, but of the upper parts there were but few remains, the enamel crowns of the teeth being in the best condition. At the left hip was a small iron knife, 4 inches long; and where the right shoulder had been was an assemblage of curious articles, the most important of which was a small bronze box, or canister, with a lid to slide on, measuring altogether 2 inches high and the same in diameter. When found it was much crushed, but still retained inside remains of thread, and bore on the outside impressions of linen cloth. Close to it

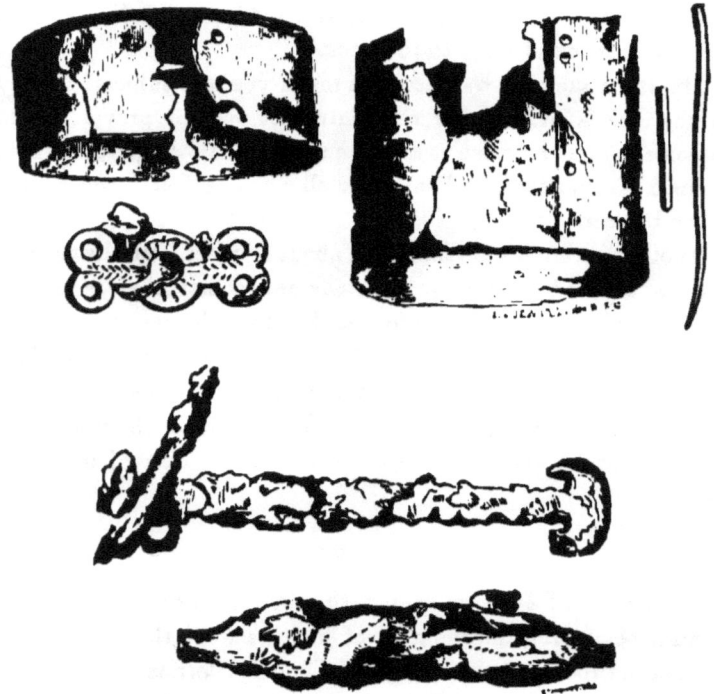

Saxon Box for Thread, and Iron Implements.

were two bronze pins or broken needles, and a mass of corroded iron, some of which has been wire chainwork connected with a small bronze ornament with five perforations, plated with silver and engraved with a cable pattern, near which were two iron implements of larger size, the whole comprising the girdle and chatelaine, with appendages, of a Saxon lady. Many pieces of hazel stick were found in contact with these relics, which were probably the remains of a basket in which they were placed at the funeral. All the iron shows impressions of woven fabrics, three varieties being distinguishable, namely, coarse and fine linen, and coarse flannel or woollen cloth. The box is very faintly ornamented by lozenges, produced by the intersection of oblique lines scratched in the metal and may be compared with one found at Stand Low in 1845 (see Vestiges, p. 75).

On the 10th of July we opened two more barrows of the same construction on the hills rather nearer Buxton; the first, 9 yards across and a foot high, composed of earth, was tempered or puddled above the grave, which was sunk a little beneath the natural level. We could not perceive the least trace of bone, but about the middle of the grave was part of an iron knife, to which adhered a mass of decayed wood, the impression of the grain being sharp and distinct upon the rust.

The other barrow, 11 yards diameter and about 18 inches high, is composed, as the two others, of earth tempered over the grave, which was dug nearly east and west. Within it, about a yard from the top, lay a skeleton extended on its back, with the left arm crossed over the body, the right lying close to the side, and the head to the west. The teeth indicated the deceased to have been a young man. The closest scrutiny of the earth for some distance around the body failed to reveal anything further, the knife so commonly found with Saxon interments being absent in this case.

MINNINGLOW.

18th of July we made a slight excavation in the large barrow at Minninglow, near the cist wherein a skeleton was found in 1843 (Vestiges, p. 39). The cutting was continued through loose stones to the depth of 4 feet from the surface, when the natural soil appeared, and through the whole we found many pieces of firmly baked Romano-British pottery that had been formed on the wheel, from clay mixed with coarse sand and small pebbles, which had acquired in baking colours varying from brick red to dark grey or purple; altogether we collected near a peck of fragments, which might have been purposely broken, as no large pieces are to be found amongst them; most of them appear to be parts of vessels modelled after the pattern of the common globular cinerary urn of the Romans. Near the natural soil we found two small brass coins in good preservation.

I.

Constantine the Great. Reverse: Gloria Exercitus. Two figures holding standards.

II.

Constantius II. Same legend and same reverse.

On the 20th of July we opened a small mound near the preceding, on the face of the hill declining towards the Brassington and Elton road. Upon cutting a section through the middle, traces of a large fire appeared, the earth forming the tumulus being changed in colour and consolidated. The natural surface in the centre was strewed with charred wood, calcined human bones, and stones which had been cracked and flaked by heat. Amongst these relics of the long quenched pile, were portions of three vessels of compact wheel-formed earthenware, precisely like the bulk of the fragments from the large barrow last described, and one small brass coin of the Lower Empire; all much burnt. One, only, of the three vessels is sufficiently complete to afford an outline of its form, which is clearly an improvement on the usual globular shape of the Roman olla: it is very elegant in outline, and measures 7 inches in height, and differs from the Roman ware in the quality of the paste, which is extremely gritty and hard, and is externally grey. One of the others has been of the same shape, but of a dark red colour. It is certain that this mound covers the place where the corpse was reduced to ashes along with the three vases and the coin, but from so few bones being found, it is rather likely that the collected remains were deposited in some part of the mound not explored, unless, indeed, they were so completely burnt as to leave but a slight residuum.

I have frequently observed the difference between Celtic deposits from tumuli, and Roman incinerated bones, to be most strongly marked; the former are almost uniformly cleanly burnt in pieces sufficiently large to be recognised as parts of the skeleton, and consequently far exceed the latter in quantity, which are as constantly reduced to ashes, and are frequently mixed with sand and other impurities from the embers of the pile. This discovery is chiefly interesting as fixing the date of a kind of pottery which might easily be mistaken for medieval ware by persons not accustomed to the critical examination of texture.

HURDLOW.

On the 21st of July we opened a small tumulus on a hill above the High Peak Railway, near Hurdlow, which had been cut through the centre, but the imperfect manner in which investigations of this kind were formerly executed, afforded a chance of our finding something. We discovered that the former excavators had removed one side of a small rectangular cist, which was placed a little to the side of their trench; its other sides were intact, and the earth inside did not seem to have been disturbed, yet we found nothing within but a horse's tooth, a bit of thin bronze, and a few imperfectly burnt bones.

On the afternoon we re-opened the barrow on Cronkstone Hill (the next eminence), which was examined by Mr. William Bateman, in 1825 (Vestiges, p. 33). A short distance east from the centre was a large irregularly shaped grave in the rock, the bottom of which was upwards of five feet below the apex of the mound, within it lay the skeleton of a full sized person who had suffered from a morbid enlargement of the head of the right humerus; as usual, in the early interments, he lay in a contracted posture, with a circular instrument of flint near the head, and surrounded by rats' bones. A few inches above this skeleton was a deposit of calcined human bones, apparently interred at the same time as it. There may probably be other interments in the mound, which is about 20 yards diameter.

MINNINGLOW.

Walking over the smaller tumulus in Minninglow plantation, on the 20th of July, I observed, as a peculiarity before unnoticed, that it consists of two distinct barrows of different structure, or to speak more correctly, that a later barrow of earth has been cast up against the side of the original mound, which is a cairn entirely of stone surrounding a megalithic cist vaen (Vestiges p. 40).

On the 27th of July, excavating as near the centre of the earthy barrow as possible, we raised three or four ponderous flat stones, beneath which the earth exhibited a crystalized appearance, resulting from its having been tempered with liquid; cutting down through it we arrived at the natural surface at the depth of rather more than 4 feet, and found that the mound had been raised over the site of the funeral pile, as it remained when burnt out. The scattered human bones had not been collected, but lay strewed upon the earth accompanied by some good flints, part of a bone implement, and a bronze dagger of the most archaic form, having holes for thongs and no rivets, all of which had been burnt along with their owner. The dagger is singularly contorted by the heat, and affords the first instance of a weapon of bronze having been burnt, and the second in which we have found one associated with calcined bones, the first being at Moot Low, in 1844 (Vestiges p. 51). But perhaps the most important conclusion to be drawn from the discovery is the corroboration of the opinion entertained in favour of the high antiquity of the cairns or stone barrows, and other megalithic remains of primitive industry, as we here find a mound containing an interment accompanied by weapons indicating a very remote period, and itself differing both in material and structure, occupying a position in relation to the cairn, which affords positive proof of its more recent origin.

BALLIDON MOOR.

On the 30th of July we opened a fine bowl-shaped tumulus,

15 yards across, situated on Ballidon Moor. The upper part, to the depth of two feet, was almost entirely of earth, near the centre presenting the appearance of having been tempered. In this stratum were a few calcined bones, and fragments of a rude urn. Immediately beneath was an accumulation of stones, large and small, forming the base of the mound, which was raised on a rocky and uneven surface, which caused the thickness of the substructure of stone to fluctuate between two feet and a yard. The limestone employed being of a friable nature had become so far decomposed as to yield sufficient sand to choke up the interstices.

After noticing the trifling remains exhumed from the upper bed of earth, we observed nothing until arriving at the sandy stone, amongst which were four skeletons that might have been slightly disturbed before, but from their contracted posture and decayed condition it was difficult to decide, with respect to three of them, whether they had or not; the fourth had certainly been either disturbed at the interment of the others, or had been buried as a skeleton whilst the bones were fresh, as all parts of the skeleton had been collected and the long bones laid side by side. The latter were still unbroken, and it is obvious that they must have been thus arranged while retaining much of their natural strength, had it been otherwise they would have been broken by the stones with which they were in contact. This skeleton was nearer the centre than the others, and a very few inches beyond it we first observed a well-defined stratum of burnt earth, with a layer of pure charcoal above it, interposed between the upper bed of earth and the sandy stone. Pursuing this favourable indication we discovered, almost simultaneously, two very interesting interments which were found by extending the cutting a little beyond the middle of the barrow. The most ancient was about five feet below the summit in a depression in the rock, which was converted into a neat lozenge-shaped cist by four flat stones placed on edge; it was the skeleton of a middle aged man in unusually fine preservation, who lay with the knees drawn up, contrary to the usual custom on his right: side his femur measures 18.6 inches;

he was accompanied by one poor flint only, suited to point an arrow. The skull, in perfect preservation, has been engraved in the Crania Britannica, it is chiefly distinguished by the rugged or strongly marked character of the facial bones, and has an internal capacity of 74½ ounces; the nasal bones have been fractured, and re-joined during life, and the teeth were much worn down. The cranium is considered by the learned authors of the Crania Britannica, as a *typical* example of the brachy-cephalic variety of the Ancient British head, and is engraved as such in Dr. Meigs' Cranial Characteristics of the Races of Men, Philadelphia, 1857.

While taking up this skeleton we met with a large flat stone lying aslant, with its lowest edge within the cist; this was most likely the cover which had given way; the upper end was embedded in stones and burnt sand, interspersed with partially calcined human bones, and others in their natural state; among the latter were some remains of an infant; close above stood a large cinerary urn in an upright position, containing calcined

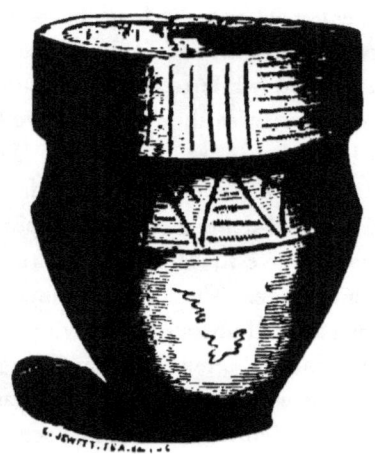

Cinerary Urn from Ballidon Moor.

human bones, and protected from superincumbent pressure by a large stone resting at each end upon an upright slab. The urn,

11¼ inches high and 9 diameter at the mouth, is ornamented by patterns impressed from a twisted thong, and is in fine preservation, having been found perfect. The bones within it were beautifully coloured by burning, and perfectly clean ; amongst them we found a piece of an animal's jaw, rats' bones, a fine bone pin 4 inches long, a fragment of thin pottery, and a flint arrow head, all (including the rats' bones) much burnt. The presence of partially burnt human bones in the sand, the discoloration of the latter, and the occurrence of calcined rats' bones in the urn, demonstrate the fact of the corpse having been consumed upon the spot. The section will render the arrangement of the interments in this curious barrow easily understood.

Section of Barrow, Ballidon Moor.

On the 1st of August we examined three more tumuli, in the same neighbourhood, all of which had most unfortunately been mutilated. The first had been encroached upon by a stone quarry, and we were told that a pitcher had been found in it some years before. By removing the loose stones and earth down to the rock, we found some bits of hard Romano-British pottery, which alone had resisted the attacks of the quarry men.

The second was in the next field but one, and appears to have been nearly all removed, though, from occupying a rocky protuberance, it looked tolerably perfect. About the middle we found the humerus of a human subject, near which was a grit sharpening stone and a cow's tooth.

The third barrow in the same field was half removed, it afforded a few animal bones, part of a sharpening stone, some pieces of ancient earthenware, but no human remains.

PARWICH.

On the 6th of August we made a section into the smallest of two mounds, near Parwich, situated in a field, called, I believe, from the owner or occupier, Saint's Low, in a low situation near a small watercourse. The composition of the mound, notwithstanding its affix of "Low," indicating no artificial origin, the investigation was relinquished without our interfering with the larger mound close by.

On the 9th of August we made an examination of the remains of a tumulus in a plantation on the summit of Saint's Hill, near Parwich, which had been destroyed by getting stone for the walls enclosing the plantation, when about 80 small brass coins of the later Roman Emperors were found scattered about the barrow.

Owing to the double destruction caused by stone getters, and persons tempted to search by the discovery of the coins, we were unable to find a single inch of undisturbed ground, and the sole evidence of former interments was afforded by two human teeth and some rats' bones.

MINNINGLOW.

On the 13th of August we opened a barrow at Ryestone Grange, close to Minninglow farm, which is a tolerably perfect mound, 11 yards across and near four feet high, but crossed by a thick stone wall which greatly impeded our operations, and which there is reason to believe prevented the discovery of the primary interment. At one side of the wall we found many bones, both human and animal; the only undisturbed skeleton being that of a child, buried about a foot from the surface, and unaccompanied by anything of interest; among the animal bones were some teeth of dogs. On the other side of the wall we found an iron knife, of the usual Saxon shape, about a foot beneath the turf; and on the natural surface below, a deposit of calcined bones containing a bone pin. By undercutting the wall as far as practicable, we ascertained that the centre of the barrow was principally of earth surrounded by large stones inclining inwards, and from this locality we drew out a piece of curiously ornamented pottery of primitive manufacture.

On the 15th of August we examined the site of a large barrow, near the last, 25 yards across, the circle being yet well defined from the foundation of the mound consisting of very large stones round the verge. The interior had been completely destroyed, about 6 inches only of factitious earth remaining, which, near the centre, was mixed with an enormous quantity of rats' bones.

SHEEN.

On the 21st of August we examined a very large barrow near Sheen, in Staffordshire, about 35 yards diameter and more than 9 feet deep, wholly composed of earth, which, near the natural surface, was mixed with charcoal, and varied by layers of moss. The latter in a great measure retained its natural colour, and contained many beetles, some of which were well preserved. About a yard from the bottom a thin ferruginous seam ran through the mound, perfectly solid and hard like pottery, which might possibly be the effect of heat. No interment was found, but there is little doubt of the existence of a deposit of calcined bones in some part of the mound.

MIDDLETON.

On the 17th, 18th, and 19th of October, and 1st of November, some further researches were made in the Flax Dale Barrow, near Middleton-by-Youlgrave, where a large cinerary urn with its deposit of burnt bones was found, in 1846. Although the present more extensive excavation was not equally successful, it afforded us an opportunity of becoming acquainted with a plan commonly adopted by the Britons in the construction of their tumuli, by first making a circle of large stones, within which the interments were placed, and then covered with an accumulation of stones, until a mound was formed surrounded by a kind of wall of one or

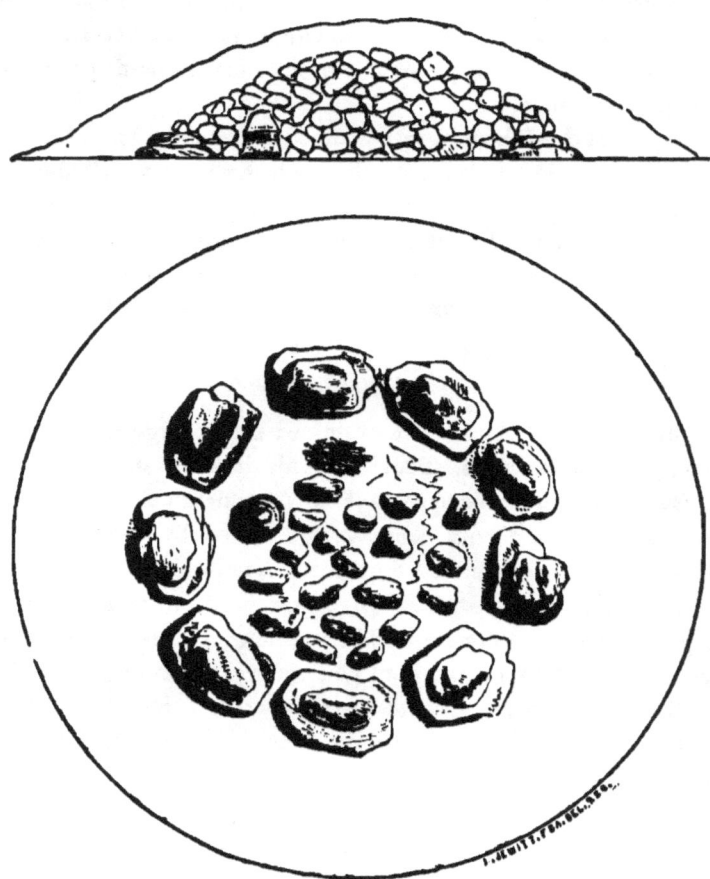

Plan and Section of Flax Dale Barrow.

two courses, consisting of the aforesaid circle; the whole was then covered with earth, which, though thinly laid on at the summit, was suffered to extend considerably further than the walled circle, thus concealing all the stonework. The earth around the circumference of the barrow was very compact, particularly near the outside, and in some places abounded with pieces of melted lead and calcined flints, which led us to think it probable that fire had been employed to harden the earth whilst moist, with the intention of rendering the mound more durable. The only interment discovered on this occasion was just within the S.W. side of the stone circle: it consisted of a deposit of calcined bones which had originally been placed within an urn so imperfectly baked as to have almost become disintegrated, the decay having been accelerated by the atmosphere, eighteen inches of loose stone only covering the deposit. Some flints, fragmentary human bones, and a chip from a stone celt were casually found in the stony part of the mound.

The adjoining field is called Foggy Lees, which may be a corruption of Foggy Low.

BARROWS OPENED BY THOMAS BATEMAN IN 1850.

On the 26th of February, another section was made in the barrow near Kenslow, called Ringham Low, which had been examined twice previously without much success. A few more pieces of Romano-British pottery like that found before, indicated that three urns had been interred in the mound, which consists entirely of earth, and is much like the small barrow at Minninglow, opened 20th July, 1849.

On the 7th of March, we opened a small barrow near Church Sterndale, mostly composed of earth, with a few stones on the level of the natural soil; without being able to find any interment.

CALTON.

On the 2nd of May, we examined some of the tumuli on Calton Pasture, near Chatsworth, of which there are at least seven, all more or less mutilated.

The first of those opened by us was a large flat barrow, about seventy feet diameter, and four high, situated in a field adjoining "The Hospital Field," consequently not in the large open Calton Pasture, though close to it. It was composed of sand and small stones, increasing in size towards the centre, where was a large cist vaen constructed of sandstones, which we found had been broken up very recently before our visit; we found only a few scattered burnt bones, and pieces of lead ore, which had undergone the action of fire.

The next, near "The Beech Plantation," had been a conical mound, covering an area fourteen yards in diameter, but was much mutilated by the centre being removed. It had originally been constructed as the last, with a central cist surrounded by stones and sand, and had contained a deposit of calcined bones, accompanied by a small vase, neatly ornamented, of which we found some fragments.

The third was a small mound connected with some earthen ridges rather lower down in the Park; it was soon found to have been pillaged, and was therefore as speedily abandoned.

The fourth and last that we examined, is near the fence separating the estates of the Dukes of Devonshire and Rutland, and is a bowl-shaped barrow, about fourteen yards across and four feet high. We worked for some time more hopefully than at the former mounds, as it did not appear to have been so much disturbed, although we ultimately found that it had. It was principally formed of stone, with but little earth, and we found that the interment had been placed in a depression in the natural surface in the centre, which had been cleared out by former excavators. From the presence of burnt lead ore, and a piece of pure lead, it is probable that the interment had been by cremation as in the others.

HASLING HOUSES.

On the 3rd of June, we opened a barrow at Hasling Houses, near Buxton, measuring about twelve yards across and three feet in height, chiefly composed of tempered earth, except in the centre, where were a good many stones, covering a grave cut from east to west, about eighteen inches deep. Within it lay at length the skeleton of a powerful man of middle age, with the head to the west, who had been buried either within a coffin, or upon a thick plank with another above him, in order to keep off the pressure of the stones. In the earth, about a foot from the skull, we found a rude instrument of flint, probably unconnected with the interment, and brought with earth from the neighbouring field as material for the mound. The femur measures 19½ inches; and both bones of the left leg had been fractured just below the knee, and strongly re-united by the formation of osseous substance many years before death. The body was most probably that of a Saxon.

In the afternoon we examined the remains on Foxlow Hill, near Buxton, where, in addition to some inconsiderable earthworks, there is the base of a large tumulus, the upper part of which had been removed to within a few inches of the rock. We found many traces of its former contents in the shape of human teeth and rats' bones, but all in the utmost confusion.

HILL HEAD.

On the 5th of June, we opened a barrow on the Hill Head, an eminence in the neighbourhood of the last. The mound is about twelve yards across, and presents the appearance of having been much reduced, the height being nowhere more than eighteen inches. The centre had been disturbed with the effect of displacing the skeletons of three or four persons and some calcined bones; the earth around did not appear to have been moved, as masses of rats' bones occupied their original level. Notwithstanding the unfavourable condition of the barrow, we collected 81 jet ornaments, composing a handsome necklace that had accompanied one of the skeletons, they comprise 53 cylindrical, and 11 flat beads, 12 conical studs, and five out of the six dividing plates requisite to form the decoration: the plates are plain, and the centre pair are perforated for eight beads to go between. It is likely that many more of the very small flat beads would have been found if the tumulus had not been before disturbed; those that were found being collected with much trouble from an area of many feet, instead of lying near the head of their owner.

In the afternoon we opened another barrow to the west of the last, on Stakor Hill, which at first appeared nothing more than a natural ridge of rock, terminating with a rounded end rather higher than other parts; but on cutting down in the centre, it was found to be a barrow, and that it had been disturbed thereabout. A grave, about a yard deep, had been cut in the rock, and roughly walled round, and had contained at least two skeletons. By removing one of the wall stones, we found a small bronze awl, similar to several others in the collection at Lomberdale, which had been inserted into a wooden handle as a tool for piercing skins or leather. The grave extended to the north, where it was both deeper and undisturbed, as we found a third skeleton lying at the bottom, having under the head a thin instrument of white flint that had been intensely burnt, but destitute of any other accompaniment except animal bones, which were plentiful in both tumuli.

On the 10th of June, we examined the remnant of a barrow at Cotes Field, near Hartington, but were disappointed by finding the interior occupied by the ruins of a limekiln; a few fragments of human bone, and bones of rats, alone testifying to the sepulchral origin of the mound.

On the 20th of June, we excavated a small mound of earth near the large barrow at Sterndale, opened in September, 1846, but failed to discover an interment.

When, to occupy the afternoon, we worked a little in the large barrow, where, in 1846, a bronze dagger was found, and made two cuttings to no purpose, as we observed only remains of animal bones and pottery, some of which was of the Romano-British period, and doubtless belonged to a late interment that was found near the surface some years before by men getting stone.

VINCENT KNOLL.

On the 25th of June, we were engaged upon a barrow on a hill facing Vincent Knoll, where we opened a barrow in 1849. Most of the elevation had been destroyed, and it was not easy to define its original boundary, yet the grave, which was cut in the rock to the depth of four feet, could not be very far from the centre. In this, two bodies had been interred in the usual contracted position, one of them lying on its left side, the other on its right, each having the head in the opposite direction. That which lay on its right side was first uncovered, proving the skeleton of a slender young person, which had at the feet a large and good instrument of slightly burnt grey flint, the use of which is not obvious.

The other was the skeleton of a much more robust person, accompanied by two weapons of flint, neither of which was so fine as that found with the other body. They lay on the rocky floor of the grave, surrounded by snail shells, and imperfectly guarded by some large stones artlessly inclined over them.

On the 28th of June, we opened a barrow on the "Upper Edge," near Sterndale, the top of which was of stone, and the lower part entirely of earth. About the centre were many pieces of charcoal, extending from a little below the turf, to the natural surface, a depth of about three feet. Amongst the charcoal were numerous pieces of calcined bone, and a few bits of flint; and from the appearance of the earth in the vicinity of the charcoal, it was judged that the process of combustion had taken place upon the spot.

BRUSHFIELD.

On the 3rd of August, we opened a finely shaped barrow near Brushfield, upon Lapwing Hill, overlooking Cressbrook valley, measuring seventeen yards across and four feet high in the centre, composed of earth, with a few stones in the middle, where a shallow grave, about a foot deep, was sunk in the rock. In it lay extended the remains of a human body, so very much decayed as to be almost undistinguishable, but which we ascertained to have been deposited with the head to the west. Beneath the remnants of bone were many traces of light-coloured hair, as if from a hide, resting upon a considerable quantity of decayed wood, indicating a plank of some thickness, or the bottom of a coffin. At the left of the body was a long and broad iron sword, enclosed in a sheath made of thin wood covered with ornamented leather.

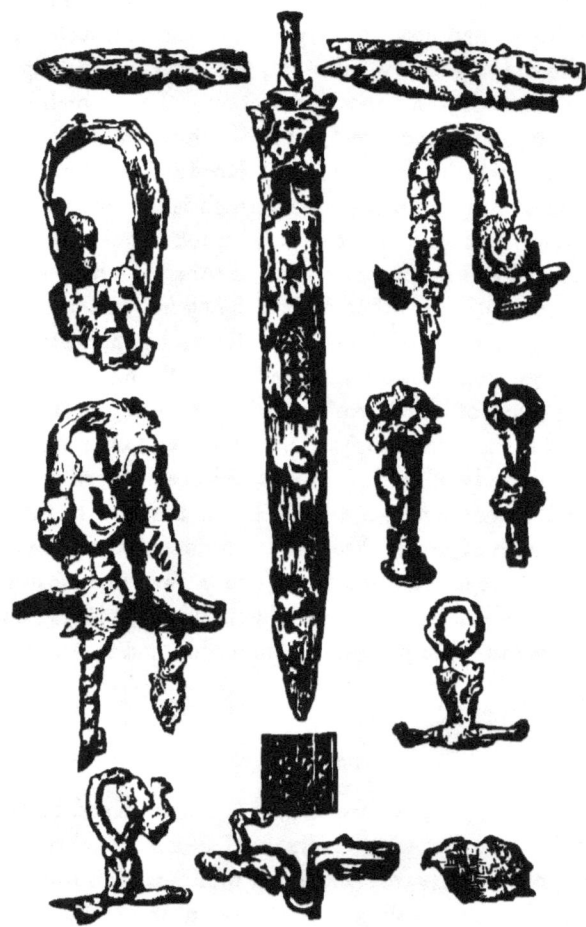

Iron Sword, Javelins, and other Instruments, from Brushfield.

Under the hilt of the sword, which like most of ancient date is very small, was a short iron knife; and a little way above the right shoulder were two small javelin heads, 4½ inches long, of the same metal, which had lain so near each other as to become united by corrosion. Among the stones which filled the grave, and about a foot from the bottom, were many objects of corroded iron, including nine loops of hoop iron about an inch broad, which had been fixed to thick wood by long nails; eight staples or eyes, which had been driven through plank and clenched; and one or two other objects of more uncertain application, all which were dispersed at intervals round the corpse throughout the length of the grave, and which may therefore have been attached to a bier or coffin in which the deceased was conveyed to the grave, possibly from some distant place. The only specimen of a Saxon sword, which was the weapon of the thegn, previously found in this part of Derbyshire, was singularly enough found with the umbo of a shield on the same farm in 1828; thus indicating the connection of a noble Saxon family with Brushfield in the age of Heathendom, the name of which is perpetuated in a document of the 16th century, preserved in the British Museum.*

On the same afternoon, we examined a mutilated barrow nearer Brushfield, called the "Gospel Hillock," perhaps from the first Christian Missionary having taken his stand thereon while exhorting the Saxons to forsake the worship of Woden and Thor; and we were much disappointed by finding nothing more than a few calcined bones and a fragment of pottery.

On the 14th of August, we excavated another barrow, near to that containing the Saxon thegn, having a tolerably perfect appearance, and crossed by two walls; but after much labour, we found that the whole of the centre had been disturbed as low as the natural surface; we consequently met with nothing more satisfactory than a piece of unburnt human skull, a few calcined bones, and some pieces of bone of different animals.

---

* Mortgage of Lands in Little Longsdon, Monsall Dale, and *Brighterighefield* (Brightric's Field,) otherwise Brushefielde, between Thomas Shakerley of Derby and Rowland Eyre of Hassoppe; dated......May. 37th Elizabeth. B. Mus: Additional MSS. 6702. fol. 45.

BARROWS OPENED BY THOMAS BATEMAN IN 1851.

TADDINGTON.

On the 22nd of April, we opened a small barrow on elevated land near Taddington, called Slipper Low, which was only about six yards diameter. It covered an irregularly shaped grave, cut in the rock, about eighteen inches deep, containing an adult skeleton, extended on its back, with the head to the north-west. The bones were much decayed from the grave having been filled with tempered earth, which led us to conclude that the interment had taken place at a late period, although no implement whatever was found to indicate the era.

On the 23rd of April, a peculiarly shaped barrow upon Crakendale Pasture, near Bakewell, was examined. Its singularity consisted in three prolongations radiating from the central mound, which was about four feet high. On digging in various places, scattered pieces of bone, both human and animal, were found; and in the centre, which had been previously disturbed, were remains of at least three adults and one child, as well as some pieces of calcined bone, bones of rats and other animals, fragments of an ornamental drinking-cup, and a small instrument neatly cut from the tine of a stag's horn. The centre of the barrow was carefully surrounded by several courses of flat stones set edgeway on the natural surface, which, if the barrow had been untouched, would have led to an easy discovery of the central cist, round which they had no doubt been placed with great regularity.

YOULGRAVE.

On the 3rd of May, we made a second investigation of the tumulus at Bee Low, near Youlgrave, which was first imperfectly opened by us in 1843, the excavation being then confined to the centre; but the mound being a bowl-shaped one, upwards of twenty yards diameter, it was thought worth while to make a further trial in it, which was begun by digging from the old cutting in the middle to the south side. The first discovery made when we had proceeded about three yards, was a skeleton lying on its left side with the knees drawn up, and the head to the east, so that the face was turned to the outside of the barrow. It was about eighteen inches below the surface of the mound, and did not seem to have been placed in a cist, although two or three courses of flat stones were carefully laid over it: near the head were three small instruments of bronze, two of them awls, and a few bits of the same metal that had been melted, and which had originally been small instruments of similar character. This skeleton having been taken up, we perceived the ground on the right or western side of the trench to decline; following this indication, we came to an irregular grave cut in the rock, the bottom about 4 feet 6 inches from the surface of the barrow: it was surrounded by a lining of small flat stones placed on edge, and within this lining was a regular pitching, like a street pavement, of clear chert stones very closely packed, extending over the whole grave; above them earth and stones had been thrown in without order, but underneath them was the skeleton of a young person resting in the usual contracted position, with the head to the south-west, the elbows almost in contact with the thigh bones, and the hands in front of the face. At the angle formed by the bending of the knees, was a beautiful drinking-cup, only $6\frac{3}{8}$ inches high, ornamented by two variations of the lozengy pattern; it still retained its upright position, and close to it was a very fine instrument of white flint, upwards of four inches long, which may have been used either as a knife or saw. While tracing out the western extremity of this grave, our attention was drawn to a very large stone, set up in a direction from S.E. to N.W., on a little higher level than the bottom of the grave, which was at length found to be one end of a rectangular cist, the other sides and cover of which were formed of similar slabs. Its internal dimensions were 3 feet 6 inches long, 2 feet wide, and 3 feet deep; and it was filled with stiff earth and small gravelly stone, amongst which, near the top, were fragments of calcined bone, and a small bronze awl or pin; removing the earth down to the floor (which was rock), we there found the bones composing the skeleton of an aged man, with a short round cranium, carefully placed in a heap in the middle, the long bones laid parallel with each other, and the skull put at the top of the heap, with the base upward. The bones being perfect, it is evident that this arrangement had been made whilst they were fresh and strong; and it is not a little singular that a similar mode of interment exists among the Patagonians, who make skeletons of their dead previous to burial. After removing these bones we found two small flints, and a piece of stag's horn at the bottom. Great quantities of rats' bones were found through the whole of the excavation, but they were observed to be most abundant and best preserved around the second interment, with which, it may be proper to mention, there was a single piece of an infant's skull, no other of its bones being found by a most careful examination. The accompanying plan represents the position of the various interments in

Plan of Interments in Bee Low.

the barrow; the flat stone shewn with burnt bones in the centre, being found in 1843.

MONSAL DALE.

On the 16th of May, we examined the remains of a tumulus about fifteen yards diameter, in a field on the left hand side of the road from Ashford to Wardlow, about a mile beyond the public-house at the entrance of Monsal Dale. Owing to the land having been much ploughed, the height of the tumulus had been considerably reduced, not more than a foot of artificial material being left. Immediately on removing the turf many fragments of human bone, detached from several skeletons, appeared, and near the centre was a skeleton not so much disturbed, lying on some large rough limestones, and having near the head a small shattered vase, still preserving an upright position in decay—it is slightly moulded and ornamented with oblique punctures. On a portion of the lower jaw of this skeleton is an osseous excrescence, of the shape and size of a small bullet. The bones of an infant, and one or two small flints were also found.

On the same afternoon, we began an examination of a large mutilated flat-topped barrow, twenty yards diameter and four feet high, on the summit of a hill called Hay Top, overlooking the manufacturing colony of Cressbrook. The mound is piled upon a naturally elevated rock, so as not to present more than two feet of accumulated material in the middle, where we began to dig, finding remains of many individuals, from infants to adults of large stature (an imperfect femur, broken off below the neck, measuring near nineteen inches), but all were in disorder except one skeleton, which appeared to lie on its left side in the centre; it was, however, so much surrounded by other bones as to be rather difficult to identify, and, from the same confusion, we cannot positively assign all the following articles to it, though there is scarcely a doubt that the flints and bone ornament were buried with it:—The objects referred to, are ten jet beads of the three common shapes, several flints, including three thick arrow points, and a curious bone ornament, with a hole for suspension round the neck, where it was found, not unlike a seal with a rectangular face. The skeleton, from the slenderness of the bones, was judged to be that of a female. We casually found pieces of two vessels, a polecat's skull, and many bones of the water-vole.

On the 23rd of May, we resumed our labour in two parties, digging at once on either side, between our former cutting and the north and south verge of the mound, and carrying on the trenches towards the west, where the barrow was most perfect, the whole of the eastern edge having been carted away. In the south cutting we found an oval cist about three feet from the surface, sunk a foot in rock and lined with a few flat stones; the diameter was under a yard, but it contained the skeleton of an aged man lying on his right side, with the knees necessarily so much drawn up as to approach the face, the head pointed to the south-west: and near it was a neat ornamented vase of imperfectly baked clay, 5½ inches high, and a perforated bone pin, about six inches long. On this side the tumulus was also found part of another skull, which had been removed from some other place.

While these discoveries were being made, the excavation on the north side was equally productive, for immediately below the grass were many fragmentary human bones, amongst which we found an iron spear, with the socket broken, yet 9½ inches long; and a blue glass bead, with a spiral thread of white running through it, which objects, we were informed, had been disturbed many years before, by a man digging in the mound under the impression of its being a mineral hillock: they must have belonged to a body interred near the surface at a late or Saxon age. Proceeding deeper, we found the rock cut away for a large space about two feet lower than its ordinary level, making the entire depth from the grass rather more than four feet. At the east extremity of this excavation there was a small enclosure of flat stones, something like that on the other side, before described, containing a skeleton much contracted, and in this case lying on its left side, with the head to the south, accompanied by one flint arrow point.

About the middle of the excavation, in the rock, were two rather small human crania, placed side by side, near a drinking-cup 7¼ inches high, ornamented with a lozengy pattern. Upon the crown of one of the skulls was a neatly chipped instrument of grey flint, and it is singular that no trace either of the lower jaws or of any other parts of the skeletons could be seen, though no disarrangement had ever taken place in this part of the mound, and it is certain that the crania alone had been buried there. At a little distance from them were the skeleton of a child, and one cylindrical jet bead. These discoveries, with the occurrence of numerous broken bones, both human and animal in the upper parts of the trenches, terminated the labours of the day. A portion of the west side of the mound intervening between the cuttings being reserved for the next day's examination, when it was cut out to the level of the rock, disclosing a grave about a yard square, sunk about three feet lower. Inside this excavation was a very neat rectangular cist, 2 feet long and 18 inches wide, formed of four flat slabs of limestone, filled with limestone, gravel,

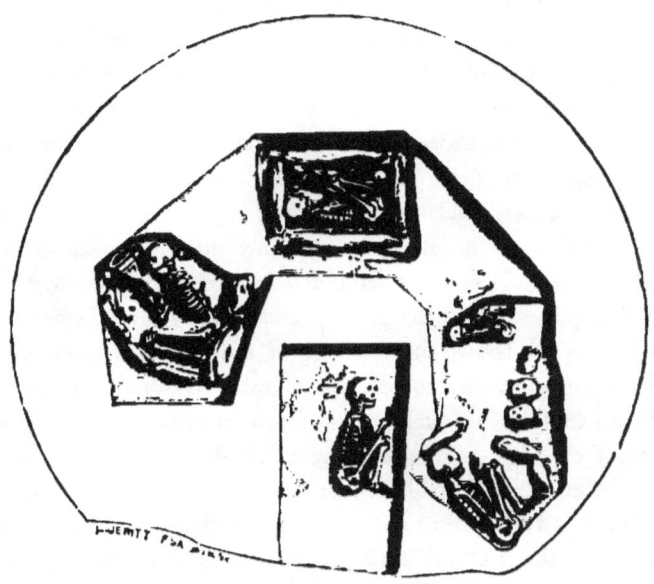

Plan of Barrow near Monsal Dale.

and rats' bones, which being very carefully removed, allowed us to see the skeleton of a child, doubled up, with the head to the south, and a most beautiful little vase, 4⅜ inches high, completely covered with a minute chevron pattern, lying obliquely in contact with the pelvis of the child, which had become thrust into it by the pressure of the grave ; the depth at which this deposit lay was about five feet from the surface of the mound. The skeleton of the child is arranged in a glass case at Lomberdale, and from the abnormal shape of the head, it is probable that death was occasioned by hydrocephalus. Many burnt bones, and disjointed bones, as before, were found in the course of the day. The plan of this interesting barrow will illustrate the foregoing account.

On the 29th of May, we made a section from south to north through another large mutilated tumulus in the same neighbourhood, but on the other side of the Wye. Not far from the centre we discovered a large sepulchral urn, 12 inches high, with a deep ornamented border, inverted over a deposit of clean calcined bones, placed upon some uneven stones on the natural surface, and having among them a calcined bone pin. The urn was quite uninjured, and owed its preservation to a large mass of limestone by its side, close to which lay a celt-shaped instrument 5 inches long, with a cutting edge, made from part of the lower jaw of a large quadruped rubbed down ; and two phalanges of a human finger. Proceeding further, we met with the skeleton of a small hog, then those of two children, all interred in a simple manner, without protection or accompaniment : beyond these was an adult skeleton that had been deposited at a late period, if we may judge from the appearance of the mound immediately above, where were many scattered bones, the skeleton of a dog, and a small bronze fibula of the most common Roman shape. By further excavation we found that the last skeleton had been interred near a very large stone set on edge from east to west, which formed the side of a cist vaen, measuring inside 3 feet 6 by 18 inches, the other sides being supplied by similar slabs, the whole placed in an excavation lower than the natural surface, the depth from the top of the mound to the floor of the cist being 5 feet 6 inches. By clearing it out, the following discoveries were made in the order in which they are enumerated :—First, a small vase of clay, neatly

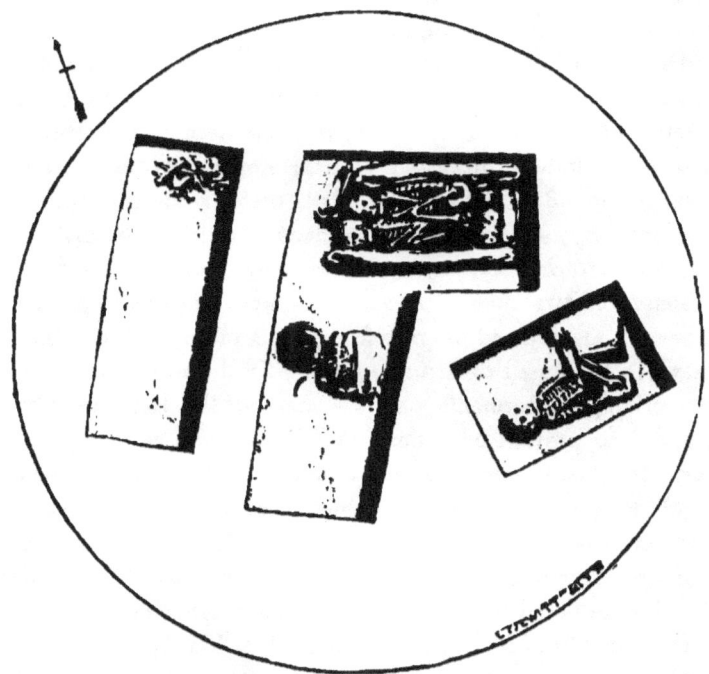

Plan of a Barrow near Monsal Dale.

ornamented, but so imperfectly baked as to have but little firmer consistency than the surrounding earth ; next, and immediately below it, were skeletons of two infants and an adult, so much huddled together as to render their respective position unascertainable ; close to these, we found a fine and sharp spear head of grey flint 2½ inches long, and two other implements of the same, one of them a small disk, near an inch in diameter : immediately under lay another adult human skeleton, which had clearly been deposited on its right side, with the head to the west, as were all the others found in this cist. This, the lowest interment, was evidently a male, the one next above presents female characteristics, and both, together with the children, presented unmistakeable evidence of having been interred at the same time, so that we have some reason to suppose that the family was immolated at the funeral of its head, as has been customary with savages in all ages and parts of the globe.

On the 3rd of June, another skeleton was found between the cist and the eastern verge of the mound, which lay in the contracted position on its left side, with the head to the south. It had been slightly protected by four stones, not very carefully arranged round it, and was quite destitute of accompaniment. On the same day, a large trench was made parallel to the first, without any interment of consequence being found. The decayed skeletons of two infants were noticed, and we casually picked up a barbed arrow-head of grey flint, and a piece of hard sandstone that had been used to triturate grain. In the accompanying plan the principal interments only are marked, the later ones being omitted to prevent confusion. While we were re-filling the excavation, Mrs. Bateman had the misfortune to drop in, unobserved, a gold ring set with an onyx cameo, representing a classical subject, an occurrence which may some day lead to the conclusion that the Romans buried in these ancient grave-hills. Many theories are based upon foundations equally fallacious.

On the 27th of June, we examined a low barrow, eighteen yards diameter, at the extreme point of the range of hills called Longstone Edge, in the direction of Wardlow. It was composed of earth and stone, heaped above a natural elevation, in the middle of which was a rock grave two feet deep, containing the remains of a full grown skeleton that had evidently been disturbed at no very remote period, and a small piece of urn.

In the afternoon, we opened another mound of the same size, situated about a quarter of a mile nearer Wardlow, chiefly composed of stone raised over a similar rock grave, which had likewise been spoiled of its contents. By emptying it we found many pieces of calcined human bone, a neat javelin-head of burnt flint, that had probably accompanied them, and another weapon point, made from a piece of animal bone rubbed smooth.

STAKOR HILL.

On the 2nd of July, we excavated the site of a barrow, most of which had been removed, on a hill near Buxton, not far from Stakor Hill. The mound had been so completely demolished, as to render it doubtful where it would be most proper to begin, and on digging in the most elevated part, we found the rock at the depth of a foot. This caused us to try in a place no higher than the level of the field, when immediately under the clods we perceived fragments of a human bone, and a little deeper a human skeleton, lying on its right side, with the knees contracted, and the head to the south. It had been deposited in a rude cist, walled round by a single course of large stones, and close to the left hip were two neatly sharpened darts of bone ; near the legs was a deposit of calcined human-bones, accompanied by a round-ended flint also burnt, and a little beyond them, and consequently further from the skeleton, were the unburnt remains of another individual, which had been slightly disturbed : two instruments of flint, and the lower mandible of a hawk, were found between the two, supplying the third instance in which we have observed the remains of this bird in tumuli. These interments removed, we arrived at the edge of an irregular grave, cut about a yard deep in rock, but rather lower at the south end, filled with clayey earth and small stones, amongst which we first found some bones of a child. Lower down was a female skeleton lying on the right side, with the head close to the south-east end of the grave, and the knees drawn up to accommodate the body to the limits of the excavation, which measured 3 feet by 2. Between the head and the knees was a broken drinking-cup of ruder workmanship than usual, lying on its side, with the mouth towards the latter ; and a neat javelin-head of flint was found in throwing the earth out of the grave, so that its position was not ascertained. Both mastoid bones were dyed green, from contact with two small pieces of thin bronze, bent in the middle, just sufficiently to clasp the edge or lobe of the ear. There were many rats' bones in the grave. This is probably the oldest interment we have found in which metal has been present—the very small quantity possessed, its application to the purpose of adornment, viewed in connection with the fact of the later interments above being accompanied by weapons of bone and flint only, bear out this opinion.

On the morning of the 4th of July, we examined an artificial mound composed of sandstone, on the top of the hill behind Ladmanlow Wharf, near Buxton, and found it to cover a small excavation in the gritstone rock, which contained no interment, although bits of flint had been observed from the first.

In the afternoon, we made four trenches in another barrow, situated on a neighbouring eminence, called Anthony Hill. It measures about fourteen yards across, and is not more than a foot in height, having been removed to within a few inches of the natural soil. Many fragments of human bone, and a boar's tusk, were found just under the turf, but no depression in the natural level being observed, it became evident that all the interments were destroyed from not having been buried deeper.

On the 4th of September, we opened a barrow on the summit of a very steep hill, called Hollings, overlooking the almost unapproachable village of Hollings Clough. The barrow, which appeared to have been previously excavated, was about twelve yards diameter and four feet high, with a concave centre like a basin. By cutting out a large hole, we found that it covered a grave cut in loose sandstone rock to the depth of two feet, in addition to the height of the mound; the grave measured about eight feet long by seven wide, and contained numerous pieces of calcined human bone, which had apparently been burnt at the south-east corner, where the sides were quite red from the effect of the fire. A piece of slate pencil, and an old-fashioned button, were found near the surface, which proved that the mound had been so far disturbed, and the scattered way in which the burnt bones were disposed amongst the stones filling the grave, led us to think that the whole had been plundered.

On the 12th of September, we examined a small mound near Pilsbury, composed of earth and stones, but found only a few pieces of burnt bone and the tooth of an animal.

MINNINGLOW.

We spent the 13th of September in excavating at the large chambered barrow at Minninglow, where we cleared out a very large and perfect megalithic chamber, on the south side, which had previously escaped a close examination at our hands, though it had evidently been explored before; as we found only one or two pieces of ancient human bone, and many animal bones of recent date. The plan shews the arrangement of the stones forming the chamber, with the interior dimensions, excepting the height, which is rather more than five feet; the largest capstone is about seven feet square.

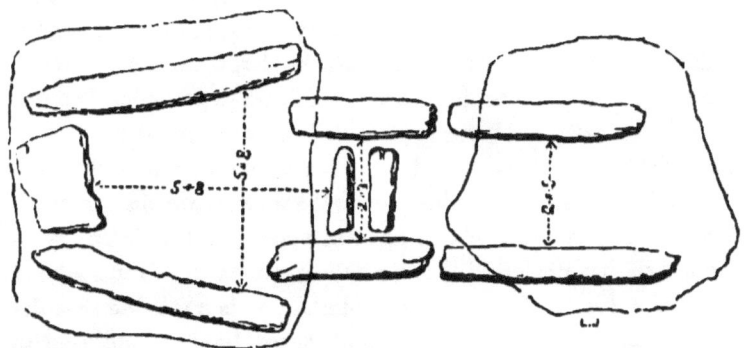

Plan of Cists at Minninglow.

There are several imperfect cists in the same barrow, and one of similar structure to the present, in the centre, which yet remains perfect, and is covered in by a capstone. At the west side of the mound we found two small brass coins of Constantine, jun., with the common reverse of two soldiers with standards—legend, GLORIA EXERCITVS,—which lay just below the turf, and numerous pieces of Romano-British pottery, which may be accounted for by the following extract from the MS. Diary of White Watson, F.L.S., of Bakewell, the friend and associate of many scientific men and antiquaries of the last century. Under a drawing of two urns similar to Roman ollæ in shape:—" 1784, April

20th. Drawing of the fragments of two urns, found in a barrow at Minninglow, by Mr. C. Taylor, Stanton."

> "Time was, these ashes lived;
> A time must be,
> When others thus may stand
> And look on thee."

MIDDLETON.

On the 24th of October, we opened a large trench in the barrow at Larkslow, near Middleton by Youlgrave, which was first examined by Mr. William Bateman, in 1825, when amongst other things were found a cinerary urn, containing burnt bones, and an "incense cup." It appeared by our excavation, that the centre of the barrow had been surrounded by large masses of chert, within which circle the interment had been deposited. We discovered the calcined bones which had been emptied out of the urn at the former opening, and a few pieces of an unburnt skeleton. From a very careful examination of the former, we find them to consist of the remains of a full-grown person, and an infant, with whom had been calcined a few small instruments of flint, a bone pin, and a tooth of some large animal. It is probable that the critical examination of all deposits of burnt bones would lead to much curious information respecting the statistics of suttee, and infanticide, both which abominations we are unwillingly compelled, by accumulated evidence to believe were practised in Pagan Britain.

On the 10th of November, we thoroughly re-opened the barrow near the railway stonepit, at Minninglow, first examined in 1843, but were not very successful, finding only a good sharpening stone, and the bones of some small quadrupeds, which were not laid much under the surface. The barrow was mostly formed of large stones placed on the surface of the land, and covered with an accumulation of small stones and earth, so as to produce a rounded outline.

BARROWS OPENED IN DERBYSHIRE BY THOMAS BATEMAN IN 1852.

STANTON.

On the 10th of April, 1852, in company with Mr. Carrington, and Mr. Glover, the Historian of the County of Derby, I walked over a considerable part of Stanton Moor, in order to survey the scene of former discoveries, and to examine the existing remains of Tumuli, Rocking Stones, &c., upon this interesting tract of land. On passing over the brow of the hill, near the Andle Stone, we noticed a small circle of six stones, four of which retained their upright position, whilst two were prostrate, the diameter being about twenty feet; in the interior were a few small pieces of pottery, and some calcined bones that had been scratched up by rabbits, the sight of which caused us to set to work with our pocket-knives, when finding the remains to become more plentiful, we borrowed a hack and spade from the adjoining farm, and cleared a considerable space in the centre of the enclosure, where a grave had been dug for the reception of three or four cinerary urns, and as many "incense cups;" all which had been emptied of their calcined contents, and broken by former diggers, who, however, left the fragments. These having since been joined, as far as possible, afford a tolerable idea of the original shape and ornamentation of the vessels, about which there is a little peculiarity, the outline of the large urns being more straight sided than common in this part of England; they approach the form of a common red garden flower-pot, and are sparingly decorated with the everlasting chevron. Most of the urns of this type hitherto discovered, have been exhumed in the South-West of England, the Deverell Barrow having afforded several specimens.

WAGGON LOW.

On the 25th of June, we proceeded to the top of a hill near High Needham, called Waggon Low, where we found some indications of an artificial mound, the dimensions of which could not be ascertained, on account of the numerous rocky protuberances around it. By excavation, we found that several interments had been placed between the masses of rock, which had originally been covered by the mound. The first discovered lay on its left side upon the rock, at the South side of the barrow, at the depth of about eighteen inches from the surface, with the knees drawn up, and the head towards the S.W.; immediately in front of this skeleton were two iron knives, respectively $5\frac{1}{4}$ and and $8\frac{1}{2}$ inches long, lying in contact with each other; there were also several tips broken from the tines of stags horns, some other imperfect animal bones, and part of a quern, which had been used as a sharpening stone, in the vicinity of the skeleton, which was that of an aged person, one of whose legs had been fractured, and reunited immediately above the ankle. Pursuing the excavation towards the north, the rock was found to have been cut out to the further depth of 18 inches, so as to form a large irregularly shaped grave; at the end nearest the first discovered skeleton, there was a large stone, under which was a deposit of calcined bones, accompanied by a small arrow-point of flint, and a rude instrument of bone, and in an angle of the rock close by, was a small vase of coarse clay, slightly ornamented, $4\frac{1}{2}$ inches high. Next to this deposit were the bones of a full-grown person and an infant, both much decayed, but we considered the former to have been laid with the head to the east, they were destitute of relics, and were very imperfect, though they did not appear to have been disturbed. Immediately in contact with them, we observed the feet of another skeleton, which being carefully uncovered, was seen to lie on its right side, with the legs gathered up, and the skull to the north; at the right shoulder were three instruments of light-coloured flint and a small bronze awl, $1\frac{1}{2}$ inch long, tapering each way from the middle, which is square—also the leg bone of a dog. The skeleton is that of a young person slightly above the middle height, the jaws containing the full number of teeth, which are but little worn; it is in beautiful preservation, and having been articulated, is preserved in a glass case at Lomberdale. Two flat stones were set up on edge behind it in the barrow, and it was imbedded in earth, to which it owed its preservation. During the progress of these researches, we observed the ground at the west side of the trench to have been disturbed yet lower, but were unable to follow up the indication, from the approach of evening; therefore, on the 28th of June, we again visited the spot, and after removing stone to the depth of 4 feet 6 inches, found that the grave assumed the shape of the letter L, the lower limb representing the western portion, now under examination, where we discovered the skeleton of a good sized man of middle age, lying on his left side with the knees drawn up, and the head towards the west, embedded in tenacious clay, above which was a thick layer of charcoal. The whole grave was carefully cleared out to its extremest limits without further result, except the discovery of numerous rats' bones, and of occasional portions of those of larger quadrupeds, such as horses' and swine's teeth.

BARROWS OPENED BY THOMAS BATEMAN IN 1853.

On the 10th of April, we examined a mound situated in a small waterless valley near the farm-house at Bank Top, near Hartington, but found that although it had evidently been cast up as a barrow, its contents had been removed at a former period, as we discovered traces of recent excavation in the presence of pieces of earthenware, such as was used in the last century, dispersed throughout the centre. The tumulus was composed of earth and stones, heaped up on the surface of the land to the height of three feet at least. We observed numerous pieces of animal bone, part of a stag's horn, and a few pieces of Romano-British pottery about the natural surface; one of the latter is the circular bottom of a vessel about three inches diameter, which appears to have had the broken edge rubbed down previous to its being buried.

BARROWS.

HOB HURST'S HOUSE.

View of Hob Hurst's House.

On the 3rd of June, we went to a conspicuous mound on the heathery, uninclosed, and most elevated part of Baslow Moor, called Hob Hurst's House, and found it to be a circular tumulus, composed of sand and gritstones, about eleven yards diameter, and four feet high; though, from its being surrounded by an embankment, inside of which the earth had been cut in the form of a ditch, the height appeared fully six feet, and it was only by digging down to the natural surface, that we were able to ascertain the actual elevation. The diameter at the outside of the embankment was 22 yards, it was formed, like the mound, of stones and sand, and was fourteen feet thick at the base and about four feet high. A trench cut from the south side of the central mound, disclosed some large upright slabs of gritstone, set on the natural level, which we at once perceived to be part of a cist or sepulchral chamber, which was soon cleared out and sketched.

It was rectangular, measuring from north to south ten feet three inches, and nine feet from east to west, and was chiefly constructed of slabs of stone each nearly a yard broad. There were traces of fire throughout the whole enclosure, the undisturbed sand having been burnt to a dirty white, or cream colour, and covered with a layer of charcoal, which was thickest towards the east side, where in the corner formed by the junction of the south boundary of the chamber, we discovered the original deposit, consisting of calcined human bones, lying in the very spot where they had been drawn together while the embers of the funeral pyre were glowing. They were in a small heap along

Cist in Hob Hurst's House.

with some thick pieces of charcoal and two lumps of burnt lead ore; and were separated or marked off from the floor of the chamber by a semicircular row of small sandstone boulders, all of which exhibited marks of fire. A few more burnt bones were found embedded in the sand near the north end of the cist, but no instrument or pottery of any kind was seen, although one of the pieces of charred wood exhibits a cleanly cut oblique surface, which must have been effected by a sharp instrument. In the popular name given to the barrow, we have an indirect testimony to its great antiquity, as Hobhurst's House signifies the abode of an unearthly or supernatural being, accustomed to haunt woods and other solitary places, respecting whom many traditions yet linger in remote villages. Such an idea could only arise in a superstitious age long ago, yet sufficiently modern to have effaced all traditionary recollection of the original intention of the mound; it likewise affords a curious instance of the inherent tendency of the mind to assign a reason for everything uncommon or unaccountable, which no extent of ignorance or apathy seems able totally to eradicate.

Many of the remaining pre-historic monuments of our land are similarly connected with names well know in popular mythology, now so rapidly vanishing, that it is probable the legends will be forgotten, while the names alone will be perpetuated as long as the structures with which they are identified exist. We may here observe, that the practice of separating the deposits within the cist by pebbles, as in this barrow, is most unusual in the Midland Counties, but is described as prevalent in the Channel Islands, by Mr. Lukis, in the Journal of the British Archæological Institute, Vol. I., page 142.

On the 22nd of September, we opened a barrow near King Sterndale, called High Low, which being situated in a rough plantation, was incapable of measurement; it did not appear, however, to have been very large even at first, and had evidently been reduced in size since. We excavated a good deal of the centre, which we found about three feet higher than the natural surface, upon which was a considerable quantity of charcoal, but found that the whole had been turned over and plundered, so that nothing but fragments were seen. From them it was clear that two interments had taken place in the mound, the traces of the most ancient being manifest in part of a large coarse urn, a calcined flint, and probably the charcoal; those of the more recent were the bones of an adult skeleton, which had been accompanied by a drinking-cup, and many broken bones of animals, including stags' horns, some of the latter having been tooled or sawed. Bones of the water rat were plentifully distributed amongst the stones in the more open part of the tumulus.

Another mound, in a field close by, had been so thoroughly destroyed that we did not think it worth the trouble of examination.

BARROWS OPENED BY THOMAS BATEMAN IN 1854.

MONSAL DALE.

In April or May, 1854, some persons engaged in getting calcareous tufa, for ornamental purposes, a little way above the foot bridge in Monsal Dale, found a human skeleton in a natural cavity in that stone, about six feet below the surface. This accidental discovery being noticed in the local newspapers, led me to visit the place on the 1st of June, and the following is the result of observations then made :—

The bottom of the valley of the Wye, in that part of Monsal Dale, like many others in Derbyshire, presents in some places large masses of calcareous deposition or tufa, many feet in thickness, which have been formed by springs strongly impregnated with earthy matter supplying streams running through the vallies at a much higher level than at present. The summit of the tufa formation, where the skeleton was found, is about fifteen feet above the surface of the stream in its ordinary state, and between the base of the tufa bank and the present watercourse, a level plain or terrain, eight or ten yards wide, intervenes. In order to quarry the tufa with the least trouble, the men made an excavation in the face of the bank towards the river, at the height of about ten feet above the latter, and after removing a considerable quantity of tufa, arrived at a cavity naturally formed in it, partly filled with earth, and having its roof adorned with stalactites; within was the skeleton of a young person, near which lay some rough pieces of limestone or chert, and a circular instrument of light-grey flint. At our visit the place was carefully cleared out, and some of the bones not having been previously disturbed, it became evident that the body had been deposited in a sitting position. A variety of animal bones occurred amongst the earth that was thrown out, the most remarkable being the lower jaw of a cat, and the same of a fish, probably the trout. The tufa being perfectly solid for five feet above the cavity, it is evident that the interment must have been deposited by means of an opening from the face of the bank, which was unobserved until the bones appeared. They were at least twelve feet from the outside, where the labourers first broke ground.

BOLE HILL.

On the 29th of September, we examined the remains of a large tumulus at Bole Hill, on Bakewell Moor, near that investigated on the 24th of August, 1843. (Vestiges, page 47.) By measurement with a tape, the diameter was ascertained to be exactly 23 yards; about eighteen inches only in height remained, the upper part having been removed at the time of the enclosure of the common for the sake of the stone. The remainder consisted entirely of small gravelly stone, the upper moiety having been much disturbed, together with all the later interments that had been deposited above the natural surface; of these we observed the remnants of at least two, some in their natural state, others calcined. We also found a few articles of different dates, the most modern being a small piece of kiln-baked pottery, of coarse texture, and red colour, and a circular stud of green glass, which may possibly have graced the centre of a fibula, as a fictitious gem; a more ancient object was the point of a very slender bronze dagger, much attenuated by frequent sharpening; it was in two pieces, which lay some distance apart: there were many bones and teeth of animals amongst the gravel, and when we arrived at a depth that left only six or eight inches of artificial ground above the natural level, we observed innumerable rats' bones, and in the gravel just below, near the centre of the barrow, we discovered the primary interment in a state of advanced decay; it was the skeleton of a man lying on his left side, with the knees drawn up and the head to the north-east; beneath the head was a very rude instrument of grey flint, nearly round, which was the only article of man's device found near him. From the unmanageable nature of the clayey soil on which the skeleton lay, and the friable condition of the bones, no measurement of the long bones could be taken, but fortunately so many pieces of the skull were recovered as to allow of its restoration. To us it appears a remarkable example, and may be described as having the calvarium long, narrow, and conveying the idea of lateral pressure; the forehead retreating, with the frontal sinuses prominent, the facial bones large, and the upper maxillaries, together with the lower jaw, strong and wide.

BARROWS OPENED BY THOMAS BATEMAN IN 1855.

FOREMARK.

On the 22nd of May, we examined a few of the very numerous tumuli situated in a plantation called "The Ferns," near Foremark Hall. The locality is a continuation of the eminence called Knoll Hill, and were it not covered by trees, would command an extensive view of the fertile vale of the Trent. The mounds, more than fifty in number, are placed without regularity, but are very uniform in appearance; their size varies from seven to ten yards across, and their average height is from two to three feet. The opening of five of them in places least encumbered with timber, afforded, it is presumed, a complete insight into the manner of interment practised throughout the whole. We found in every instance, that the mound had been raised over calcined human bones, which lay in the same place on the natural surface as they occupied when the funeral pile was smothered out by the casting up of the tumulus. The bones and black ashes of the pyre, reduced by compression to a layer about an inch thick, generally covered a space about four or five feet diameter in the centre; above were accumulated stones bearing marks of fire, which had been first thrown on the glowing embers, and over these earth was heaped to form the bowl-shaped mound. The only indication of man's workmanship brought to light by these researches, were two very small fragments of iron, found with two separate interments, one only having the definite form of a very slender pin, 1¾ inches long.

The origin of this tumular cemetery is enveloped in obscurity, and I fear to express an opinion upon a subject so uncertain, where opinion can be but mere conjecture; the absence of pottery and weapons affording no clue to the age or people to which the sepulchres should be attributed. Yet, taking it for granted that all the mounds would, if opened, reveal the same mode of burial, it would be natural to suppose that no great variation of date, if any, existed as to their age. Inferring further, from the lack of remains of a primitive character, and the presence of the iron fragments in two out of the five mounds opened, I should hesitate in assigning to them a high antiquity; and would rather seek to connect them with the eventful period in which tradition affirms the place to have been the scene of a sanguinary conflict between the Saxons and their Danish enemies, of whose successful forays in the Vale of Trent we have evidence in the name of the adjacent village of Ingleby, as well as in that of the still nearer domain of Foremark.

On the 23d of May, the two circular mounds within the curious embankments in a field called the "Buries," near the Saxon town of Repton, were excavated with a view to ascertain their real character, and that of the earthworks with which they are connected. As an ample description of the place, accompanied by measurements and a ground plan, may be seen at page 259, of Dr. Bigsby's elaborate History of Repton, 4to., 1855, it will be sufficient to place on record, that the present investigation left the question of the intention of the mounds wrapped in as much mystery as ever, with the sole exception of our ascertaining that they covered no sepulchral remains.

The largest was composed of extremely compact earth, which appeared to have been tempered with water when it was cast up, the natural pebbly gravel, mixed with clear sand, was found at the depth of about six feet below the summit of the tumulus. One or two small pieces of coarse kiln-baked pottery, similar to that often met with amongst Romano-British remains, which had evidently been accidentally mixed up with the earth, occurred in the progress of the excavation.

The smaller mound presented results exactly similar as to structure; the only article found was a large iron nail, apparently modern, which lay about a foot from the surface.

RINGHAM LOW.

On the 7th of June, we went to the large chambered tumulus near Monyash, called Ringham Low, some of the cists in which

94 BARROWS.

had been examined in 1847 (Vestiges, p. 103,) for the purpose of investigating a cist that had been accidentally discovered. It was rather north of the centre of the mound, with the ends east and

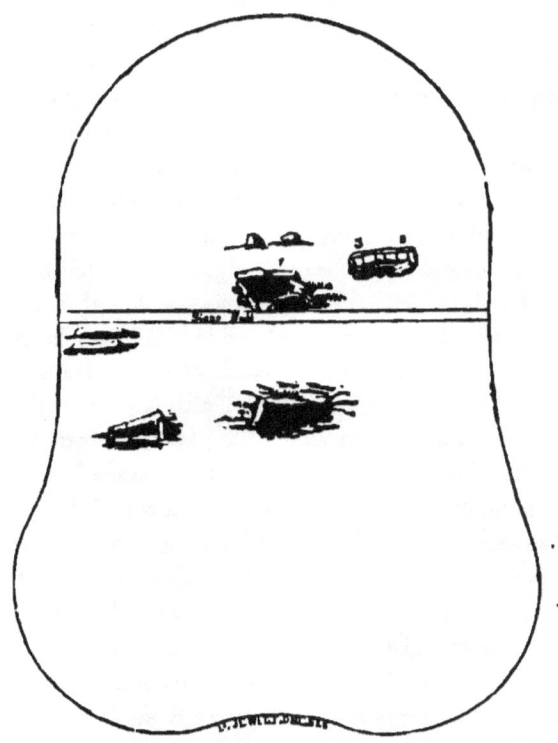

Plan of Ringham Low.

west (No. 1 of the Plan,) and was rhomboidal in shape, measuring eight feet six inches in length, by four feet in width, the sides were mostly formed by four very large stones, one of which was upwards of nine feet long ; the bottom was paved with five slabs of limestone pretty well fitted to each other, the average depth was about eighteen inches. It was filled with limestone gravel, and small stones, covering a large quantity of human remains, most of which were in the utmost disorder, though near the bottom they had been less disturbed, and perhaps, in one or two cases, retained their original position. These have since been ascertained to include the remains of twelve individuals, comprising two infants and ten adults, mostly exhibiting the lengthened form of skull I have before observed to be constantly found in tumuli of the same description as the present.

The lower part of the gravel, and the interstices between the paving-stones, abounded with rats' bones; and on removing part of the floor we found that many human bones had been drawn beneath it by these restless creatures. In clearing out these joints we found three very beautiful leaf-shaped arrow points of white flint, one of which, considering the material, is of wonderful execution; it measures 2¼ inches in length, is an inch broad in the middle, and weighs less than 48 grains, although it is not made from a thin flake, but is elaborately clipped all over both surfaces. We observed fragments of the skulls of oxen, teeth of horses, dogs, &c., but no trace of pottery, although a little charcoal was mixed with the clay on which the pavement rested.

On the 9th of June, we made several cuttings in the northern half of the mound, one only affording traces of interment. A little to the east of the cist examined on the 7th of June, we met with another enclosure constructed in like manner, with three large stones, one end being absent. (No. 2 on the Plan.) It contained the imperfect skeletons of four persons, and the only instrument found was part of a bone pin. This cist having the same orientation as the former, was connected with another similar enclosure extending from its western end, which, owing to the wetness of the day, was not then opened. The dimensions of No. 2 are :—

	ft.	in.
Presumed length, one end being absent	5	0
Width at east end	2	8
Ditto west end.....	4	0
Average depth	2	0

like the cist of the 7th of June, it was paved with limestone slabs.

On the 21st of June, we cleared out the other cist in connection with the last. (No. 3 on the Plan. Like the others, it had been previously disturbed, and the paved floor had been removed; we found in it the remains of two full-grown skeletons, which had been much broken up, and two very beautiful leaf-shaped arrow heads of white flint, that had escaped the observation of the former diggers. The measurements of this chamber were—

	ft.	in.
Length	8	4
Average width	3	0
Depth	3	6

On the same day we examined a low mound a short distance east from Ringham Low, in the direction of Ricklow Dale, measuring about 14 yards across. It was so much destroyed as to yield no remains, except two pieces of an extremely thick human skull, and the usual rats' bones; in fact, the whole mound had been removed to within a few inches of the natural surface, on which lay some flat stones.

On the 5th of July, we opened another cist on the south side of the wall, which will be seen from the plan to cross the mound at Ringham Low. This (No. 4 on the Plan) when emptied, exhibited a fine and perfect specimen of primeval architecture, measuring in

	ft.	in.
Length	9	0
Width at east end	5	6
Ditto at west end	2	6
Depth	4	0

Six stones only were used in its structure, no pavement having been laid down. We left it in the same perfect state as we found it, having discovered only a few human bones, and a roughly chipped block of hard stone, which were embedded without order in a layer of stiff clay, immediately above the natural rock on which the chamber was based; and a little charcoal at a higher level near the west end.

All the enclosures have been made by large slabs of limestone from the immediate vicinity, set on edge in narrow channels cut in the natural soil to the required shape of the chamber, and then secured in their respective positions by small stones firmly wedged between their sides and the solid earth. The tumulus in which they are distributed is composed of a vast accumulation of stones of all sizes, and is of irregular shape, as will be seen from the plan; its size may be stated as about 50 yards by 30, and its average height 4 feet.

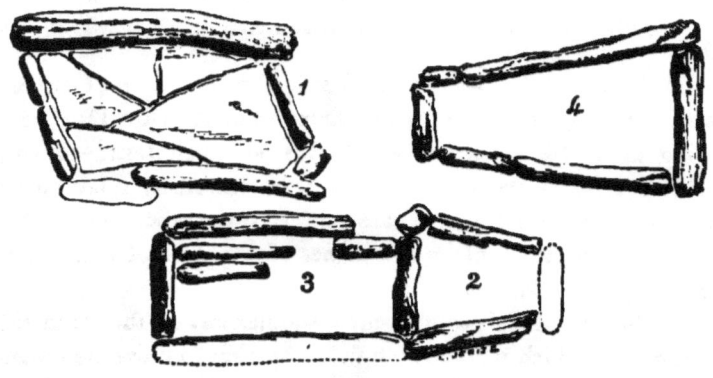

Cists in Ringham Low.

BARROWS OPENED BY THOMAS BATEMAN IN 1856.

ELDON HILL.

On the 9th of July, after a very long and cold drive through a mountainous country, we opened two barrows on Eldon Hill, about a mile from the village of Peak Forest, the mountain, in the side of which is the famous chasm called Eldon Hole, formerly considered unfathomable, celebrated in Latin verse by Hobbes, and in English by Charles Cotton.

The first mound, placed east of the highest point of the hill, measures not more than 5 yards in diameter, by about 2 feet in height, and is composed of small stones and earth. It yielded rats' bones, the root of a stag's horn, and the lower jaw of a small dog or fox, but produced no human remains, very probably from having been reduced in size.

The other tumulus on the highest point of the mountain, measures 16 yards across, by about 4 feet in height, and is composed of large stones and earth. We found that the centre had been previously disturbed; nevertheless we there met with an immense quantity of rats' bones, a few portions of the skeleton of a child, a few bones from the extremities of a full grown person, and a rhomboidal article of bone, 2¼ inches long, with a hole through the middle, most likely intended to attach it to the dress as a button or fastening of some kind. In the undisturbed part, immediately south of the centre, were eight tines or points from the antlers of stags, some showing marks of tooling, also where they had been partially sawn through before they were broken off; accompanied by the lower jaw and bones of a cow, and other splintered animal bones, all lying about 18 inches from the top. Further south was a scattered deposit of calcined human bones, accompanied by the unburnt skeleton of an infant, a fine spear head of flint much burnt, 2 inches long, and a small vase of the usual imperfectly baked clay, 4¾ inches high, very nicely ornamented, but partly disintegrated. The interments lay about 18 inches above the natural surface, among some large stones which were not arranged so as to guard the deposits, indeed the latter appeared to have been carelessly interred at a period subsequent to the formation of the tumulus.

WINSTER.

On the 13th of October, in consequence of information kindly communicated by Miss Worsley, I went to Winster, a small town about six miles from Bakewell, to see an interment that had been accidentally discovered by removing a bank of earth in the garden of that lady. There was no external indication of such a deposit having been made, and if any mound had existed it would probably be levelled when the garden was laid out. The bones had been disturbed by the labourers previous to my visit, but it was observed that the body had been placed on the natural surface in a contracted posture, with the head to the north-east; by examining the contents of the grave, it appeared that the deceased had been accompanied by an iron spear head and the lower stone of a quern or hand-mill, the former was broken by the finders. The body was covered with large stones of the same sorts as may be met with in the neighbourhood, yet evidently collected from different places, there being grey waterworn limestones from the surface of the land and other black limestones of a shaly texture that had clearly been quarried. The earth whereon the skeleton lay, exhibited traces of a large fire, and among the ashes were a few particles of calcined bone, together with the remains of wood; many of the stones, including the quern, had also been in the fire. The height of the earth above them was near 5 feet, and it appeared to be quite free from any other stones. I observed the lower jaw of an ox lying about, which was found during the progress of the work, but could not learn that it was connected with the interment, though from discoveries of former years, I am induced to think that it would be. A second interment of similar character was discovered on the following day, about 3 yards further in the bank of earth; the mode of sepulture was in every way identical with the former, and the bones having been, by the judicious kindness of Miss Worsley, preserved untouched for my inspection, I was enabled by removing them myself to make the following observations as to the manner of burial:—A large wood fire was made upon the natural surface, in which the stones used for covering the body, and part at least of the weapons of the deceased, were first burnt, as is abundantly clear from their present condition; after the fire was exhausted, the body was laid on the spot where it had been kindled, upon its right side with the knees drawn up, and the head pointing to the north-east; at the head was placed a small vessel of very coarse and unornamented pottery, much decayed when found; and at the back of the skeleton were laid a very large iron spear head of coarse workmanship, of the unusual length of 2 feet, found with the point towards the feet of the skeleton; a small curved instrument of iron, 5 inches long, originally inserted in a wooden handle, the bone ferule of which still remains; and a bead-formed ring of stoneware or porcelain, 1½ inch diameter, slightly ornamented with two incised lines round the outer edge, and two recessed places, which, but for its brittleness, might have received a pin to constitute it a fibula. After the completion of these arrangements, the stones having been burnt, were carefully placed over the corpse, and earth was finally heaped over the whole to the height of between 4 and 5 feet. It is very remarkable, that amongst the stones around this interment, was found the upper half of the same hand-mill, the lower stone of which was buried with the first skeleton; it is a very neatly wrought example of the bee-hive shaped quern, having both a funnel shaped hopper for the reception of the grain, and a hole at the side for the handle; it is made from the millstone grit of the neighbourhood, obtained probably from Harthill Moor, not more than two miles distant, a locality where numerous pieces of similar querns have been from time to time turned up by cultivating the land. From the great heat to which it had been exposed it was split into several pieces. The human bones were much decayed in consequence, I think, of the corpse having been interred whilst the grave and the surrounding stones were hot; perhaps, however, some more recondite cause must be sought to account for their nearer approximation to their original dust, than those of the other skeleton, which were undoubtedly of contemporary date.

As far as I can judge, both skeletons were of men of ordinary stature, and it is singular that interments of this late period should have been deposited in the ancient contracted position.

I noticed in the last grave one or two bits of calcined bone, and the unburnt tooth of a sheep. The jaws and other bones of a dog, and some shapeless fragments of iron, were found in the earth a little above the interment, before my arrival; and I would observe that another specimen of the large and heavy spear, which consists of a wide socket terminating in a blade, the section of which is rectangular, found in the Thames near Kingston, is in the collection at Lomberdale, where the foregoing relics are also deposited, by the liberality of Miss Worsley, and her brother, Charles Worsley, Esq.

EXCAVATIONS BY THOMAS BATEMAN IN 1857.

ROWSLEY.

On the 8th of April, I went to Rowsley, to see an ancient burial ground, brought to light by the alterations required to convert an old farm-yard into a garden, the situation of which is in an angle of land at the confluence of the Wye and Derwent. The skeletons were found by digging trenches to bury stone from the old buildings, then being pulled down: they lay in tenacious earth, about 3 feet from the surface, with the heads to the northwest, extended at length on the back, with the arms straight by the sides as in modern burial, but without any trace either of wood or nails to indicate that they had been enclosed in coffins. I carefully examined a skeleton that was uncovered, in the presence of several gentlemen, and found its position to agree with that of those previously found, as described by the labourers.

There is a tradition in the neighbourhood that a chapel formerly stood on the spot, and that this was its graveyard; but I am unable to refer to any documentary or recorded confirmation of it, still it is most probably true; and the presence of a sandstone stoup or vessel for consecrated water, which had lain about the place from time immemorial, adds greatly to the credit of the tradition; this object (latterly used for feeding the cats), is something like a mortar, but of globular shape, 6 inches high by 8 diameter, ornamented by four projecting ribs, two of which are enlarged so as to form ears or handles; it may be of the Norman or early English period.

SMERRILL.

On the 3rd of June, we opened the first of three barrows upon Smerrill Moor, near Middleton-by-Youlgrave, situated on the edge of the hill forming one side of a rocky but waterless valley. It measured about 11 yards across by 3 feet in height, was composed of earth and stones, and exhibited signs of former disturbance in the external appearance of a large stone in the centre, that had been removed from the side of a cist, which we afterwards found to consist of two compartments. The first had been plundered, and its contents were re-interred in confusion: they comprised bones from no fewer than twelve skeletons, of ages varying from infancy to senility, intermixed with a few pieces of calcined bone, charred wood, rats' bones, potsherds, &c., including jaws of two foxes or dogs, and a good spear head of white flint.

The second compartment was made by three large limestones placed on edge, their upper part appearing above the surface of the mound. It contained the skeleton of a female of rather low stature, who had been placed on her left side with the knees drawn up, and the head towards the north-east; a plain flake and a knife of flint lay at the head, and the bones were embedded in earth that had acquired a dark colour, apparently from the decomposition of wood; particles of charcoal, rats' bones, and fragments of earthenware of two sorts, were also present. The skull is remarkably small, and elevated in its contour, the occipital bone being much flattened, possibly by artificial compression in youth; the teeth indicate an age not exceeding 18 or 20 years, and the long bones are slender in proportion to the length; the femur measures $16\frac{1}{2}$ inches.

On the 13th of June, we opened the second barrow on the contrary side of the ravine, a mound about 9 yards across and 2 feet high, surrounded by an irregular circle of large limestones, and showing the grey surfaces of many others that jutted through its grassy covering. We began our cutting on the west side, and continued it to the centre, where, after much labour, we uncovered a large grave of irregular shape, sunk in the rock to the depth of 5 feet; its average dimensions were 8 feet by 6; it was filled with stones, and had upon its stony floor, a coating of stiff clay in which was embedded the skeleton of a tall young man, who lay on his left side with his knees drawn up, and the head in an easterly direction; owing to the wetness of the clay, the bones

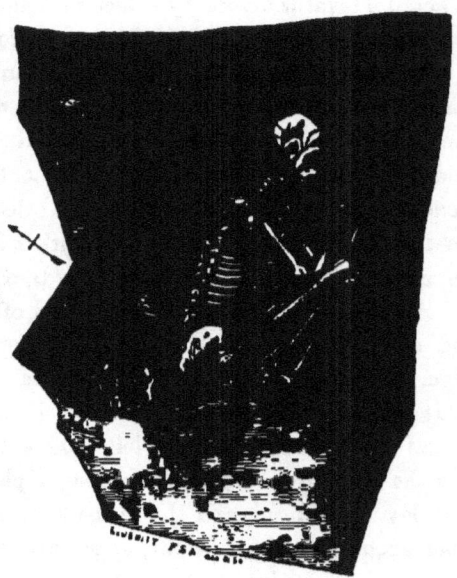

Rock Grave, Smerrill Moor.

were in an advanced state of decomposition, having become of the consistency of cheese; the skull was narrowed and otherwise posthumously distorted by the pressure of the overlying mass; and the femur measured $19\frac{1}{2}$ inches, the tibia 16. Behind the pelvis lay a very beautiful drinking cup, $8\frac{3}{4}$ inches high, the exterior entirely covered with ornament: it lay on its side upon an assemblage of implements, consisting of a bone netting rule or modelling tool, 12 inches long, made from the rib of a large animal (horse or cow), neatly rounded off at each end, and reduced to a regular breadth and thickness throughout; a dagger $4\frac{3}{4}$ inches long, a spear head 3 inches long, and four other instruments of flint, all whitened by the action of fire. The usual rats' bones were present in this undisturbed and interesting tumulus.

On the 15th of June, we opened the third of the tumuli on Smerrill Moor, which is situated rather lower down the course of the valley, on the same side as the last, and is about 10 yards diameter by 18 inches high. The centre afforded no deposit, but a little to the west of it we found a skeleton slightly guarded by two large stones, one at the head the other at the feet: it was not more than a foot beneath the turf, and owing to that circumstance, was not in good preservation; it lay on the left side with the knees drawn up, the hands near the face, and the head pointing south-east. The skull is rather globular, and is of dense texture, though thin; the femur measures $17\frac{1}{4}$ inches. No instruments were found in immediate contact with it; but we found some bones from a former interment, a small piece or two of white flint, and a sharpening stone, in the earth just above. The mound was composed of earth and stones in pretty equal proportion, plentifully mingled with rats' bones around the skeleton.

BARROWS OPENED BY THOMAS BATEMAN IN 1859.

BOLE HILL.

On the 25th of May, we opened two stone cists on the site of the ruined tumulus at Bole Hill, Bakewell Moor, where some remarkably elongated crania were found in 1843.

The first we examined did not appear to have been disturbed, although the skull therein discovered lay in one corner, apart from the skeleton to which it belonged. The body had been deposited in the usual contracted position upon its left side, and was surrounded by small stones, having above an artless covering of large flat slabs. The shortness and slenderness of the bones indicate the female sex, the femur being but $16\frac{1}{4}$, and the tibia 13, inches long. The skull is decidedly long in the fronto-occipital diameter, but from the fulness of the parietal prominences, this peculiarity is not so obvious at a first glance as in other crania from the same mound. The obliteration of the sutures, taken in connection with the general smoothness of the calvarium, and the abraded state of the teeth, show that the age at death would not be less than 50 years.

The second cist-vaen had been so thoroughly dug over at a former period, as to yield nothing more than detached bones of two or three skeletons, one of them that of a young person. No instruments or pottery were found in either enclosure. The cists consisted of rectangular compartments, made by placing massive blocks of limestone on edge upon the natural surface of the land, the unoccupied space between them being levelled up with stone collected in the neighbourhood.

CHELMORTON.

On the 9th of September, we opened a small grave mound near Chelmorton Thorn, Derbyshire, measuring about 9 yards across and 2 feet high. By cutting a trench through the middle we found it to consist of puddled and tempered earth mixed with a few limestones, the latter more plentiful about the centre; beneath these, and very slightly lower than the natural surface, on a very uneven floor of rock, lay a tall but slender skeleton, evidently of a young man of the Anglo-Saxon race, who had been carefully deposited at full length on his back, with the head due west; the arms lay along the sides, but the hands had been placed upon the lower part of the person, the phalanges of the fingers being found in the hollow of the pelvis, which had become flattened by pressure from the earth above. Close to the left side of the pelvis we found two short knives and a buckle of iron, all very much corroded by the destructive action of the puddled earth, which had also decayed the skeleton so much, that it was impossible to obtain accurate measurements of any of the long bones.

It is rather remarkable, that the place has the reputation of being haunted: on the occasion of our visit a person was pointed out who had actually been favoured with a sight of the apparition, which was manifested in the form of a man of unearthly stature, who walked before the seer for some distance, about the hour of four on a summer's morning.

In the afternoon of the same day, we went to a mutilated barrow, situated in a romantic spot close to the verge of some limestone rocks, overhanging a waterless valley near Chelmorton, called Deepdale, about a mile north-west of the village; but found that the whole remains had been turned over, most likely to extract the stone for building purposes. Of objects indicating its original intention, we observed traces in the presence of comminuted bone, rats' bones, and shreds of flint.

BARROWS OPENED BY THOMAS BATEMAN IN 1860.

HADDON FIELD.

On the 20th of August, after repeated disappointments from the unusual wetness of the summer, we opened a barrow on Haddon Field, near Bakewell; for access to which we were indebted to the kindness of the Rev. Frederick, and Lady Adeliza Norman, who also attended during the opening. The mound was of a regular convex form, about 16 yards diameter and not more than 4 feet high. A cutting through the centre passed downwards through about 12 inches of earth, succeeded by large limestones disposed without regularity or any apparent design, although their removal disclosed the only interment that was found: this, owing to a natural rise in the land about the middle of the barrow, was not more than 2 feet 6 inches from the surface. The skeleton lay on its left side in the usual contracted attitude, upon a thin bed of charred wood strewed on the natural level of the land a few inches only above the rock; the head pointed west south-west; the elbows were bent so as to allow the hands to be brought in front of the face; and near the lower part of the back was a small earthen drinking cup, 6½ inches high, very neatly ornamented with a vandyked pattern; close beneath which were three useful implements, an arrow head of flint that had acquired an opaque grey tint from partial calcination, a mesh rule for netting or else a potter's modelling tool, 6¼ inches long, rounded at the ends, cut from a horn of the red deer, and a very small brazen awl, which, when found, showed slight but distinct traces of its wooden handle. These objects would seem more appropriately to have accompanied a female than a male corpse, yet the size and general appearance of the bones indicate the latter as the sex of the deceased. The measurements of the long bones are—

	Inches.
Femur	18½
Tibia	14¼
Humerus	13

The skull (see No. 237 of the list) is that of a man of upwards of forty years of age; it is a characteristic example of the ancient British type, and being more fully described in the list, calls for no further remark in this place than to observe that it possesses a peculiar flattening of the hinder part, extending from the upper edge of the occipital bone to those of the parietals adjoining the lamdoidal suture, a feature by no means uncommon in crania from barrows of the same remote antiquity, and which may be attributed to some prevailing method of nursing during infancy.

One or two teeth of animals and the least possible trace of rats' bones, with one small bit of primitive earthenware, were found in the digging, but no indication of other interments could be seen, although much of the centre of the mound was cut away in the hope of making some further discovery.

CALVER LOW

Having been informed, on the 30th of August, that some skeletons had been discovered the day before, by men baring the rock preparatory to quarrying it, at the verge of the cliff overlooking the limekilns at Calver Low, I immediately went to the place and found that there had been five skeletons buried in a line side by side, a few feet apart, in graves sunk down to the rock which is there about two feet below the turf. The bodies were all extended at length with the heads to the west, so as not merely to admit of the corpses facing the east, as is the Christian custom of burial yet observed, but in this case also to face the village, and the pleasant valley extending towards Baslow—either motive may have prompted the arrangement, as there is reason to believe the interments to be of the Anglo-Saxon period, although it was suggested at the time, in one of the local papers, that they were remains of some who perished during the ravages of the plague at Eyam in 1666.

In returning to the narrative, it will be best to describe the several skeletons, numbering from the north, premising that the legs of all had been cut away, owing to their being so near the border of the cliff, which descends for a considerable distance almost perpendicularly, having long been quarried for lime burning.

1.—A young person with very slender bones, the femur $17\frac{1}{2}$ inches long, undisturbed with the exception of the skull, which had been broken and robbed of the teeth previous to our visit; a small bit of coarse red pottery was picked up amongst the earth near the bones.

2.—Removed before our arrival, but from the few bones preserved, it appears that the person was older than the first, although the femur measures $16\frac{1}{2}$ inches only—the skull thin, a good deal decayed and very imperfect.

3.—Removed—the skull very perfect when found, since despoiled of the whole of the facial bones. The calvarium and lower jaw have been recovered. The former presents, when viewed from above, an oval outline with a very full occipital protuberance; the latter is well formed, and the state of the teeth indicates an early adult age. Imperfection in the thigh bones prevents measurement, they do not however appear to have been very long. A small iron knife, of the common Saxon shape, lay upon the pelvis of this skeleton, and has imparted a ferruginous tinge to the bone from contact during oxidyzation. It is the only instrument found with any of the interments, and alone furnishes a clue to their date.

4.—With the exception of the legs, was quite undisturbed, as it lay beneath a wall on the extreme edge of the hill. By working on the other side of this fence, the skull was extracted in such a state as to be capable of restoration; it is oval, platycephalic, and like the other three—that of a young individual whose thigh bones, imperfect at each end, are large and much stronger than the appearance of the head would lead one to expect. The skull is very much distorted by pressure, also producing fracture, posthumously applied to the left side of the frontal bone, most likely from stone filling the grave, as no care had in any instance been taken to protect the bodies from the overlying weight.

5.—This, the most southern of the row, was entirely removed, most of the bones having been thrown down the precipice before attention was excited by a recurrence of the skeletons.

There are some indications of a tumulus in the field a few yards further back from the wall, which, if opened might disclose something to substantiate the inference drawn from the presence of the iron Knife with one of the skeletons, which, however, we think is alone sufficient to determine the Saxon origin of the cemetery.

SALTBY HEATH, LEICESTERSHIRE.

By the invitation of the Rev. F. Norman, the writer went, on the 21st of September, to assist at the opening of two large barrows, situated on what was formerly called Saltby Heath, now an enclosed and cultivated tract of breezy upland, a few miles from Belvoir Castle. Near them is a long earthwork, consisting of a wide ditch running parallel with a vallum formed of the earth excavated from it, called King Lud's Intrenchment, which with another similar work in the immediate vicinity, named Foulding Dyke, and the two barrows in question, are laid down in a plan, engraved on plate 53, of vol. i. of Nichols' Leicestershire, page 305.

The first opened mound is that nearest the intrenchment on the plan: since Nichols' time it had been planted, and after having been overshadowed by half-a-century's growth of larch, was again exposed to view by the timber being felled; it measures at least 25 yards across, and has an actual elevation of 5 feet, but, from earth having been collected for its formation from round the base, it seems much higher. Soon after removing the turf, we found pieces of a very large and thick urn of coarse Celtic pottery, burnt to a brown colour outside, and black within, and having a very simply ornamented border, the pattern consisting merely of diagonal lines, intersecting in opposite directions at wide intervals. Shortly after, we observed the disconnected bones of a human skeleton of full growth, those of a dog, and a few of other animals, all which had clearly been disturbed by planting, though nothing seemed to have been taken away from the spot. After digging through sandy earth, to the depth of 5 feet without further discovery, we arrived at the natural surface here, in the centre of the barrow, burnt and blackened by the action of a large fire, ample evidence of which still remained in masses of charred oak, the grain of the wood perfectly retaining its specific character. Just before touching this layer of charcoal, we found the tarsal bone of an ox, slightly tinged with red from contact with the burnt earth that had been thrown upon the hot embers. Although the area covered by the ashes was fully cleared, no portion of calcined bone or other indication of interment was found in this part of the mound, whence the conclusion, that the fire was kindled either to dress the funeral feast, or to bake the sepulchral vessel that accompanied the unburnt remains found at the summit; or else, as is equally probable, to serve both purposes. The hunter chief, who, with one of his dogs, was deposited high up in this considerable mound, was interred in accordance with a previously observed custom, not unusual in cases where large tumuli of earth have been raised in localities where stone is either scarce or not easily collected. Barrows of this class rarely repay the labour expended in opening them, and are most commonly found in comparatively low situations.

The other barrow was upwards of 30 yards in diameter, but the height was about the same as that of the former. We were not so fortunate as to discover any interment in it; nothing but a few slender animal bones occurring at intervals in the progress of digging through the dense mass of sandy earth, of which, with the exception of a very few stones near the summit, it was entirely composed. On reaching the natural surface, in the centre, 5 feet below the top of the mound, we found that it was baked quite hard, and had assumed a black tint, changing to red lower down, from the effect of intense heat, but presenting a variation from what was observed in the other mound in the absence of charcoal. Now as this is a substance that resists decay so long as to be almost indestructible, it becomes evident that all remains of the fire must have been carefully swept up and removed before the task of raising the mound began, most likely with a view to their being deposited along with the calcined bones they had prepared, in some part of the barrow not examined by us, owing to lack of time for more thorough excavation.

BARROWS OPENED IN STAFFORDSHIRE, BY MR. SAMUEL CARRINGTON IN 1848.

ECTON HILL.

On the 18th of May, we commenced by opening a barrow on a hill near the celebrated Ecton Mine, called Hanging Bank. The tumulus is about 20 yards diameter, 4 feet high, and concave in the centre like a bowl. In the middle was found a deposit of calcined human bones, with those of the water-rat in abundance, close to which lay part of the skeleton of an adult, the other part of which had been removed as recorded by Plot, in his History of Staffordshire, 1686 folio, page 330.—"In digging open a Lowe on Ecton Hill, near Warslow, in this county, there were found mens' bones, as I was told, of an extraordinary size, which were preserved for some time, by one Rev. Mr. Hamilton, Vicar of Alstonefield." The burnt bones had also been disturbed at the same time. Both interments lay on the natural surface, unprotected by any cist; the calcined bones were accompanied by a large bone pin, upwards of 5 inches long, two spear points, and two arrow heads of flint, all of which had passed through the fire. A piece of stag's horn was found in another part of the mound.

THROWLEY.

May 20th, opened a barrow about 30 yards diameter, on Arbor Hill, near Throwley Hall. Proceeding towards the middle from the south side, through very compact earth, to the depth of from three to four feet, in which were bits of charcoal and chippings of flint, we found the ground on the right hand side of the cutting, about the centre of the tumulus, to be more open and stony, and intermixed with rats' bones: following these indications, a cist was soon discovered, constructed of flat slabs of limestone, six of which placed edgeways in a rectangular form served for the basement, whilst above them the sides of the structure were continued by a neat wall, terminating with large flat stones which covered all in. On removing a portion of the wall, the contents, consisting of burnt human bones, amongst which was a flint arrow point, were found covered with fine earth which had penetrated in the course of ages. Adjoining the eastern end of this cist was erected a smaller one, composed of three flat and two rounded stones, so securely covered over that no earth had penetrated through the joints; this also contained burnt bones. The ground on the west side of the trench appearing loose also, we directed our attention that way, and found two more interments of a different character, namely:—two entire skeletons which lay in a contracted position very near to each other; one of them, a young person, had a slender arrow head of flint. A few more human bones and an iron spike about 3 inches long which had been inserted into wood, were found in another part of the tumulus.

May 23rd, opened another barrow situated a few hundred yards from the last, and measuring about 20 yards across, but found nothing of any importance; much vegetable earth having a dark appearance like ashes or charcoal, was intermixed with the soil in alternate layers; and one chipping of flint was found.

MARE HILL.

May 25th, we opened a barrow on the top of Mare Hill, near Throwley Hall, by sinking by the side of a mass of natural rock which approached the surface near the middle of the tumulus. About three feet down we discovered a grave, cut in the rock, covered, more especially about the sides, with charcoal: in it were two skeletons, near the shoulders of one was a spear point of calcined flint; in the earth, near the grave, were found a small piece of pottery and a piece of lead, having the appearance of wire, which subsequent researches prove to have been accidentally fused from metalliferous gravel present upon the spot where either a corpse was burnt or an urn baked, which was generally the site afterwards occupied by the tumulus.

Carrying the excavation to the further side of the before-named rock, we found that the artificial ground extended much deeper, and was mingled with fragments of human skeletons and rats' bones; and about four feet from the surface was a cist of flat stones placed on end, which contained three interments on different levels: the uppermost was the skeleton of a child, the next a deposit of burnt bones, among which were some animal teeth; the lowest was an entire skeleton. Immediately above the burnt bones was found a small bronze dagger about 3 inches long, perforated at the lower end with two holes, which did not present the usual rivets for attaching the handle, and which must therefore have been secured by ligatures. Outside this cist were found, pieces of human skull, sherds of pottery, flints, animal bones, and a piece of lead of conical shape.

At this point we continued the excavation at right angles, being induced to do so by observing another declination in the earth, which led to another deposit of calcined bones. Further on at the depth of about two feet from the surface, was the skeleton of a child, laid as usual on the left side, with the knees drawn up, in a state of decay, accompanied by a very neatly ornamented vase 5 inches high, which was placed by the side of a flat stone set on edge for its protection. Half a yard further we found another incinerated interment, the bones, amongst which were a good arrow head of flint and a perforated bone pin, having been placed within a small inverted urn much decayed, which lay in the midst of a heap of burnt earth and charcoal. Near the same place were a piece of fused lead and the skeleton of a child, without any relics.

WATERFALL LOW.

Waterfall Low, a large tumulus on an eminence overlooking the village of Waterfall, was opened on the 10th of June. It is a very conspicuous object, being 20 yards diameter and 9 feet high. We began by cutting across the centre through a mixture of earth and stone; at the north end of the trench was a thick stratum of red earth, which had evidently been burnt, under it the barrow was composed of loose stone, intermingled with pieces of human bone, stags' horns, rats' bones, and in some places with dark coloured earth containing charcoal. Near the middle, about eight feet from the surface, was a cavity three feet long and eighteen inches wide, cut in the rock to a further depth of between one and two feet; although this was plainly the grave, it contained only a few fragments of bone, having evidently been examined by barrow diggers of a former age. A large part of the centre of the barrow was turned over, with no more successful result than the finding of horses' teeth and chippings of flint.

DEEPDALE.

Round Low, near Deepdale, was partially investigated on the evenings of the 15th and 16th of June; one-half of the mound being under tillage, could not be explored. It is situated near one opened in 1846, and is of no great elevation, though about 30 yards across. In digging through the midst, we found a few scattered bones, some of which were calcined, a few instruments of flint, a piece of a fine urn, a few animal teeth, a piece of fused lead, and a number of pebbles and sandstone boulders not indigenous to the soil. The remaining half of the barrow has since been excavated without success.

June 17th, we opened another barrow at Deepdale, called Top Field Low, which had been previously much disturbed, so that we found nothing but some burnt bones, pieces of pottery, and flint flakes.

June 19th, we opened another barrow at Deepdale, in the immediate vicinity of the others. The field in which it is situated is called Burnet's Low, the prefix being derived from a late occupier of the land. The mound was 17 yards across, and having no great elevation it promised an easy task; but having dug to the depth of two feet, we arrived at the side of a very large grave, about six feet wide, cut at least three feet deep in the rock; it was filled with stones without any earth, except what had been washed in during the lapse of ages. We cleared it out for the distance of ten feet from the southern end, without meeting with the other extremity, which time would not allow of our doing. The sides were cut down perpendicularly, and were blackened by charcoal. On the west side within the grave, was a skeleton, deposited on the left side with the head to the south, and the knees drawn up; under the shoulders of which was a well preserved bronze dagger, with three rivets for the purpose of fastening the semilunar handle, which had imparted a green tint to the bones with which it had been in contact. The earth above was mixed with pebbles and bouldered pieces of sandstone, and in it we found an arrow point of flint.

MOUSE LOW.

June 21st, opened a barrow between Deepdale and the village of Grindon, called Mouse Low, fourteen yards diameter and not more than two feet high; the lower part composed of stiff clayey soil, plentifully interspersed with small pebbles; in the centre was a cist constructed of three large flat stones, the fourth side being left open; it was paved with very thin slabs of blue limestone, and contained the skeleton of a very large and strongly built man resting on his left side in the usual contracted posture, near whose head was a peculiarly elegant and well finished drinking cup, 8¼ inches high, inside of which were two implements cut from the ribs of a large animal (compare with those found with a similar interment at Green Low, in April, 1845, Vestiges page 69), a spear head, and two beautiful barbed arrows of white flint; outside the cup were two more arrows of the same kind. The skull is very large, and is remarkable from the presence of a frontal suture, although by no means that of a young man; the teeth are in fine preservation; and the skull is of the platy-cephalic variety, occasionally found amongst Celtic crania. In other parts of the mound numerous pieces of human bone, stag's horn, and a neat circular ended flint, were found. And as far as our trench extended, which would be about five yards, it exposed a row of large boulders of hard red grit, laid on the surface of the natural soil in a direction coincident with the longest side of the cist; the smaller limestones near these were almost turned to lime from the effect of heat, and were mixed with burnt bones and charcoal.

CASTERN.

On the 24th of June, a small barrow called Green Low, situated in the same field as the large barrow at Castern, opened in July, 1846; was opened by cutting three parallel trenches through it. In the middle cut were no perceptible traces of human remains, but several articles of different periods were found in it, as a small celt of green hone slate, a round ended flint, a piece of coarse pottery, and a very perfect harp shaped bronze fibula, of a type with good reason considered as Roman. These articles were to all appearance of casual occurrence, not having been deposited with any interment, or even in connection with each other. In another of the cuttings, near the edge of the mound, we found the skeleton of a child, with a flint arrow point. In the remaining trench, another juvenile skeleton, much decayed, was discovered. In the course of the day, pieces of stags' horns, animals' teeth, rats' bones, numerous pebbles, and some flints were found.

WETTON.

June 29th, a barrow was discovered at Bincliff, near Wetton, that had escaped previous observation from having been nearly levelled by agricultural operations, although it still retained its circular form and regular curvature. On examination, human remains, mixed with bones of the water rat, were found about a foot from the surface. The ground in the midst of the barrow appeared to have been dug out to the depth of four feet and filled in again, with the addition of stones and charcoal; but no interment was found.

WINKHILL.

July 1st, examined the site of a barrow, near Winkhill, called Martin's Low, which had been some time removed; where we found only a spear point of grey flint. We observed, as a rather remarkable circumstance, that, after making a hole to the depth of a foot, the earth appeared perfectly dry, notwithstanding the abundance of rain that had fallen; whilst, on sinking a little lower, the excavation suddenly filled with water, although the barrow is placed on the highest point of the land.

GRINDON.

July 3rd, excavated a barrow upon Grindon Moor, close to one much larger called Hurst Low. This one, though apparently of considerable elevation, promised an easy task, but, after cutting from the edge to the centre to the depth of six feet, through clay of various colours, intermixed with stones, until, in the middle of the tumulus, we came to a space filled with stones without any admixture whatever except charcoal, we gave up the search without finding more than half of the upper stone of a quern or hand-mill of grit. It is, however, possible that the interment may remain in some part of the barrow yet unexplored.

July 4th, spent another unsuccessful day at Grindon in opening another barrow, eighteen yards in diameter, by two trenches, each two feet deep, intersecting the centre. In all parts were scattered pieces of human bone, some calcined pieces of earthenware, and flints.

MUSDEN HILL.

July 5th, began upon the first barrow on Musden Low, near Calton, originally about twenty-seven yards diameter, but mutilated at one side. We made two excavations intersecting each other about the former centre of the mound, and reached the natural surface at the depth of about four feet from the summit, where lay a skeleton completely embedded in rats' bones. It is singular that this body, which had been buried in an entire state, had been partially blackened by the action of a fire kindled close by, for the purpose of burning another corpse, whose ashes were deposited near the same place; some of the rats' bones were charred in the same way, thus proving that a very long time had elapsed between the two interments, as the rats must have resorted for many generations to the place before any considerable quantity of their remains could have accumulated previous to their becoming blackened by the fire. Several pieces of fused lead had been gathered up with the deposit of burnt bones. Some pretty good instruments of calcined flint, and pieces of three urns, ranging apparently from the Celtic to the Romano-British period, were found in indeterminate positions.

CALTON MOOR.

July 13th, a tumulus on Calton Moor, called Thorncliff, about a mile from the village of Calton, was opened. It is a large bowl-shaped barrow, 26 yards diameter, considerably elevated in the middle. We commenced a section four feet wide through the centre, cutting first through a mixture of earth and small stones, in which lay a very slender skeleton, measuring 5 feet 6 inches in length, which had been deposited at full length on its right side, about four feet east of the centre of the barrow, and not more than a foot beneath the turf, probably an interment of much later date than the barrow itself; we next encountered a stratum of clay 4 feet thick, below which were loose stones, then small stones mixed with clay down to the natural surface, where we found a rock grave extending under the east side of the mound, which was cleared out to the depth of three feet without our arriving at the bottom. Being now four yards from the summit, at an advanced hour in the day, we attempted to reach the floor of the grave by undermining the stratum of clay forming an arch over the grave, but having undercut it to the extent of six feet, we very fortunately abandoned the work as unsafe shortly before it fell in, and terminated both the day's labour and the chance of discovering the original interment. Animal bones and pieces of flint were found below the clay. Although the arrangement of this volume is chronological, we may be allowed to deviate from it in this instance, for the sake of finishing the account of the contents of the grave; which were discovered on the 29th and 30th of August, when the direction of the grave being known, we sunk down upon it, and after working upwards of a day and a half, had the satisfaction of finding, at a depth of more than four yards from the surface, the primary deposit in this difficult barrow; namely, the remains of a large skeleton, accompanied by a neat instrument of flint and a bronze dagger, with three rivets of the usual form, but broken, perhaps by the pressure of some very large stones with which the grave was filled, and in consequence of which our labours were rendered much more arduous.

MUSDEN SECOND BARROW.

July 18th, investigated a second barrow on Musden Hill, about a hundred yards from that opened on the 10th inst.; we cut two transverse sections through the centre, where a few burnt bones were found. More to the east was a skeleton with the head to the outside of the barrow, near it was a lump of flint devoid of form; and above and around it were fragments of two globular narrow-necked urns, ornamented with a few projections upon the shoulders, which had contained burnt bones. These are of the kind attributed to some of the Saxon tribes, many examples having been found in various cemeteries in this country, as well as on the Elbe, by the late Mr. Kemble. Below the calcined bones that had filled these urns was a thin layer of gravel, which had been exposed to heat sufficient to melt the small particles of lead ore usually found in it. Many pieces of flint were picked up in this part of the barrow, and part of a medieval pitcher, with vertical streaks of green glaze, was observed. None of the interments had been protected by cists.

CASTERN VALLEY.

20th of July, opened a large tumulus in a narrow valley by the river Manifold, between Castern and Throwley, called Cow Close Lea. The mountainous scenery through which the river winds its serpentine course (whence the name) is most picturesque, the hills, on the Throwley side especially, rising to a great height. On account of the barrows in this district being for the most part on the tops of the hills, this one had been previously overlooked by us. The search was commenced by a section through the midst of the barrow, which, to the depth of four feet was composed of boulders from the bed of the river; next was a layer of clay and soil mixed with stone, a foot in thickness; below this was sand like the bed of the river, into which we dug for two feet without perceiving any mixture, as would probably have been the case had it been before disturbed : and as the remains of human bones, and those of the rat which we found, were confined to the level of the clay, we took advantage of the hole made by digging in the sand, to remove by undermining, a very large stone from the centre of the barrow, by the side of which were piled several smaller ones.

No trace of interment was observed near these stones, which lay within a foot of the surface. Confining the depth of the cutting to the level of the clay, we discovered at the side a skeleton and a few burnt bones; pursuing the same direction about five feet further, we found another skeleton, lying on its left side in a contracted posture, having with it burnt bones, a round-ended instrument and a pebble, both of flint. An arrow-head and some chippings of flints were found in other parts of the mound, and the earth on being turned over, emitted an odour so fragrant as to cause us to look about more than once to see whether there were not many flowers close by.

WETTON.

Longlow, near Wetton, opened on the 22nd of July, being encompassed by mineral hillocks, much like barrows in form, had also been overlooked by us, but had been disturbed by miners digging in the centre to find a shaft, they having mistaken it for what is locally termed a "groove hillock," *i. e.*, a mound composed of earth and stone accumulated by sinking mines for lead. Having ascertained that there was no interment remaining in that part of the barrow disturbed by the miners, we directed our search to the west side, where we found a skeleton wanting the head, surrounded by rats' bones, which lay in a stratum of small stones and gravel, about two feet beneath the surface. The barrow was composed of loose stones to the depth of seven feet, amongst which were fragmentary bones both human and animal; but neither the primary interment nor the interesting nature of this tumulus were discovered on the present occasion.

ALSTONEFIELD.

On the 11th and 12th of August, and on one day in the week preceding, excavations were attempted in the great barrow at Steep Low, near Alstonefield, without much greater success than in 1845 (see Vestiges, p. 76); as from the large size of the tumulus, and the stony material employed in its construction, it is impossible to lay bare any part of the surface of the land on which it stands without employing timber to secure the sides from running in. The diggings on this occasion produced only one instrument, cut from a tine of stag's horn, with a hole drilled through the base; and a number of small brass coins of the Lower Empire, all of the most common types except one of Claudius Gothicus. Reverse—CONSECRATIO. An Eagle with expanded wings. The following is a list of the coins, in all amounting to 47:—

Victorinus, 265, A.D.	1
Tetricus, 267, A.D.	1
Claudius Gothicus, 268	1
Helena, first wife of Constantius Chlorus, 328, A.D.	3
Theodora, second wife of Constantius Chlorus	1
Constantinus II. Cæsar, 317, A.D.	10
Constans, Cæsar, 333, A.D.	10
Constantius II. Cæsar, 323, A.D.	5
Constantine Family.—Urbs Roma. Reverse, Wolf and Twins	6
Constantine Family.—Rev., Constantinopolis	6
Illegible	3
	47

READON HILL.

September 4th, opened a barrow nineteen yards diameter and three feet high, on Readon Hill, near Ramshorn, which is mentioned by Plot, Hist. Staff., fol. 1686, p. 404. It contained two skeletons extended at length, about the centre, without any protection from the earth of which the mound was formed, with the exception of a few stones in contact with one of the bodies, which was possibly interred at a subsequent period to the other, as it was not more than two feet from the surface of the barrow, whilst the other lay on the natural level, at least three feet from the turf covering the mound. Vestiges of the hair of the former were perceptible about the skull, which was that of a young man, and in perfect preservation; and a small pebble was found at the right hand (compare Barrow opened 30th May, 1845, Vestiges, p. 67). The other, and probably earlier interment, was covered with a thin layer of charcoal. The skull is that of a middle-aged man, the vertex much elevated, the left side completely decayed from lying in contact with the floor of the barrow. At some distance from either of the skeletons, but nearest to the higher interment, from which, however, they were full two yards, lay an iron spear, thirteen inches long, with part of the shaft remaining in the socket, and a narrow iron knife, eight inches in length. An examination of these by the microscope, enables us to add the further information that the spear has been mounted on an ashen shaft, about one inch of which yet remains, owing its preservation to being saturated by the ferruginous matter produced by the decomposition of the iron—outside the iron are numerous casts of grassy fibre, and the larvæ of insects, apparently flies—the grass must have been present at the time of interment in considerable quantity. The knife shews fewer traces of the vegetable, and more of the animal structures, the tang where inserted into the handle, shews the impression of horn. It is fortunate that metals in a state of oxydization have the property of taking, and retaining, the most delicate casts of substances the most perishable with which they lie in contact; we thus gain much valuable information as to the materials of dress in times of pre-historic antiquity, and are enabled to describe the circumstances under which the dead were committed to the grave, with an exactitude resulting from a strictly inductive method of reasoning. For example, we find that the early Celtic population, whose chief men were armed with the bronze celt and dagger, not only wore the skins of animals during life, but were enveloped in the same after death, and were thus laid upon a bed of moss or fern, before being buried out of the sight of their friends beneath the sepulchral mound. In later times, when the use of iron became so general as to supersede the more ancient metal bronze, we find a corresponding advancement in the materials of clothing, the impression of woven fabrics, of varying degrees of fineness, being almost invariably distinguishable on the rust of weapons found in the barrows; although the old custom of providing a grassy couch for the remains of the deceased was still retained, from an intuitive feeling beautifully expressed by Sir Thomas Browne, in his Hydriotaphia, when referring to the sepulture of the ancients, he writes—" that they have wished their bones might lie soft, and the earth be light upon them. Even such as hope to rise again would not be content with central interment, or so desperately to place their reliques as to be beyond discovery, and in no way to be seen again; which happy contrivance hath made communication with our forefathers, and left unto our view some parts which they never beheld themselves."

On the following day we examined another barrow in the same neighbourhood, about 21 yards diameter. It is called Wardlow, and is constructed over a lump of rock, in the middle of which was cut a grave, which we found had been previously disturbed, it had originally contained a skeleton with burnt bones, and chippings of flint. A cutting through the side of the mound where there was the greatest accumulation of factitious earth, produced many fragments of human bone, together with those of the water rat.

STANTON.

On the same day we opened two more barrows in land near Stanton, called Thor's Wood, or Back-of-the-Low. The first was 14 yards across, and two feet high, wholly composed of earth intermixed with charcoal and flakes of flint. No interment was discovered by two cuttings which crossed each other in the centre of the tumulus.

The second barrow, about a hundred yards from the last, appeared to have been disturbed before. It is about 28 yards diameter and of considerable elevation, not however wholly artificial, a protruding rock having been rendered available as a nucleus by the mound builders, who added flat stones and clayey earth to complete the tumulus. Beneath many of the stones that happened to lie hollow, we observed a limey efflorescence, amongst which were innumerable snail-shells, both certain indications of the great antiquity of the mound. The natural level was found at rather more than three feet below the turf, with no better result than the discovery of one human tooth, and a few bits of bone.

September 6th, opened a barrow at Dale, in the same township as the preceding, about a mile from Calton Moor House. It is irregular in form, being 13 yards diameter from North to South, and 16 from East to West ; the height about three feet, and the components flat stones and earth. On the natural surface lay two skeletons in a line, one at the feet of the other, which presented a mode of sepulture different to any yet found in our researches, from having been intentionally subjected to the action of fire upon the spot, in such a manner as to preserve the bones in their natural order, entire and unwarped by the heat. They were surrounded by charcoal and earth, to which a red colour had been imparted by the operation, themselves exhibiting a curious variety of tints from the same cause. All deposits of burnt bones previously found by us have been strictly calcined, and reduced to fragments by the process, and have generally been gathered into a heap, or placed within an urn, so that here we find an exception to the rule perfectly inexplicable — we may observe that the bones are evidently those of different sexes. Portions of human skull and some teeth found near the burnt skeletons, indicate that a former interment was displaced to make way for the new comers. No implements were found with them, but chips of flint, and one piece of primitive earthenware occurred near the top of the barrow.

ALSTONEFIELD.

Stimulated by the want of success attending former excavations, we determined to make one more effort to disclose the primary interment in the large barrow at Steep Low. To effect this purpose, two men were constantly employed for a fortnight at the end of September and beginning of October, to penetrate to the centre, which, to a certain extent, they succeeded in doing ; but owing to the immense accumulation of stone, it was found impossible to clear a passage more than three feet wide at the natural surface, consequently affording but a very slight chance of our hitting upon so small an object as an interment in an area so large as that covered by the mound. Charcoal in profusion, and a few calcined bones were observed at the bottom—higher in the tumulus, amongst the large stones, was the skull of an ox—and on the natural soil we picked up a small brass coin of Tetricus the elder, which had probably slipped from near the top of the barrow, through the interstices of the stones, although it appears from the patina to have been some time buried deeper than those formerly discovered near the top. Close to the surface, beneath the foundation of a stone fence which had been built across the hill, the writer picked up an iron spear-head, which had doubtless been deposited with the remains disinterred in 1845 (Vestiges p. 76), but which being under the wall, not at that time taken down, escaped observation. We have since received an iron arrow-head, an article of great rarity in tumuli, that was picked up by a looker-on when we first opened the barrow; it is devoid of socket, though otherwise well-shaped, and must have been secured in a slit cut in the arrow.

20th of October, we examined the site of a barrow which had been removed from an eminence near the last, but the whole having been destroyed, we found nothing but imperfect bones and one piece of stag's horn.

HURST LOW.

21st of October, we made another attempt to find an interment in this barrow, which was unsuccessfully opened on the 3rd of July. Having previously examined the middle by a trench from one side, we made a cutting through the opposite and hitherto undisturbed side, and on approaching the termination of the former diggings, found two large sandstones, foreign to the soil, one of which was about three feet square by one foot thick; the other was of a round form. Our section exhibited strata of variously coloured clay, which underneath the stones was greenish blue, unlike any other part. An arrow-head, and a rude instrument of yellow flint were picked up, but no interment was found, although we observed charcoal mingled with the clay.

STANTON.

28th of December, we opened a barrow called Over Low, placed on the side of a hill, on the summit of which are some earthworks, near the village of Stanton. The tumulus, about 28 yards diameter, is composed of small sandstones and sand; near the middle were two contracted skeletons, very much decayed, lying within a yard of each other: a few flat stones placed on edge, so as to form a sort of cist, were placed round one of them, which was also accompanied by a few mean implements of flint, and one piece of thick coarse pottery.

RIBDEN LOW.

29th of December, a barrow was opened between the villages of Cotton and Cauldon, called Ribden Low, about 30 yards diameter. In cutting through the centre, we found a large flat stone covering a rudely walled cist, built upon the natural surface, about three feet from the top of the barrow, containing a much decayed skeleton, which reposed in the usual flexed position, on its left side, accompanied by a remarkably beautiful spear-head of flint, and some other pieces of the same material, all of which had been slightly burnt; at the feet was a human skull much decayed. The ground continuing to sink by the side of the cist, we were led to another interment, which consisted of a deposit of calcined bones, placed in a hole dug two feet lower in the natural soil, and paved with flat stones. Amongst the bones were found three large instruments, and three barbed arrow-heads of flint, remains of about five bone implements, some of which appear to have been modelling or netting tools; others pointed at each end are perforated through the middle. They are all in bad preservation, owing to their having been calcined along with the corpse of the owner. The barrow was thickly strewn with burnt bones, fragments of pottery, and rats' bones; and two very small pieces of bronze, slightly ornamented, were found near the capstone of the cist.

BARROWS OPENED BY MR. CARRINGTON IN 1849.

CALTON.

On the 12th and 20th of January, we examined a barrow close to the village of Calton, of a form rarely found in this neighbourhood, but occurring more frequently in Wiltshire, where it is denominated by Stukeley and Hoare, the "Druid Barrow." (Compare Elk Low, Vestiges p. 45). It consists of a level plateau 18 inches high, encircled by a high verge 4 feet above the natural level, its diameter 16 yards. We found that repeated interments had been deposited within the area. The first discovered, was rather South of the centre, and was a skeleton with the legs bent at a right angle, with the trunk reposing on a quantity of charred wood placed on the natural level, from whence six pieces of calcined flint were taken, four only having the definite shape of instruments. From the head of this skeleton the ground inclining to the East, our trench was continued in that direction for about four feet, when we met with a large black stone placed on edge, near which were a few burnt human bones, and not far from them part of the unburnt skeleton of a very young person, with numerous rats' bones about it. At a short distance West from the centre, was another skeleton, also of a young person, placed in a flexed position, in a depression in the earth, accompanied by two neatly chipped instruments of calcined flint, and in some degree protected by a flat stone placed on edge parallel with the body. From following up these discoveries, the excavation had assumed an irregular shape, leaving the N.W. part of the area unexplored, which occasioned us to devote another day to the examination of that portion, where we discovered another skeleton of an adult, of slender proportions, lying extended on the back, with the head pillowed upon a flat stone, which afterwards proved the cover of a small cist. By the side of the body was a short thick-backed iron knife, which had been inserted into a wooden haft. The cist covered by the pillow stone, was sunk about a foot lower than the natural level; it was made by five flat stones placed on edge, some of them having pointed ends had been driven lower into the natural soil: it was small, measuring only 2 feet by 16 inches, and it was altogether about three feet beneath the turf. It contained a confused heap of badly preserved human bones, which, from the remains of the cranium (the best preserved amongst them) were pronounced to be the vestiges of a young person.

On an eminence near Calton, called the Cop, is a barrow about 20 yards diameter, and now two feet high, but probably lowered by the plough, which we opened on the 29th of January and 3rd of February; and which furnished an example of the careful interment of part of the head of an ox, a deposit we have found in a few instances before. (Vestiges, pp. 82—85—86, and Steep Low, Sept. 1848). The outside of the mound was of stiff red earth, which was replaced by stones as the centre was neared, where we found the first interment, consisting of calcined bones simply placed on a flat stone, about a foot below the surface. About a foot lower, two flat stones appeared, covering a small quadrangular cist 2 feet 6 inches square, and 2 feet deep; three of its sides formed of stones placed on edge, the fourth neatly walled up to the same height, and having the floor roughly paved with small stones. It contained the skeleton of a young person about twelve or fourteen years of age, in good preservation, accompanied by two flints that had been wrought into form, with others more rude. Near this cist was another of circular shape, formed by stones placed on end, which appeared to have been disturbed; it contained the remnants of another skeleton, and a round flint. Proceeding a short distance further towards the edge of the mound, we came to a small cist, constructed by four flat stones, inclined together at the top, so as to protect the contents without a horizontal cover-

I

ing; within was the right half of the upper jaw of an ox, wanting the teeth, and a rude piece of flint which may be imagined to be an arrow-head. Near the surface, in the middle of the mound, was a heap of fine charcoal, in which was a piece of coarse pottery, and during the excavation we found tines and other parts of stags' horns. This, the fifth instance, of the *intentional* burial of the whole or part of the head of the ox, goes far to prove the existence of some peculiar superstition or rite, of which no notice has reached modern times.

THROWLEY.

On the 10th of February, we investigated a tumulus midway between Throwley and Calton, 17 yards across and 3 feet high, wholly composed of earth of a burnt appearance throughout. The principal interment was found about a yard from the centre, and consisted of a deposit of large pieces of calcined human bone, which lay within a circular hole in the natural soil, about a foot deep, of well defined shape, resulting from contact with a wooden or wicker work vessel, in which the bones were placed when buried, the vestiges of which, in the form of impalpable black powder, intervened between the bones and the earth. Upon the bones lay part of a small bronze pin, and a very beautiful miniature vase, of the "Incense Cup" type, $2\frac{1}{2}$ inches high, $3\frac{1}{2}$ diameter, ornamented with chevrons and lozenges, and perforated in two places at one side. Among the bones were two small pointed pieces of flint, and a common quartz pebble; and below the deposit was the shoulder-blade of a large animal, which has been designedly reduced to an irregular shape by the use of flint saws, or other instruments equally inefficient. At one side of this interment, were four other deposits of calcined bone, placed on the floor of the mound, here of rock, intersected by veins of clay, without any protection from cist or urn, but evidently deposited at one and the same time, as the heaps were quite distinct and undisturbed, though very near to each other. They had been so thoroughly calcined as to be comminuted, and had almost reached the inevitable catastrophe of "dust to dust."

WETTON.

In the first week of April, we made a second effort to open the Longlow Barrow, situated on a mineral vein that has been so extensively worked as to render the extent of the tumulus almost undistinguishable amidst the mine hillocks. Owing to this, we missed the centre, although the mound was excavated to the depth of seven feet at least. We nevertheless found parts of two human skulls, one of them infantile, together with bones of the usual animals, calcined flints of good form and workmanship, and the points of a bone spear, and pin.

WATERHOUSES.

On the 7th of April, we opened a barrow in a field called Stonesteads, a quarter of a mile from the village of Waterhouses, measuring 17 yards across, composed of earth, limestones, and boulders. Slightly South-East from the centre of the barrow, upon a pavement of thin flat stones raised 6 inches above the natural level of the land, lay the skeleton of a tall and strongly-built man, apparently beyond the middle period of life, who had been placed in the common flexed posture, with the head towards the outside of the tumulus. Near his feet was the tusk of a large boar, rubbed down on the inner surface to about half the natural thickness, near the shoulders were two instruments of burnt flint, one round ended, the other, part of a neat arrow-point; and a section about half-an-inch long, cut from a large rib, and neatly dressed round the edge of the cut surfaces. On the floor of the barrow were indications of fire, and a few pieces of calcined bone, which render it probable that there had been a more ancient interment in the barrow, which was about eighteen inches in central elevation.

LOMBERLOW.

The remainder of the day was occupied by another barrow on a rocky and elevated ridge in the neighbourhood, called Lomberlow. The mound, about 16 yards diameter, is crossed by a hedge and double stone wall, so that we could not dig out the middle, but we worked as near to it as practicable. It is composed of stones broken from the upper beds of the rocky masses around, mingled with soil just sufficient to fill the interstices, and stands upon a very uneven floor of rock, in a depression of which, enlarged by artificial means, a cist was erected of well-defined, rectangular form, composed of four massive stones, measuring inside three feet by two feet, and covered by three large stones laid across, two being of limestone, each a yard long by eighteen inches wide and six thick; the other, covering the joint, was a slab of sandstone, brought from the bed of the river Hamps, which flows through, and gives the name to the village of Waterhouses, about a mile from the barrow. The cist was south of the centre, and its covering stones not more than eighteen inches below the turf, though its floor was four feet; it was built with the longest diameter East and West, and was filled with earth, amongst which lay the skeleton of a full-grown young person, with the head to the West, and necessarily in an extremely contracted posture. At the shoulders we found a very good spear-head of mottled grey flint, and an uncertain instrument of white flint, very highly polished. Above the cist were numerous small pebbles, the leg-bone of a large dog, and a little charcoal.

CAULDON.

On the 14th of April, we examined the remnant of a barrow on the summit of a very high hill, called Cauldon Low. It is about 22 yards across, and is planted with stunted fir trees, for the protection of which a wall has been built round the tumulus, the stone having been supplied by its spoliation. Owing to this, we were unable to find more than a few calcined bones, pieces of pottery, rats' bones, and two instruments of flint, all which occurred near the centre.

On the 1st of April, another barrow in the same neighbourhood, called Farlow, was opened. It is 21 yards diameter, consisting of a level area surrounded by an elevated border, as the "Druid Barrows." Digging to the depth of four feet in the centre, through earth and stones, we discovered the skeleton of a young person laid upon the ribs of an ox or other large animal placed transversely to the human bones, at regular intervals side by side. At the North side of the barrow was a rock grave, the bottom of which was about two feet beneath the turf, containing the skeleton of another young person, accompanied by a very neatly ornamented vase, five inches high, and nine instruments of white flint, eight of which lay altogether in a corner of the grave, whilst the ninth was found near the middle. The vase retained its upright position, having been placed upon a flat stone, and likewise protected by another standing on edge by its side. On the South and East sides of the mound were remains of two other bodies, neither of which yielded any article worthy of notice. Part of the barrow had been disturbed about a year before by treasure-seekers, who having found a large urn with the upper part ornamented by chevrons, broke it to pieces, in order that each bystander might possess a memento of the discovery.

GRINDON.

28th of April, opened a barrow, 13 yards across, and two feet high, situated in land called Ellmeadows, near Grindon, which appeared to have been previously disturbed. We made trenches in various directions, but found only the fragments common to all spoliated tumuli, namely, human bones burnt and unburnt, teeth and bones of rats and other animals, pieces of flint, coarse pottery, and pebbles.

SWINSCOE.

The 5th and 12th of May were spent in opening an elliptical or "Long Barrow," near Swinscoe, called Top Low, measuring about 15 yards long by 7 wide. From the section made in the course of our researches, it appears probable that it was originally constructed of the common circular shape, and that it had been lengthened by the accumulation of earth heaped over numerous interments that had taken place from time to time, as the mound was full of human bodies. This being the case, to avoid confusion, we will narrate the discoveries in the order in which they occurred, and refer to the Plan, where each deposit is numbered so as to correspond with the description.

I.

The first interment was discovered about four feet from the top of the barrow, in a shallow grave, three feet long, cut about six inches deep in the chert rock, having a stone placed on edge at each end. It was the skeleton of a young person, in a contracted position on the right side. The skull is well formed, and suggests no idea either of undue length or the contrary. It is thin and not large, the teeth are perfect, and but little worn; the bones are those of an adult of small size, the femur measuring 16¼ inches. In the earth a few inches above the skeleton, we found a very small bronze clasp, which has been riveted to a strap, and a three-cornered piece of flint.

II.

The second interment lay about three feet from the turf, on its right side, with the feet towards the flat stone at the head of the first skeleton; it had also an upright stone at the head, and a round ended flint was found near the feet. The skull is that of a young adult, thin in substance, and decidedly short in diameter between the frontal and occipital bones; the teeth are quite unworn. Length of femur 18½ inches.

III.

The third skeleton had been partially disturbed, it was not far from the last, and lay with the face upwards, a large flat stone having been placed by its side as a guard. A neatly chipped spear-head of flint, turned grey by heat, was found near the shoulders; the head, thin in substance and a good deal decayed, is also of the brachy-cephalic type, the obliteration of the sutures and the abraded state of the teeth, indicate a person of middle-age. The femur measures 17½ inches.

IV.

The fourth deposit, which we found between the first and the third, consisted of the skeleton of a young hog, inside a roughly built cist, one side of which we destroyed before we were aware of its nature, the opposite side was supplied by a single flat stone, but the ends were built of rounded masses of rock. Along with this animal was a tine from a stag's horn.

V.

No. 5 consisted of calcined bones, which had been deposited in a cinerary urn, ornamented with a chevron pattern, and was much broken when found; amongst them were portions of two neat bone implements, perhaps modelling tools of the potter, which had not been burnt, and part of a fine flint which had been destroyed by the action of fire.

VI.

The sixth was a skeleton which lay with the legs drawn up, on its left side, upon a thin layer of charred wood, about four feet from the top of the mound, in a slight depression of the surface, and was accompanied by two flakes of flint, one of which may have served to point an arrow. The skull is that of an aged man, the teeth much worn down, and sutures indistinct; of the longer variety of the Celtic form. Femur 18 inches.

VII.

No. 7, a deposit of calcined bones with remains of flints, placed near the surface of the barrow, above the feet of No. 6.

VIII.

The eighth was not far from the sixth. It was a skeleton very much decayed, buried three feet beneath the grass, having with it a very pretty arrow-head of white flint, and some pieces of a small and neatly ornamented vase.

IX.

The ninth was a double interment, comprising two skeletons, with a flat stone on edge by their side. The lowest, which was four feet deep, was the skeleton of a full grown person, much decayed; by its side, but slightly higher, lay the skeleton of a child a few months old.

X.

The tenth skeleton was found in a grave cut in the rock to the depth of three feet below the floor of the barrow, consequently above six feet from the summit; it had a circle of upright flat stones round the edge, and was filled with earth and large stones, covering the skeleton of an aged man, who was deposited in the customary fashion with the knees up, behind the pelvis lay a handsome drinking cup, $7\frac{1}{4}$ inches high, decorated with a lozengy pattern, and a few chippings of flint were found in the grave. The skull is very thick, and unusually narrow or boat-shaped naturally; the latter peculiarity is increased by posthumous distortion, caused by the settling down of the large stones in the grave, by which one side of the calvarium has been broken and curled inwards.

XI.

The presumed site of the eleventh interment (not marked in the Plan), was near one end of the ellipse formed by the mound, which being chiefly composed of stone, was here heaped over a space consisting of earth alone to the depth of four feet, amongst which were numerous rats' bones, pebbles, and a long triangular flake of calcined flint.

XII.

The twelfth was a pentagonal cist, about 18 inches diameter, and 18 deep, made of flat stones and covered by a broad and thin slab; it was filled with earth, beneath which were some decayed bones, including part of a skull.

XIII.

The thirteenth was close to the last; it was a very young skeleton, placed close to an upright flat stone, and accompanied by one chipping of flint.

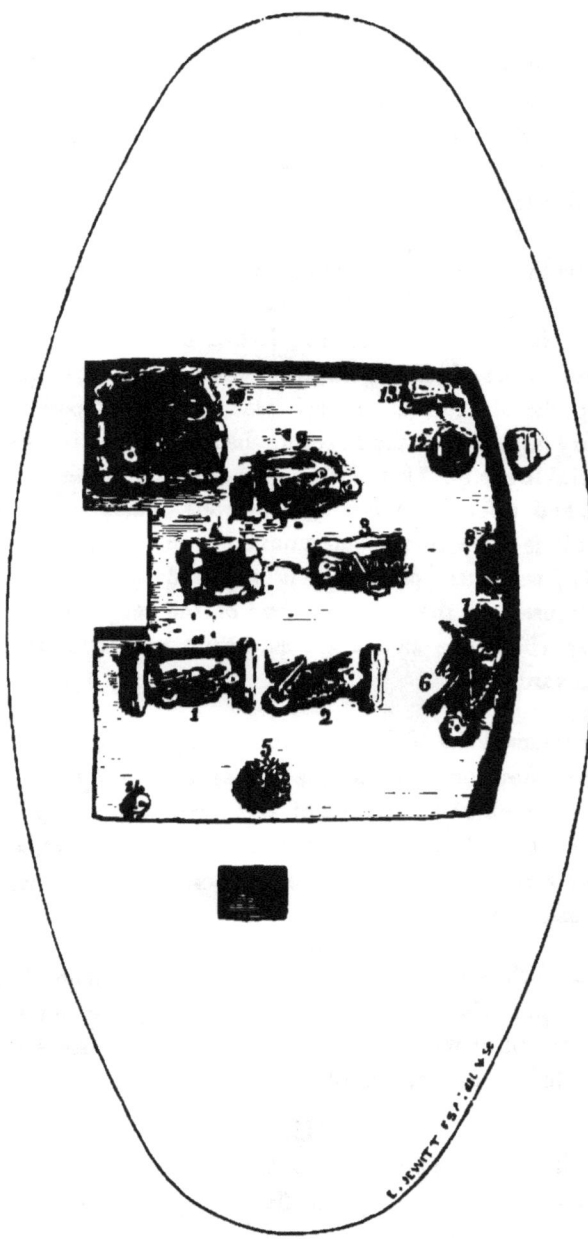

Plan of Interments in Top Low, Swinscoe.

XIV.

The last interment was found at a short distance from the burnt bones forming the fifth, it presented no feature of interest, the skull being far gone in decay, and one piece of burnt flint only being found with it.

On a review of the facts, we are inclined to assign the post of honour to the cist containing the hog, which was placed nearest the centre, and which may be considered as a deposit analagous to the encisted heads of oxen before deposited. If this opinion be deemed incorrect, and a human interment sought for as the most ancient deposit, we must take the tenth in order of discovery as the first in order of time, as well as of importance, and conclude, that with the exception of No. 1, 2, and 3, which were probably interred simultaneously, the remainder were buried at intervals more or less distant from each other.

ALSTONEFIELD.

We next examined a small mound on the highest point of land near the Load House, in the neighbourhood of Alstonefield, where we found no perfect interment, but many small pieces of human and animal bone, including numerous rats' bones, and a few pieces of calcined human bone.

MUSDEN THIRD BARROW.

On the 19th of May, we opened the third of the group of barrows upon Musden Hill, which is a fine regularly shaped mound eighteen yards diameter, and five feet high, composed of nothing but stiff clayey earth. The natural soil was touched at the depth of four feet, and was changed to a red colour by fire, the traces of which, in the form of charcoal, strewed the surface for a considerable length. A round hole had been sunk about a foot through the upper stratum of rock, near the centre of the barrow, which was filled with small stones and clay; a few burnt bones and some pieces of burnt flint, one of them part of a large instrument, were found about this part of the mound, but no interment was discovered, although extensive trenches were made. There is little doubt of an interment by cremation being yet in some part of the barrow, which is one of the same class as those near Longnor, opened in 1848.

WETTON NEAR HILL.

At page 83 of Vestiges, is a notice of an excavation made at one side of a barrow on the summit of Wetton near Hill, when after having found one interment, we desisted through meeting with the natural rock in front of our cutting. Mr. Carrington thinking it probable that something might yet remain, made a cutting from the opposite side on the 23rd and 24th of May, having previously made trials in different parts of the mound, which showed that in some places the materials were large stones, and in others gravel, both favourable indications. After removing stones to the depth of about a yard, we found a skeleton accompanied by one rude flint arrow; it lay on the left side, with the knees drawn up, and was that of a strong man in full vigour. The skull, with the exception of the left side, which was decayed from contact with the earth, is perfect, and of a shape very unusual amongst Celtic crania, being remarkably short and elevated, like the Turkish skull. It is amongst the number selected for publication in the Crania Britannica, as an example of the acro-cephalic variety. Proceeding forward, we found another skeleton, the feet of which were very near the head of the first, deposited in the contracted posture in a cist, roughly made of large limestones, and partly covered with others of the same kind. Before the face was a very beautiful vase, 4½ inches

Vase from Wetton near Hill.

high, with a fluted border and four perforated ears, which will be understood from the cut. A piece of flint and a tine of stags' horn lay close behind the skull, and a few more pieces of flint were found near. The skull, in perfect condition, is that of an old man, some of the teeth wanting, the alveoli being absorbed, the rest exceedingly worn; it is essentially square and massive in appearance, and is of the platy-cephalic variety. It is engraved and fully described in the Crania Britannica, where its internal capacity is stated to be 80 ounces. When cleaning it, on the day after its discovery, the cricoid cartilage, in a state of ossification, fell from the interior through the foramen magnum, where it had probably been conveyed by the rats which hibernated in the tumulus.

The femur measured 18 inches. The occurrence of two crania of the most opposite extremes of aberration from the ordinary Celtic type, in one tumulus, is most remarkable, and cannot fail to interest craniographers.

ILAM.

On the 26th and 30th of May we opened a barrow in the midst of a plantation on the top of Hazleton Hill, above Inkley Wood, at the back of Ilam Hall. It is a flat barrow, with a level summit 20 yards diameter, and varying from a foot to 18 inches in thickness, according to the inequality of the ground on which it stands, chiefly composed of earth, except round the edge, and where interment had taken place. The first discovery was at the West side, where a grave 6 feet long by 2 wide, had been cut 18 inches deep into the rock, then surrounded by flat stones placed on edge, and lastly, divided into two equal compartments by the same means. In one division was a deposit of calcined human bones, accompanied by two inferior arrow points of flint, and a broken pebble, also burned. The other contained wood ashes, earth which had undergone the action of fire, and a few bits of bone. From the appearance of the place, it is likely that the grave was first used as the place of cremations, and afterwards arranged as we found it, in order to hold the collected remains more compactly. A few feet from this deposit, and about 8 yards from the centre, we found a plain urn of thin pottery, about 7 inches high and 5 diameter, inverted over a few burnt bones which lay upon a flat stone—this very small cinerary urn was broken by a tree having been planted above it. Eight yards from the middle, towards the South, in a depression of the floor, was a flat upright stone, by the side of which were some small pieces of a coarse urn, black ashes, burnt earth, a fine circular instrument, and numerous pieces of calcined flint: many large stones had been used in this part of the mound. Eight yards from the centre, towards the North-West, was a very similar deposit in a depression of the rock, surrounded by large stones; the articles were, a few calcined bones, a fine round instrument, and chippings of flint, and a piece of lead, either native or molten, weighing more than $3\frac{1}{4}$ ounces.

Many more flints, including four more circular instruments, numerous pebbles, and a piece of iron ore, were scattered through the central part of the barrow, where not a trace of unburnt bone was found from first to last.

GATEHAM.

On the 31st of May we examined a flat barrow near Gateham, about 15 yards diameter, much reduced in height by the frequent passage of the plough, which was formed of stones firmly embedded in earth. On the natural surface, in the centre, about two feet from the top of the mound, there was much charcoal, and a few feet West from it was the only interment found in the barrow, consisting of a few crumbling remains of calcined bone, placed beneath a broken urn, the upper part of which was ornamented with the chevron pattern in dotted lines; they lay near the surface, and below, on the floor of the mound, was a block of flint, which, with a chipped instrument and some pieces from other parts of the tumulus, was in its natural state, and not burnt, as barrow flints commonly are.

BLORE.

2nd June, we opened a barrow near Blore, in a field called Nettles (Net Lows?) formed around a natural elevation, which is only slightly covered at the top; the entire diameter is 13 yards. On the S.W. side we found a cist, the outer side formed of a long stone placed on edge, the inner being walled from the surface to the bottom, which was paved with flat stones; the depth was 2 feet. On the floor was a deposit of calcined bones, and in a corner was a broken urn of red clay, containing a small vase, or "incense cup," in better preservation.

The large vase, originally about 9 inches high by 5 diameter, is of clay, plentifully mixed with sand and imperfectly baked, whence the surface is much disintegrated. It has been of good form and workmanship, having a deep border ornamented with diagonal lines disposed in triangles in alternate directions. The cup is of similar clay, 2½ inches high, 3 inches across the mouth, and quite plain. Nearer the edge, on the same side of the barrow, we found some remains of an unburnt skeleton, which had been previously disturbed, and not far from it were two articles indicating the interment to have been of late period: namely, the bottom of a kiln-baked vessel of blue clay, showing marks of having been turned on the potter's wheel, and a small iron ring 1¼ inch in diameter. Fragments of bone, burnt and unburnt, rats' bones, teeth of oxen, and pebbles were found throughout the cuttings.

STANSHOPE.

A singularly-constructed barrow on Stanshope Pasture, partially opened by us on the 20th July, 1846, was more carefully examined on the 1st, 4th, and 5th of June. The former excavations showed the mound to be almost all of natural rock, levelled and trimmed into a tumular shape. On the present occasion we succeeded in finding several interments, all of which had been deposited in clefts of the rock, in a way difficult to describe without reference to a plan, the clefts being quite natural, and running in different directions from the centre of the mound, which was altogether solid, except in these places, which had been successively occupied. The first contained two deposits of calcined bones; one, high up in the cleft, had been contained in an urn much broken, the other lay on the floor, which was partly burnt to lime, indicating, perhaps, that the corpse had been consumed on the spot.

The second place of burial was a cleft communicating with the first, four feet long, three feet deep, and one foot wide at the top, decreasing to six inches at the bottom; it contained a large quantity of calcined bones, accompanied by two instruments of flint, and two neatly made bone pins, one of which is partly drilled at the broadest end, they are, contrary to the usual custom, unburnt.

The third grave was a kind of cist, formed on one side by a ridge of rock two feet wide, separating it from the last, and on the other by a large long stone; it was covered by several large stones wedged in between the sides, and owing to the shape of the rock was widest at the bottom, where lay two skeletons, the largest of which had been slightly disturbed by the interment of the other, which was that of a young person. Innumerable snail shells and rats' bones covered the bottom of this grave.

The last interment here discovered, consisted of a very large and coarse sepulchral urn, inverted over a deposit of burnt bones, placed upon a flat stone; it was in some degree protected by an angle of the rock, in which it was placed, but being very near the surface the lower part was decayed by atmospheric action. It measures eleven inches in diameter at the mouth, and is quite unornamented.

BUNSTER.

6th of June, we opened a barrow in a plantation on the brow of Bunster Hill, by the side of Dovedale; it was fourteen yards diameter, and three feet high, composed of earth with but few stones, and was completely honeycombed by rabbit burrows. The only interment was a full-grown skeleton laid on the natural surface, South of the centre, on the left side, with the knees drawn up, and the head to the outside of the mound; the femur measures seventeen inches, and the skull exhibits a frontal suture, although it would appear to be that of a person in middle life. Close to the head lay a small arrow head, and some chippings of flint, two larger pieces lying nearer the surface; just above the feet was a large flat stone, beneath which were a few pieces of burnt bone. We observed neither rats' bones nor the customary fragments of those of other animals in any part of the mound.

WETTON.

Several unsuccessful attempts to open the barrow at Longlow, near Wetton, are noticed in the preceding pages, which failed from a great part of the mound being surrounded by mine hillocks, under which it extended much further than was at first anticipated, in fact, a shaft had been sunk very near the centre of the tumulus. From a careful measurement of part of the barrow still remaining in its original condition, it appears to have had a circumference of ninety yards. It is chiefly composed of flat stones, many of which are large, and set on end, inclining towards each other at the top, by which mode of construction many vacancies are occasioned. Near the surface and at the edge the stones are smaller, and the interstices are filled with gravel and earth; the depth in the highest part was more than seven feet. Convinced that we had not yet found the principal interment, and as the presumed centre had been examined down to the rock, we excavated the S.E. side of the mound in the month of March of the present year, without finding more than detached pieces of human bone, and lumps of flint amongst a quantity of charcoal near the surface; and laying bare at the bottom, a low wall of square stones, altogether about four feet long and eight inches high. At length, on the 8th of June, after having expended part of the preceding day in excavation, we had the satisfaction of discovering a very large cist, or chamber, the first indication of which were two large stones lying parallel to each other in an inclined direction. They had originally constituted one stone only, forming one end of the cist which had been displaced, and each was seven feet long by five broad. At the foot of these appeared the end of another stone of almost equal size placed on edge, which proved to be one side of the sepulchral chamber; it was seven inches thick. The opposite side was formed by a stone equally long, but about a foot narrower, and eleven inches in thickness. The stone forming the end inclined inwards, having given way; it was five feet broad by six feet long, thus rendering the chamber, as originally constructed, six feet long, five wide, and about four deep. Excepting

Cist in Longlow, Wetton.

at a little vacancy at the end first discovered, where human remains were seen scattered amongst the stones, the chamber was filled in the upper part with earth and stones, below with stones only, which being removed, exposed a well-paved floor, covered from end to end with human bones, which lying altogether in the primitive contracted position, appeared to be in great confusion, though not so in reality. Two skulls lay close together, in contact with the side of the cist, beneath another skull (shortly to be described; in the middle lay the leg bones of one skeleton and the arms of another. One skeleton was situated rather higher up amongst the stones. Bones of the ox, hog, deer, and dog; also three very finely chipped arrow-heads, and many other pieces of calcined flint accompanied the human remains, which, as well as we could ascertain, represented at least thirteen individuals, ranging from infancy to old age, and including several females.

K

This is the first opportunity we have had of exploring an undisturbed cist in a chambered cairn of this peculiar structure, most of them having been destroyed for the sake of the stone, whilst this had one end only displaced, without injury to the deposits. It is on this account a discovery of unusual interest, and when compared with the results of previous and subsequent excavations in similar grave hills, yields to none in importance. A few general observations will render this clear.

The mound, composed of stone, enclosing a chamber or cist formed of immense slabs of stone, occasionally double, or galleried, indicates, in this part of the country at least, a period when the use of metal was unknown, the sole material for the spear and arrow being flint, which is often carefully chipped into leaf-shaped weapons of great beauty. The interments within these cists have in every case been numerous, and apparently long continued; they are marked by a strongly defined type of skull, styled by Dr. Wilson, kumbe-kephalic, or boat-shaped, the more obvious features being excessive elongation, flattening of the parietal bones, and squareness of the base, producing, when viewed from behind, a laterally compressed appearance, which is enhanced by the sagittal suture being sometimes elevated into a ridge. The adult male skull found in the centre of the Longlow cist has been selected to

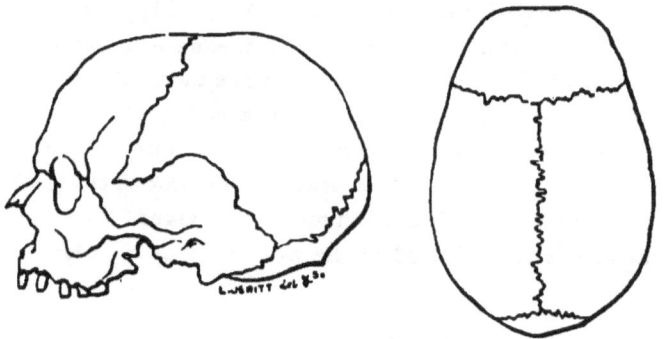

Kumbe-Kephalic Skull, from Longlow.

appear in the "Crania Britannica," as a typical example of this form. The crania of a female, and of a girl about seven years old, from the same cist, exhibit the same form in a remarkable degree, as do the others which are more imperfect. Crania from the chambered barrows at Bole Hill, Bakewell Moor (Vestiges, p. 47), Stoney Low, Brassington Moor (Vestiges, p. 46), Ringham Low, near Monyash (ditto, p. 103), Five Wells Hill, Taddington (ditto, p. 91), are of the same type, which it has been suggested may not be Celtic, and which Professor Nillson places second in the order of antiquity of the ancient inhabitants of Scandinavia, where it seems they are found occupying similar cairns. Our observations seem to indicate a period more strictly primeval. The other bones are not large, though well formed; the points of attachment of the muscles are remarkably distinct.

ECTON.

On the evenings of the 11th and 12th of June we investigated a barrow on Ecton Hill, which was partially opened on the 18th of May, 1848. On the south side we found a deposit of burnt bones, which had been placed in a large urn, with a projecting border ornamented with diagonal lines, accompanied by two unburnt tines of the antler of the red deer. The urn was much broken when found. Towards the east side was a skeleton much broken and decayed, the head towards the outside; accompanied by a few burnt bones, fragments of earthenware, a few pieces of flint, and animal bones, including a boar's tusk. At the southwest side of the mound were more human bones, which had been disturbed by miners, who finding lead in the tumulus, had concluded it to be the site of an ancient bloomery or smelting-place, such being formerly established on hills for the sake of the draught; their locality is yet indicated by the word Bole, as Bole Hill, &c.

GRUB LOW.

13th of June we opened a small barrow, three feet high, and not more than ten yards across, called Grub Low, situated between

Grindon and Waterfall. It was mostly composed of the red earth of the neighbourhood, sparingly mixed with stones. In the middle were remains of two persons: one had been interred in the natural state, with the knees drawn up; the other had been reduced to ashes, which were distributed about the first, along with much charcoal; beneath the bones were two very neatly chipped leaf-shaped arrows of white flint, one of which had suffered much from the fire. The natural surface was much blackened with charcoal, and above the deposits fine gravel had been heaped almost to the summit of the barrow.

MUSDIN FOURTH BARROW.

The fourth of the group of barrows on Musdin Hill was opened on the 16th of June. It is a flat-topped barrow, 25 yards across, about three feet high, and composed of earth, with a few stones about the various interments. About half way down, in the centre, we found a skeleton, near to which was a second much decayed, but apparently of a young person; by the side of the head was a pebble, and a circular ring of bronze, with a ribbed front, which, from the remains of the iron pin, we conclude to be a brooch. Beneath the head was another like it, in better preservation. The rust from the iron pins retained impressions of woven cloth and hair, but whether the latter results from contact with a skin garment, or the hair of the corpse, it is impossible to decide: the last is, however, most probable. Under the body was much charcoal.

Slightly further on, we found a large thin instrument of grey flint, which probably belonged to a decayed skeleton reposing near upon some stones, surrounded by rats' bones. A beautiful bronze dagger, five inches long, $2\frac{1}{4}$ broad, with a rib up the centre at each side, and three rivets for the handle, the polished patina of which rivals malachite in colour, was found, in no very determinate position with regard to any of these interments, though nearest to the first; if, however, we take former discoveries as a guide, we should attribute it to the owner of the flint instrument.

Of the fourth interment nothing remained but some of the smaller bones. The fifth deposit, found in a bowl-shaped cavity in the natural surface, about nine feet from the centre, consisted of bones which had undergone the process of cremation on the spot where they were buried, the depression being lined with charcoal. They were accompanied by the remains of a peculiarly ornamented vase, with perforated bosses, which had been placed near a stone. The sixth was a skeleton, accompanied by two flints, one round, the other pointed, which lay about three yards from the last.

The small bones and teeth only remained of the seventh.

The eighth had also been buried entire, though part of the skull, the teeth, and the bones of the extremities, were the only remains. Near the head were two flints of mean quality, and a small neatly-ornamented vase, 4½ inches high, which stood upright about eighteen inches beneath the surface. The latter has been partly broken for ages, without coming to pieces, as there is a crack half an inch wide down the side.

The ninth was the most perfect skeleton in the barrow. It lay on its left side, with the knees drawn up, and the head to the centre. The upper part was much decayed: length of femur eighteen inches.

Of the tenth little was left.

The eleventh consisted of calcined bones and the remains of an urn.

The twelfth and last was another decomposed skeleton, lying on an accumulation of stones, and accompanied by some flint flakes. Most of the interments were within a little distance of the centre of the barrow, and were surrounded by small stones laid on a stratum of charcoal; they were unusually decayed, although the bones of rats found in contact with them were well preserved.

18th of June we opened a flat mound, with an uneven surface, 25 yards across, on the moor near Gateham. It consisted of loose black earth to the depth of two feet, next a bed of stiff white clay containing charcoal, and lastly a stratum of red clay. No interment was found, although there is a tradition in the neighbourhood that it is a place " where dead men lie."

HOLME END.

On the evenings of the 20th and 21st of June, we opened a barrow near Holme End, called Lousy Low, which has originally been of some magnitude, but is now reduced, a cottage of one storey having been erected upon it. We made three parallel sections through the middle, where it is four feet high, and found in the centre one, upon the natural level, some pieces of an ornamented urn and two unburnt instruments of flint. The sections showed the materials of the barrow: the natural surface consisted of red sandy clay, on which was a layer of hard white clay, as in the preceding barrow, which, from being plentifully strewed with charred wood, we considered to have been partially baked. On this lay large stones, again covered with clay from eighteen inches to two feet in thickness, which formed the outside of the tumulus. No interment was found.

CAULDON HILL THIRD BARROW.

The third barrow of the Cauldon group was opened on the 30th of June. From its corresponding with the slope of the hill it is difficult to ascertain its diameter, but it had a depression in the centre, surrounded by an elevated circle seven yards across, and as far as the cutting extended the depth of artificial material varied from two feet to a yard. At the south-east end of our trench we found a broken cinerary urn, slightly ornamented, and some burnt bones; beneath this deposit was a small hole in the rock, filled with charcoal, which substance was likewise scattered throughout the barrow, and the earth was in some places burnt red. One flint arrow-point and some chippings occurred during the day.

BLORE.

Lady Low, near Blore, a bowl-shaped tumulus, 21 yards across and four feet high in the middle, was opened on the 2nd of July by carrying a trench six feet wide through the centre, without finding the interment, a few flints and some charcoal being the result of our labour.

CALTON MOOR.

On July the 5th we made an ineffectual attempt to open a barrow at Waterings, near Calton Moor House, 25 yards diameter and four feet high, composed of very compact earth, which was rendered more difficult of removal by being traversed in all directions by the roots of about a dozen large sycamores growing on the mound. We found only some pieces of flint, traces of fire, and an iron ox-shoe, which, though comparatively modern, was found eighteen inches from the surface. We perceived, in one part of the rock, a depression at least two feet lower than the natural surface, which would probably have led to the interment had it been possible to follow it up, but the trees prevented this being done. On the same day, we made two small cuttings in the first of the Musdin barrows, previously opened by us on the 5th of July, 1848. Near the edge we found a small cist, formed of four flat stones, reinforced by an outer range of others, all set on edge, and covered over by two larger slabs: around were rats' bones innumerable, and within was a deposit of calcined bones, accompanied by two flint instruments, also burnt, one of which is a very neatly chipped lance, made of rather unusual shape, three inches long, made from a large flake, smooth on one surface from being struck from a block, and laboriously chipped to a convex shape on the other. This is a type always found well finished, as in the specimen found in Ribden Low, which is one of the most beautiful flints we have seen. The usual fragments of bone, &c., were found in the other cutting but no interment.

SWINSCOE.

On the 7th of July, we opened a barrow on the Near Hill, Swinscoe, thirteen yards diameter, with a basin-like depression in the middle, five yards over and three feet deep. Having sunk to the depth of five feet from the basin, through earth and stone, a skeleton was found, the lower part of which only was undisturbed, the head and upper portion having apparently been long removed. Their fragments, with small pieces of burnt bone, Samian ware, and a piece of iron of no great antiquity, were found throughout the cutting from the surface downwards. The femur of the skeleton, wanting the joint at the knee, measures 18½ inches, and must have been near two inches longer.

MAYFIELD.

On the same day, we excavated Mayfield Low, a flat barrow, eighteen yards diameter, composed of sand and pebbles, in which a stone cist, containing an urn, had been discovered some years previously. We made numerous cuttings without much success, finding only a few pieces of an urn and some burnt bones near the eastern edge.

CASTERN.

On the afternoons of the 18th and 19th of July, we opened a barrow between Bitchin Hill and Castern, eighteen yards diameter, and only about eighteen inches high, a great deal of the top having been removed for the sake of the stone. On the first day we removed a considerable area from the centre towards the south-east, the whole of which was strewed with human and animal bones, and other trifling remains common in most barrows. Amongst them was the decayed skeleton of a young person. The next day we continued our excavation in an opposite direction, where, about two yards from the middle of the barrow, was an oval grave, seven feet long by 3½ feet wide, cut in the rock to the depth of about two feet. It was filled with earth and stones, covering a large skeleton lying at the bottom, on its left side, in the usual contracted posture, with the head to the north. Near the shoulders was a large and highly-polished stud, of jet or coal, 1¾ inches diameter, with two oblique holes meeting at an angle behind. A small piece of calcined flint was also found near the same place.

The femur measures nineteen inches. In the grave were many rats' bones, and above it were the remains of a young person, with bits of earthenware and burnt flints.

28th of July, we went to a mound at Windy Harbour, on the Morridge range, near Cotton, which, although originally a barrow, had been completely destroyed by a limekiln made in its centre, as we soon found by excavation.

CAULDON HILLS.

We afterwards opened a barrow on Cauldon Hills, in a lower situation than those before examined there. One-half had been removed down the level of the adjacent land, but its area was distinguishable by the smoothness of the turf and its freedom from thistles, which grow luxuriantly around: the height of the part remaining is near three feet, and the original diameter about eighteen yards. We cut through the higher part towards the centre, where rock appeared, but continuing forward to the part removed, many loose stones were observed, which were ultimately found to occupy a grave nine feet long by four wide, sunk four feet deep in the rock, which had unfortunately been disturbed by those who had removed a moiety of the barrow. We found, however, the remnants of a skeleton, the slender femur of which measures seventeen inches, and fragments of a plain globular, narrow-necked vessel of firmly-baked sandy ware, with a polished black surface, produced mechanically, and not by the application of glaze, which may be of Roman-British, or even Saxon manufacture.

30th of July, we examined one of a series of natural protuberances on the crest of a hill, near Stanshope, called Ottcliff Knoll, which seemed to possess a barrow-like aspect. There was a depression about a foot deep at one side, completely filled with small pieces of the bones of different animals, among which those of the rat were conspicuous; but in all other places the mound presented a rocky mass, thinly overspread with wiry turf, so that no other deposit could have been made.

DEEPDALE.

4th of August, we made a more complete investigation of the barrow at Deepdale, which was partially opened in 1845, when one extremity only of the grave was examined. It was now found to measure twelve feet in length by five in breadth at the widest end, and somewhat less at the other; its depth was 6½ feet, three feet having been cut out of the rock. The skeleton of a young person, and a few more pieces of the broken drinking cup found in 1845, were discovered at the broadest end; and some bones of a child, with casual flakes of flint, were found at the side, outside the grave. The skull of the young person who occupied the grave is remarkable for its elevated form.

August 9th, we were disappointed, on excavating a small barrow on Archford Moor, called Smeetlow, to find that the whole centre was destroyed by a limekiln.

August 11th, having been repulsed in an application for liberty to open a mound in a heathy field at Eaves, near Cotton, we amused ourselves with some unsuccessful digging in the Cauldon Hill group of tumuli, which on this occasion yielded only charcoal and pieces of bone.

THROWLEY.

18th August, we opened a barrow on the hill behind Throwley Moor House, the dimensions of which are not ascertainable, from the greatest part of the mound being natural. We commenced digging on the north-west side, through earth one foot deep, beneath which was rock. We soon, however, arrived at a flat stone, placed upright beneath a wall that crossed the barrow; and having removed sufficient of the latter to allow us to proceed, found immediately below its foundation a large sepulchral urn, which, contrary to general usage, stood with the mouth upwards in a hole in the rock eighteen inches deep; the upper edge, from having been long exposed to the influence of the atmosphere from being so near the surface, was so much disintegrated as to be at first taken for charcoal, but we ascertained the diameter to be about fourteen inches; it is quite plain, and composed of coarse friable clay, of a brick red outside and black within. It contained calcined human bones, amongst which were the following articles — two fine pins, made from the tibia of an animal probably not larger than a sheep; a short piece cut from a tubular bone, and laterally perforated, possibly intended for a whistle; a bronze awl, upwards of three inches long, which has been inserted into a handle, and is now covered with a very dark and polished ærugo; a flint spear head; and a bipennis, or double-edged axe, of basaltic stone. All these, except the whistle and the awl, have been submitted to the fire, by which the axe had been so much injured that it was difficult to extricate it from its position under the bones at the bottom of the urn without its falling to pieces. The urn itself, being very thin and adhering to the rock, was taken out in small fragments. The few stone axes found during our researches have uniformly been associated with the brazen daggers, and were replaced by the plain axe-shaped celt at a slightly later period, but in no other instance have they accompanied an interment by cremation; indeed the instances in which the brass dagger has been found with burnt bones bear so small a proportion to those in which it accompanies the skeleton, that we may conclude there was a marked, though gradual change in the mode of burial introduced about the time when the knowledge of metallurgy was acquired. There is, however, evidence that the ancient rite of burial was resumed at a later period, dating but little, if at all, previous to the occupation of the country by the Romans.

MAPPLETON.

In a field called Callow, at Mappleton, near Ashbourne, are three tumuli placed in a line about eighty yards from each other; they are all formed of sandy earth and pebbles. We opened that nearest to Ashbourne on the 28th of August; it is fourteen yards diameter, and two feet six inches high. On the natural surface, the earth was darker in colour and finer than elsewhere, and mixed with a little charcoal; near the centre was a piece of an urn, some burnt bones, and flakes of flint. On the same day, we cut into that at the opposite extremity with no better success, finding only flints and charcoal, but no bones. The height of this mound, which has been frequently ploughed over, is two feet only.

1st September, we opened the centre mound, which had not been so much reduced by the plough; it is twenty yards across, and 3½ feet high in the middle, where is a large tree. The occupier of the land told us that he had some years ago dug down by the roots of the tree, and found what he considered human ashes and charcoal spread all over the floor of the mound, in the midst of which he discovered a piece of iron about four inches long, since lost. We examined the natural surface at the same point without detecting the least particle of bone, but noticed a thin layer of light-coloured sandy clay spread on the natural surface, which was the substance mistaken for human ashes. By undercutting the tree a few calcined bones were found, and in another direction were some pieces of an urn, a few more bones, and chippings of flint.

BLORE.

On the 15th of September we opened a barrow called Lady Low, near Blore, not far from that examined on the 2nd July. It is twenty yards across, and has a central elevation of three feet and a half, formed of compact earth, burnt red about the middle, below which the earth was ash-coloured and plentifully mixed with charcoal down to the natural surface, where the latter was so abundant as to form a layer in some places several inches thick. A deposit of calcined bones occupied the exact centre of the mound; they were raised a few inches from the floor, and were embedded in charcoal. Amongst them were an arrow-head of white flint, a bone pin, and some fragments of very thin bronze, all much burnt. Higher up we discovered, by cutting with the spade, a small oval cavity, eight inches long by four wide, surrounded by charcoal, which was quite empty, but suggested the idea of a wooden or wicker vessel that had been partly consumed and covered with earth. A few instruments of flint, and some very minute and indeterminate pieces of bronze, were found at no great depth below the turf, in the centre of the barrow.

September 22nd, we opened a barrow near Cotton, called the Round Knoll, of the diameter of eighteen yards and five feet high, composed of clay, with a few sand stones, near the natural level. A kiln for burning lime had been made at the end, but as it did not seem to extend to the centre we made it the base of operations by cutting a trench to the centre of the mound, on a level with the bottom of the kiln. The rest of the barrow seemed never to have been disturbed, yet we discovered nothing but charcoal and rats' bones, which lay near the bottom of the kiln, which no doubt occupied the place where the interment had been deposited. On the same day we partially opened another mound nearer to Cotton, less than the last, and not more than eighteen inches high. We cut down in the middle, between two large stones placed on edge, which at first appeared to form a cist, but which we soon found had been converted into a limekiln by some utilitarian occupier of the land

29th of September, we examined a tumulus at Pike Low, between the villages of Waterhouses and Waterfall, which had likewise been destroyed by lime burning.

THROWLEY.

On the same day we opened another barrow on Throwley Moor, which, like the last in the same locality, is formed on an uneven protuberance of rock; it is thirteen yards diameter. About two feet from the surface, near the centre, we found a shallow rounded grave, about three feet in average diameter, the bottom covered with black ashes, amongst which were a few dislocated bones, above which were some large pieces of a plain globular urn of considerable size, which had been perforated at the side with two small holes, like a similar vessel found at Steeplow, near Alstonefield, in 1845. At no great distance was another depression in the rock, seven feet long and just wide enough to receive a human body, the broken remains of which were accompanied by a few calcined bones and one chipping of flint. A piece of the urn was found in the earth above.

COTTON.

October 13th, we opened a barrow at Three Lows, between Cotton and Ramshorn, which is a flat mound, sixteen yards across. We first removed a large space in the centre, where it was much intermixed with stone. At the natural level was a layer of grey earth a few inches thick, so compact as not to be penetrable by the spade, which was succeeded by soft red earth, covering a pavement of flat stones, where we found a small piece of fused lead. Proceeding northward, we perceived the stratum of grey earth to be broken up and mixed with charcoal, and found a good instrument of flint. Abandoning the north side, we excavated towards the south, and shortly discovered an interment of calcined bones, spread upon a layer of charcoal; they contained a spear-point of calcined flint, and two arrow-heads of the same material, unburnt.

STANSHOPE.

On the 17th and 24th of November we opened a barrow in the Ram's Croft Field, at Stanshope, which is more than usually concave in the middle, the depression being thirteen yards across and almost three feet deep; the entire diameter of the mound is forty yards. We commenced digging in the middle of the bason, finding rock at the depth of two feet, whereon lay two parallel rows of rugged stones, about three feet asunder, which had probably formed a cist, as part of a skeleton, pieces of pottery, and a flint arrow-point, together with rats' bones and charcoal, were found between them. On the rock was a thin layer of ash-coloured earth, as we thought resulting from the soil being saturated with water that had been poured upon a fire in which some bones had been calcined near this part of the barrow.

About three feet south-east of the centre was a deposit of burnt bones, lying in the earth about a foot beneath the turf, without protection. In the rock below were two circular graves, each about a yard diameter, and about four feet in depth from the surface of the mound; they were about a yard asunder, and that to the south, being first examined, was found to contain two skeletons — one, which was that of a young person, lay at the bottom, and a little higher was the other, the remains of a child. Between the two was a large instrument of grey flint, rounded at each end, with other chippings; and close to the vertebræ of the child was a very beautiful drinking cup, 6¾ inches high, with parallel bands or hoops of ornament, which stood upright when found. Above these interments, and within two feet of the surface, were the remains of another elegant drinking cup, ornamented with a chevrony pattern, the fragments of which, although lying altogether, and being carefully gathered, failed to supply more than two-thirds of the whole vessel. It is therefore probable that it had been broken before the interment for some reason with which we are unacquainted. An arrow-head of flint was found with it.

The other grave also contained the skeleton of a child, accompanied, like the former, by a neat spear-head of slightly burnt flint, and an equally elegant drinking cup, 6¼ inches high, ornamented in a different style. In this case, it was placed at the head. The three cups are of the same clay, and are altogether so identical in fabric, though varied in ornamentation, that we may safely conclude them to be the work of the same artist. The graves were filled up with earth and stones. On the north side of the area, to which the labour of the two first days was confined, we found part of another skeleton, accompanied by bones of the water rat.

On the 2nd of September, we resumed the examination. Whilst still within the central bason, we found, near to its western limit, some bones of a full-grown human skeleton, a horse's tooth, one instrument of calcined flint, and many unburnt flakes of the same. The lower part of the barrow in this direction was chiefly composed of large stones, with but little earth amongst them, which led us to suppose that there was no interment in their vicinity, as all the other skeletons were surrounded by small stones, mixed with earth. The east side, untouched before from want of time, was next examined, where, at the depth of two feet six inches, we found the disturbed remains of a young person, covered with small stones and earth, lying on the natural surface, and accompanied by rats' bones, a piece of earthenware, and some small flints. We found that this skeleton had been disturbed by the formation of a grave close to it, cut nine inches deep in the rock, for the reception of a later interment, which was discovered immediately after. This grave was irregular both in form and depth, being deepest in the middle, so that the skull and opposite extremities were on a higher level than the rest of the bones. The skeleton, which was that of a tall young man whose femur measures $19\frac{1}{2}$ inches, lay on the left side in the usual contracted position, embedded in earth which presented the appearance and was actually of the consistence of mud, arising from the percolation of water through the overlying mound. A rude piece of black flint lay under the upper part of the body, and at a higher level, above the right shoulder, was an elegantly-shaped bronze dagger, $4\frac{3}{4}$ inches long, with two rivets attached, between which are two holes that have never been filled with metal, but which may have served to bind the dagger more securely to its handle, by thongs of leather or sinews of animals. It presents the corrugated surface usual on bronze instruments that have been buried in their leather sheaths, and is further enriched by the impressions of a few maggots or larvæ of insects. Several small pieces of flint were found in this grave, which at one point was only about a yard from the second discovered by the first day's excavation.

WETTON.

On the 8th of December we reopened the smaller of the barrows at Three Lows, which was examined, without any decisive result, in the summer of 1848. We now discovered two interments in it, the principal being deposited in a cist made of four thin stones in the centre, close to where the former cutting was discontinued. Its dimensions were twenty inches long, seventeen wide, and twenty deep. It contained a deposit of calcined bones, with which were two neat pointed instruments of flint, a bone pin, and part of a small vase of dark-coloured clay, 3¾ inches diameter, with a broad border two inches deep, very carefully ornamented: all these, including the vase, had passed through the fire — that, probably, which had consumed the dead; and it was owing to this that the whole of the vase was not to be found. South from the cist was the skeleton of an aged person, lying within a foot of the surface, surrounded and covered with stones, the head pointing north-west. Nothing was found with it. Outside the cist we observed two pieces of pottery and two flints. The mound was composed of earth, sprinkled with charcoal in all parts except where the interments had been laid.

WARSLOW.

On the 24th of December we examined a barrow on an eminence near Warslow, called the Cops, having a wall built across the middle. We found the floor of the mound depressed in the centre, where, at the depth of four feet from the summit, were two skeletons of young men, lying on their left sides, about a yard asunder. One of them possessed a single instrument of flint, the other had two; and in both cases they were deposited under the skull.

Calcined bones were found from the surface downwards, but not in any quantity except about half way from the surface, where some lay together, with a flint arrow-point amongst them. Small pieces of pottery, fragments of human bone, tines of stags' horn, and a piece of animal bone, artificially pointed, were picked up at a higher level than the place where the skeletons lay. The interior of the mound was of stone, with some earth; the outer parts were of more unmixed and compact earth.

BARROWS IN STAFFORDSHIRE, OPENED BY MR. CARRINGTON IN 1850.

THROWLEY.

On the 16th of February we opened a barrow at Rushley, near Throwley, twelve yards diameter, and two feet six inches high. We found no interment, but near the centre were fragments of bone, horses' teeth, burnt flint, and rats' bones.

We afterwards re-examined the mound behind Throwley Moor House, where an urn and stone axe were found in 1849, but found it to consist almost entirely of natural rock, the inequalities having been smoothed over into barrow form by the addition of a little earth.

WARSLOW.

On the 23rd of February, at Blakelow, near Warslow, we opened a barrow, twenty yards across and two feet deep in the middle of our section, composed of stiff earth of different colours, inclining to clay. Not far from the centre was a deposit of calcined bones, mixed with charcoal, lying on the natural surface, covered and surrounded with stones placed with but little attention to regularity, excepting a few on the level which seemed to have been arranged in a row. The bones were accompanied by two neatly-wrought instruments of flint — one a spear-head, the other oval — which, contrary to the general custom, had not passed through the fire. Several other trenches were made without further results.

STANTON.

On the 16th of March we opened Scrip Low, a barrow near Stanton, composed of sandy earth and pebbles, and measuring about fourteen yards diameter. We found the interment, consisting of calcined bones, about eighteen inches from the surface, some distance north from the centre, surrounded by sandstones, which only occurred in that part of the barrow. A considerable space in the middle was uncovered, down to the natural surface, about two feet beneath the summit, where a layer of dark-coloured earth was observed, but nothing of importance found, a broken instrument of flint, two small pieces of plain earthenware, and a few burnt bones only being observed.

On the 6th of April we opened a barrow, called Green Low, near Beresford Hall, where Charles Cotton entertained his friend, Isaac Walton, but found nothing beside one piece of burnt bone and a circular implement of flint, as the greatest part of the mound was natural, where otherwise, we found the natural surface at the average depth of two feet, increasing in the centre to a yard, where was some charcoal.

LADY LOW.

On the 13th of April we made a cutting in the south-east side of the tumulus, at Lady Low, near Blore, first examined on the 2nd July, 1849, and discovered a heap of calcined bones buried in the earth, without any provision having been made to enclose them. In their midst lay a bronze dagger, of the usual shape as far as regards the blade, but having a shank or tang to fit into the handle, which was secured by a single peg passing through a hole in the former; the handle, where it overlaid the blade, was terminated by a straight end, and not by a crescent-shaped one as usual. The dagger had been burnt along with the body, furnishing the second instance of the kind, and the third in which that instrument has been discovered with calcined bones in our researches. We also made a further search in the other tumulus at Lady Low, where burnt bones were found on the 14th of September, 1849, but found nothing but two blocks of flint.

20th of April, we reopened the third barrow on Musdin Hill, examined on the 19th of May, 1849, by making a wide section through the middle. This time we cut a circular trench around our former excavation, and found some burnt bones near the surface, with a small piece of an urn and two flints. The upper part of the barrow was composed of differently coloured earth from the lower, in which we found no interment, although it showed no traces of having been disturbed by former digging.

The next barrow is situated in a plantation between Ramshorn and Cotton, near one opened in a field called Three Lows, on the 30th of October, 1849. The present barrow measures 22 yards in diameter, and is about 18 inches high in the middle, but is encircled by a more elevated ring, varying from 3 to 5 feet in height. On the natural level, in the centre, were a few burnt bones, with charcoal; and beneath the south-east segment of the ring were more calcined bones and charcoal. Only one small piece of flint was found. The mound was composed of earth and stones, the latter forming a kind of pavement.

ECTON HILL.

On the 9th of May we opened a barrow on Ecton Hill, a few hundred yards south of that examined on the Hang Bank. We cleared a space about 13 feet square, in the middle, beyond which there was not more than a foot of raised earth, so that a more extensive cutting was needless, and within this limited area we found eight interments, deposited on the rocky surface of the land, about 18 inches below the turf covering the barrow, which had probably been reduced in elevation by repeated ploughing. The general arrangement of the interments may be simply explained by the statement, that in the centre was a skeleton lying in a contracted posture upon the *right* side, surrounded by six skeletons all lying contracted upon the *left* side; and a deposit of calcined bones placed against a stone. They were discovered in the following order. First, the burnt bones; second, a skeleton, beneath which were two rude flints partially calcined; third, a skeleton; fourth, skeleton, accompanied by a round flint; fifth and sixth, two skeletons, lying opposite ways, with the skulls in contact; seventh, skeleton, with a small wrought flint; eighth, a skeleton. With the fifth were a few burnt bones, and the fourth was the central interment.

On the 18th of May we opened a barrow at Thorswood, near Stanton, which we had discovered in returning from that opened on the 6th of September, 1848. The diameter of the present one in 13 yards, with an elevation of 5 feet, presenting an unmutilated appearance. On digging down in the centre the rock was found at the depth of 3 feet, as the tumulus had been raised on a natural prominence and had been previously rifled. A few pieces of an urn, with the usual chevron pattern, were found about a foot below the turf; lower down were some pieces of bone, and at the natural level, in the centre of the barrow, were black ashes and charcoal, with a few pieces of calcined bone and flint. There were also some large stones about the same place, one measuring 3 feet each way, which had no doubt formed a cist for the protection of the urn and calcined bones before the barrow was disturbed. We afterwards examined a circular rise in the next field, but found nothing.

On the 25th of May we examined a barrow upon Morridge, opposite the village of Winkhill, 13 yards diameter and 18 inches high, of the so-called "Druid Barrow" shape, flat in the middle, with an elevated ring surrounding it. We turned over the greater part without finding any thing but a small arrow, and another instrument of burnt flint; a little charred wood was seen on the natural surface.

BITCHINHILL.

On the evenings of the 29th and 30th of May we made further search in the second barrow at Bitchinhill Harbour, previously opened on the 8th of July, 1845, and turned over much of the tumulus without finding any interment. The following notes were taken at the time. The East side was formed of stone mixed with earth, the rest of the mound being of earth only; the rocky floor was also lower on the East than elsewhere, and in this depression we found part of two Romano-British vessels, an iron awl 3½ inches long, which has had a wooden handle, and some charred wood. At the North-West side were numerous pieces of melted lead, some of which had run into forms like thick wire, probably from the heat of the funeral pile, as all the bones we noticed, as well as the pieces of flint, had been calcined. The lead was about a foot beneath the turf, and amongst the usual unimportant objects found in disturbed barrows were fragments of imperfectly baked pottery, pieces of stags' horns, pebbles, and a sharpening stone.

CASTERN.

The large barrow at Castern, near Wetton, first opened on the 14th of June, 1845, was again investigated on the evenings of the 5th, 6th, and 11th of June. On the former occasion, a trench was dug from the south-west side, towards the middle, and on the present a supplementary cutting was made parallel with each side of it. In the western one were no signs of any interment; some human bones, evidently removed from another situation, and some chippings of flint, alone being observed. In the other trench we found the disturbed skeletons of two persons, the skull of one exhibiting the frontal suture, and the usual fragments of flint, pottery, charcoal, and rats' bones. The advancing shades of evening now compelled us to relinquish our labour, and the want of success induced us to fill up the cutting; but on after-consideration we determined to make another attempt in the same direction as where we left off, as that part of the mound was stony to the summit, and mingled with charcoal and detached human bones, whilst elsewhere the superstructure was of earth, resting on a foundation of stone. Hence the inference that a later interment had taken place, the stone dug up in making the grave being thrown in again above it. Accordingly, on the 11th June, we resumed our labours, and were soon rewarded by the discovery of a skeleton upon the floor of the barrow, accompanied by several instruments of flint, three of which lay under the head and shoulders. A more uncommon article, a bronze armilla, was found beneath the edge of a stone that lay upon the skeleton, and in contact with the pelvis, into which it was slightly forced by the pressure, which had likewise broken it into two pieces. It is made of a flat ribbon of bronze, half an inch broad, with overlapping ends to preserve elasticity, ornamented outside with a neatly engraved lozengy pattern, and has a span of 2⅜ inches diameter. The body appeared to have been laid on its back, with the head to the west, but the bones were so imperfect as to render this not quite certain. Wherever we dug in the barrow there were broken human bones and numerous remains of rats.

WETTON.

The largest barrow at Three Lows, near Wetton, opened, as far as the central part is concerned, on the 7th of June, 1845, was now fully investigated on the evenings of the 4th, 10th, 12th, and 13th of June, by a trench cut round the former excavation, so as to expose a considerable space between it and the outside of the mound. We began at the west side, and found, first, an imperfect armlet of thick bronze wire; next, a noble pair of red deer's horns, with part of the skull attached to one of them, and having with them a neat arrow-head of flint. Proceeding onward, we found many pieces of a large urn, with the burnt bones it had contained; and on the 13th we discovered the place where it had been first placed, part of the bottom still remaining in situ. Amongst earth blackened by the admixture of ashes, here were found a very neat barbed arrow-head, and a remarkably fine spearhead or dagger of flint, upwards of five inches long, without the point, which is missing. The latter has been so much calcined as to present a dark-coloured vitrified surface, exhibiting numberless cracks precisely similar to Cracklin porcelain; where broken, it shows a white interior. We had before found two calcined flint spear-heads of smaller size, and a round instrument which may also have been originally deposited with the burnt bones. Fragments of many urns, some tastefully ornamented, burnt and unburnt human bones, large pieces of stags' horns, and flakes of flint, were found in all parts of the mound, but most plentifully on the south and west sides. The unusual number of stags' horns of the largest size found in this barrow on both occasions is very remarkable. They indicate the hunter-life of its occupants, naturally resulting from the facility with which a regular supply of large game could be obtained before the country was to any great extent brought under cultivation.

CASTERN.

There is a small tumulus in the same field at Castern as the large barrow lately described, which we slightly examined on the 12th September, 1846, but abandoned on finding the centre converted into a limekiln, which was, nevertheless, occupied by a human skeleton extended at the bottom, which we were convinced was a modern addition, afterwards explained by information afforded by two aged persons living in the neighbourhood, who stated that the skeleton was that of one Francis Brown, who lived in a house near at hand, and who was one day found suspended by the neck from a beam, with a stool overturned near his feet, upon which discovery he was buried as a suicide in the old limekiln, which was very near and convenient. In the sequel, it appears, however, that poor Brown was unjustly suspected of self-destruction, as it is said that two criminals, executed at York some years after, confessed that they were the actual perpetrators of the murder, and that they had arranged the corpse and stool in such a manner as to convey the impression that the slain man was a suicide.

Notwithstanding all this, we were confident that the mound was a barrow, and as it was full fourteen yards across and four feet high, thought that there was room to find an interment somewhere. We therefore removed a space four yards square between the kiln and the south-east edge, finding at the natural level a pavement of flat stones, whereon were many disjointed human bones belonging to several skeletons, mixed with numerous instruments of calcined flint. The most perfect skeleton lay in the middle of the pavement, with the head towards the interior of the barrow, and was accompanied by a knife, a spear-head, and other instruments of white flint. Nearer to the centre of the barrow was a deposit of burnt bones, and one implement of flint; and not far from the outside we found the remains of a finely ornamented cinerary urn, with its contents, the calcined bones lying broken and disturbed a few inches under the turf.

In the course of the excavation, we found many bones of animals, fragments of vessels (one of which had been a drinking cup), a flat piece of sandstone rubbed hollow at one side, and a round piece of ruddle, or red war paint, which, from its abraded appearance, must have been in much request for colouring the skin of its owner. In the few instances in which this substance has been found in our tumuli, it has uniformly been associated with weapons of flint of good workmanship. Most of the very numerous flints picked up in this barrow are fair specimens.

BAILEY HILL.

On the 3rd of August we opened a barrow on Bailey Hill, between the Dove and Bostorn, on the Derbyshire side of the stream. It was raised upon a very irregular protuberant rock, which in the middle was cut through the loose upper beds into a kind of grave, the bottom of which, conforming to the dip of strata, was three feet deep at one end, whilst it diminished to nothing at the other. In this were three interments, the most primitive of which had been disturbed by the later deposits, its bones being found at intervals from the surface downwards. The bones were those of a full-grown person, and much decayed. A second skeleton was found undisturbed at the bottom, on which it lay on its right side, with the body slightly curved, the knees contracted, and the head to the west. Before the face was a small plain vase, lying on its side, and at the back of the skull was a very large tusk from the wild boar. The femur measures about $16\frac{1}{2}$ inches. About a foot below the surface was a deposit of calcined bones, containing a very neatly made pair of tweezers of bone, unburnt, and perforated for suspension. The grave was

Bone Tweezers.   Bailey Hill.

filled up with stone, and the artificial part of the mound consisted of similar materials, amongst which rats' bones so much abounded as to fill up most of the interstices from the surface to the bottom of the grave. A few pieces of two vessels were picked up during the day. The following remarks upon the barrow, made by Mr. Carrington immediately after the opening, are valuable. He says — "I consider this to be the most primitive barrow I ever opened, as the small instrument of bone may have been deposited with the burnt bones at a much more recent period than that in which the mound was originally constructed. The coarse urn, without any decoration — the absence of every other article, with the exception of the boar's tusk — serve to strengthen this supposition. The contents of the cist were examined with the greatest care, yet nothing more was discovered, except one small round piece of ironstone — not a sandstone, or pebble, or charcoal (which are all commonly found in Celtic barrows) — not even one bit of flint was to be seen. This is the first barrow I have opened in which the latter material has not been present."

On the 11th of August we went to examine some mounds on elevated land, near Bostorn, Derbyshire, which looked like barrows, and in which we found large loose stones, with numerous snail shells beneath them; but as they were not promising, we soon left them. We next dug a hole within a rude circle of stones, on a hill side facing the river Dove, where, finding a piece of a stag's horn and a bit of an urn, with some charcoal, we were induced to make a fair trial. The circle, which is not complete, is eight yards diameter, and formed of stones irregularly heaped together for the purpose of retaining the earth within it, which would otherwise be washed down the declivity by heavy rains. The earth in the inside is about a yard deep, and is succeeded by a deep bed of shingly stone, unmixed with earth, common to the bases of many of the Derbyshire hills, being the gradual accumulation of debris from the limestone rocks above. The earth in contact with the shingle was black, and intermixed with fragments of bone and charcoal, yet yielded no interment beside one piece of calcined bone, and a quantity of black ashes upon a flat stone, intermixed with what we thought might be the dust of burnt bones. A few chippings of flint, numerous animal teeth, and a few rats' bones were observed.

ELKSTONE.

August 31st—On the summit of a hill, south-west of Elkstone, are two barrows, near each other, both of which were examined on the same day. The first, sixteen yards diameter and one yard in central height, was opened by a section through the middle, three yards long and one wide, cut through stiff earth and clay, mixed near the surface with stone. The trench was afterwards enlarged by cutting about a yard more from one side, when a few burnt bones and two small flints were found. Continuing this extension down to the natural surface, we found a full-grown skeleton, with the legs drawn up, lying on its right side, with the head to the north-west. The bones, which were much decayed, had become embedded in clayey earth whilst sound, and now appeared more like a cast or impression than a real skeleton. It had been laid on the floor of the barrow, on which was a thin coat of ashes, causing the superincumbent earth to separate so perfectly as to leave a level surface round the bones, thus aiding the illusion. A stone placed lengthway at each side afforded the only protection, and in the earth above we found a bronze awl, rather thicker than usual, a few instruments of flint, two animal teeth, pieces of human bone in calcined and natural state, and rats' bones in small quantity. The second barrow is twenty yards across and only one foot high. In the centre was a large rubbing-post for cattle, which had been set up in the midst of a deposit of calcined bones buried about a foot beneath the surface. They were spread over a space a yard long by about a foot wide, from whence a great many were collected, though some were left closely imbedded in clay, forming a light-coloured seam about an inch and a half thick, out of which they were with difficulty to be taken. They were accompanied by part of a very beautifully ornamented vase, which had been destroyed by the rubbing-post, and a few pieces of calcined flint, three only of which can be called instruments. A little lower, and to the side, were the decayed remains of a young person, accompanied by a large boar's tusk and some unimportant flints. Underneath we found a large grave, cut four feet deep in the rock and filled with stones, which were emptied out for the length of three yards, without showing either end of the grave; its least width was four feet, but it appeared to increase the further we went. On the rocky bottom lay a skeleton in a contracted posture, with the head to the north-west, much in the same manner as that in the other barrow. The closest scrutiny failed to reveal any thing beyond rats' bones as an accompaniment. The femur measures 18½ inches. A large sandstone, with a small bowl-shaped cavity worked in it, was found near the burnt bones. A similar stone was found at Stanton, Staffordshire, and other examples will occur in the course of the volume.

WETTON.

On the 9th of September, we opened a mound nine yards across, near Thor's Cave, Wetton, situated midway between that object and the road to Grindon. Owing to its very slight elevation it is not easily seen, and a wall crosses it some distance from the centre. We turned most of it over, finding it to consist of red earth, mixed with chert, and to show near the surface charcoal, bits of bone, burnt and unburnt, and pieces of stags' horn. Near the centre, about a foot below the surface, we found two very curious vessels; one of rather globular form, four inches high, is carved in sandstone like some of the Irish urns, and is ornamented by four grooves round the outside. About a foot from it was another equally curious vessel, which may be styled a bronze pan or kettle, four inches high and six diameter, with a slender iron bow like a bucket handle. It has been first cast and then hammered, and is very slightly marked by horizontal ridges. The

Vessels of Stone and Bronze, Wetton.

stone vessel was found in an upright position, and the bronze one was inverted: above it were traces of decayed wood. It is probable that a deposit of burnt bones was placed near the centre of the mound, the greatest part of which was in a field that had been often tilled, so that they might easily have been so far removed by the plough as to leave only the few traces which we observed near the surface. Stone vessels of this kind are rarely found in England, but are common in the north of Scotland and the Shetland Isles, where they are not unfrequently provided with handles.

STANSHOPE.

In a meadow by the road side, between Stanshope and Dam Gate, are three tumuli, two of which are within thirty yards of each other: the third is at a greater distance from either. They are composed of different coloured earth, grey being the prevailing tint. That nearest Stanshope was first opened on the 16th of October, by cutting out a portion of the middle, five yards square, to the depth of three feet six inches, but without corresponding success, as nothing was found to indicate the nature of the mound but a sprinkling of charcoal. It is 28 yards diameter and three feet high, and in all probability contains calcined bones.

The second (about thirty yards from the first) is the same height, but about two yards less in diameter. It was opened on the afternoons of the 2nd and 5th of November, by digging a circular hole in the middle, and several trenches in the south and east sides, with but little more satisfactory results than in the former case. The charcoal was more abundant, and we found a rudely formed spear-head and some chippings of flint, and near the surface some animal teeth and bones.

The third (nearest to Dam Gate) is neither so high nor so large as the others, as it measures only sixteen yards across. We made a section nineteen feet long by eight wide, from east to west, through the middle, and found only a few particles of calcined bone, and numerous chippings of flint, two of which have been intended for instruments; one of the latter has been burnt.

On the 27th of December we opened a barrow in a field to the right of the road from Load Mill to Alstonefield, which is eleven yards diameter and three feet high in the centre, composed of earth, with a few flat stones near the surface. The earth in the lower part was darker coloured than above, and much mixed with charcoal, amongst which were a few calcined bones and two blocks of flint. Nearly the whole mound was turned over without further success, and still the lower part had evidently never been disturbed. It is pretty clear that the interment of burnt bones had been enclosed within a small cist, erected near the surface with the flat stones we there found, and which had been pulled to pieces.

BARROWS OPENED BY MR. CARRINGTON IN 1851, PRINCIPALLY IN STAFFORDSHIRE.

On the 1st of March we resumed our labours for the season, having obtained permission to excavate two barrows near Broad Low Ash, in a field to the right hand of the road leading from thence to Ashbourne, from which town they are about two miles distant. They are not more than ten yards asunder, and their diameters are respectively seventeen and twenty-two yards. We selected the least for examination first, and found it to consist of stiff earth, with many large stones in the centre. On sinking down at this point, we found human bones that had been displaced to make room for a later interment; beneath was a grave cut one foot deep in the natural soil, which was about a yard from the summit of the mound. The first undisturbed interment lay on the natural level, close to the north-east side of the grave. It was a skeleton reposing on its right side, with the head to the north, having with it a small spear-head of flint, and near the skull a deposit of calcined human bones, containing two neatly chipped flints, both fractured from having been burnt with the body. We have here a double interment, by inhumation and cremation, suggesting a barbarous rite. Within the grave was the skeleton of a young person, lying on the right side, in the same direction as the others. Before the face was a very neatly ornamented vessel of clay, $5\frac{1}{2}$ inches high, inverted upon the smooth side of a large boulder; and a small spear-head of flint. The ornamentation of the vase has been effected in part by a flat-sided pointed instrument, and partly by the thumb nail.

On the 8th of March we examined the largest barrow at Broad Low Ash, which is so near the road as to have lost a part of one side by the fence, although the centre remained perfectly intact. By digging a trench, nine feet wide and eighteen feet long, through the middle, we found it to be entirely composed of earth, except in a place about two yards from the roadside, where there were a number of stones about a foot beneath the surface, and near them some charcoal, with burnt bones in small quantity, and flakes of flint. No other trace of interment was found.

In other barrows similarly composed of earth, flat stones and scattered bones have been found near the summit, all below being formed of solid earth, frequently in strata of different colour, which have evidently never been disturbed, whilst the most careful search has failed to discover any deposit in the usual situation on or below the natural soil; whence we may conclude that in this by no means unfrequent class of tumuli, the interment (generally by cremation) was for some reason placed near the surface, where it was so liable to destruction by cultivation and other causes so as to render it a matter of surprise that *any* remnants should have been preserved to the present day.

CALTON MOOR.

On the 26th of April, we opened a barrow near Calton Moor House, thirty yards diameter, consisting of earth only, which, though much lowered by ploughing, and further mutilated by a driving-road for cattle having been cut through it, was fortunately not sufficiently injured to affect the original interment, which consisted of a simple deposit of calcined bones, placed exactly in the centre of the barrow, without either cist or accompaniment save charcoal, which spread out from the bones over the natural surface for some distance. We dug in other parts of the mound without meeting with further interments, but we found a few flints, including a barbed arrow-head, and a flake from an instrument which has had a polished surface.

ECTON HILL.

On the evenings of the 12th and 13th of May, we opened a second barrow upon Hang Bank, about 300 yards east of that previously examined. The diameter is about sixteen yards, and the mound appears perfect; but notwithstanding its promising exterior, nothing of importance was discovered, a small deposit of burnt bones only being laid in a depression in the natural soil. About a foot from them were two pieces of flint — one a rounded, the other a pointed instrument which seems designed for an arrow-head. The barrow being raised on a ridge of rock was not so deep as it appeared, having an elevation of about two feet in the centre. It was found to be composed throughout of earth, although the neighbourhood abounds with stone, and was so completely excavated that we are satisfied no other interment has ever been made.

On the 24th of May we examined a mutilated barrow, near Ballidon, Derbyshire, in a field called Back Low Close, having in the middle a large stone, which being removed we found the remaining depth of the mound to be about two feet. From this point we extended our excavation around till it became evident that the whole had been plundered. We merely found the remnants of an urn, with bones and teeth of animals, and a little charcoal.

Another barrow in the same field had been removed some time before, when a skeleton, accompanied by a vessel, and lying in a cist, was found, and of course destroyed. At the time of our visit one edge only of the mound remained, from which we obtained burnt bones, charcoal, and rats' bones.

On the 14th of June we made several cuttings in the conspicuous barrow on Wolfscote Hill, which was opened in 1844, the first of which was from the south west side. We continued it for about four yards, and found the actual height of artificial material to be six feet, consisting entirely of stone, small above and increasing in size towards the base, where the stones were arranged so as to incline to the centre. Another opening was made at the east side, where the stone was intermixed with earth abounding in rats' bones, splinters of human bone, and flakes of flint.

SHEEN.

On the 21st of June we made an excavation in the centre of a large tumulus, at the Brund, near Sheen, measuring 38 yards diameter and nine feet high, composed of earth. About half way down we found a deposit of calcined bones, much decayed, the teeth being most conspicuous amongst the fragments. Near them was a triangular sandstone, in which a circular cavity had been artificially worked, like that found at Elkstone on the 31st of August, 1850. By filling up the cutting, we found a flint that had been chipped to a circular form.

On the 16th of July we made another parallel trench, near four yards long, which at the north end was two yards deep, and gradually increased to three at the other extremity, before reaching the undisturbed surface. We found no interment, but observed a little charcoal, and picked up two chippings of flint, and another of the sandstones, with a cup-shaped cavity worked in it. The stone in this case was too large for carriage, so we cut out the part with the cup. Capsular stones of this kind are not uncommonly found in tumuli on the Yorkshire moors, especially in the neighbourhood of Pickering, as will be seen further on in this volume. I was also told by Mr. Rhind that he had found the same inside the primitive structures called "Picts' Houses," in Caithness. We were told that the apex of this barrow had been much lowered some time since, when a bronze weapon, half a yard in length, was found.

On the 11th of July we examined a third barrow, at Three Lows, Wetton, in a line with the two previously opened. It is a large shallow mound, and yielded nothing but charcoal, although several trenches were made in it.

On the 15th of July we made an excavation, four yards long by three wide, in a barrow in the garden at Newton Grange, near Tissington, Derbyshire. The mound measured fifteen yards diameter and four feet high, and is composed of stiff earth, mixed with chert, amongst which we observed charcoal and a few chippings of flint at intervals from the surface to the natural level, where there were some pieces of calcined bone, a piece of coal, and an iron nail, the two last showing that the barrow had been previously opened. On the same day we dug a hole in the middle of another barrow, on a hill at Newton Grange, looking towards Parwich, the dimensions of which were twenty-eight yards diameter by two feet six inches in height, finding it composed of earth and gravel, but making no discovery.

On the 18th October we turned over a space of about twelve square yards in the centre, for the most of which we found the natural level strewed with charcoal and burnt earth, where were also a few rude flints, but no trace of interment. We likewise tried other parts of the barrow without success.

SHEEN.

On the 17th of July we opened a barrow, close to the road from Sheen to Holme End, measuring 28 yards diameter. It was lowered about four feet in 1837, and is now two feet high, constructed of sandstones and earth. Several trenches were cut, and at length a deposit of calcined bones was found on the natural surface, about ten yards from the south edge of the barrow. At a little distance were two arrow-points, and a circular-ended instrument of flint. A little further from the bones was a small piece of the edge of an urn. A great deal of charred wood was found upon the natural surface, about the south-east side.

NEW INNS.

On the 9th of August we examined the remains of a barrow which had been raised upon a rocky mound near New Inns, Derbyshire, finding only broken human bones, teeth of rats and other quadrupeds, with flakes of flint and pieces of earthenware.

We then proceeded towards Cold Eaton, where in a pasture field, between Green Low and Net Low barrows, opened in 1845, are two more large flat barrows, previously unnoticed. That opened on the present occasion was nearest Net Low. It was about twenty yards across, with a central elevation of eighteen inches, and was entirely composed of earth. The original deposit was placed in a circular hole, eighteen inches diameter, sunk about six inches in the stony surface of the land on which the barrow was raised, so that the entire depth from the top of the latter was two feet. The interment consisted of a quantity of calcined human bones, which lay upon a thin layer of earth at the bottom of the hole, as compactly as if they had at first been deposited within a shallow basket, or similar perishable vessel. Upon them lay some fragments of iron, parts of two bone combs, and twent-eight convex objects of bone, like button-moulds.

The pieces of iron have been attached to some article of perishable material; the largest fragment has a good-sized loop, as if

180

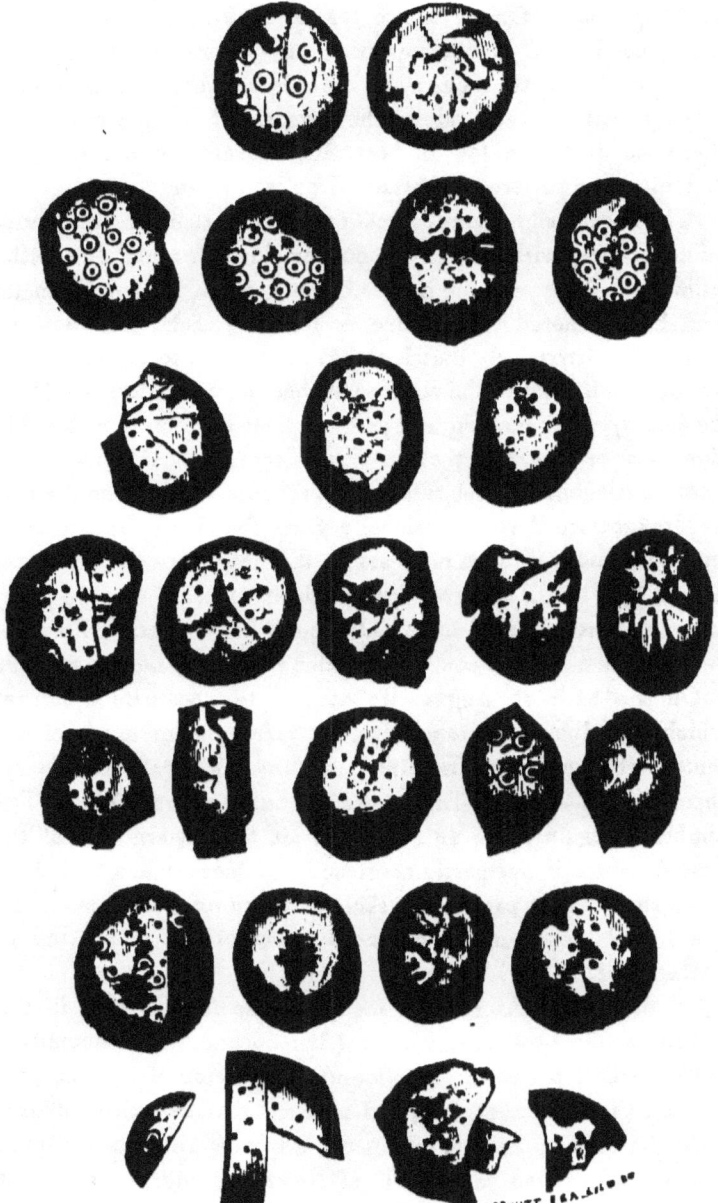

Bone Draughts from New Inns.

for suspension. One of the combs has been much like the small-tooth comb used in our nurseries, and is ornamented by small annulets cut in the bone; the other is of more elaborate make, having teeth on each side as the former, but being strengthened by a rib up the middle of both sides, covered with a finely-cut herring-bone pattern, and attached by iron rivets

The twenty-eight bone objects consist of flattened hemispherical pieces, mostly with dots on the convex side; in some, dots within annulets. They vary from half an inch to an inch in diameter, and have generally eight, nine, or ten dots each; but these are disposed so irregularly that it would be difficult to count them off hand, which leads to the conclusion that these counters would not be employed for playing any game dependent upon numbers, like dominoes or dice, but that they were more probably used for a game analagous to draughts. This is most likely to be the fact, as draughtmen have occasionally been found in Scandinavian grave mounds; and we must assign this interment, if not to the Danes, still to the Pagan Saxons, whose customs were in many respects identical. All the articles found in this barrow have undergone the process of combustion, along with the human remains.

On the 14th of August we opened the companion-barrow, which was about the same size, by turning over much of the centre, when we found nothing but three pieces of late pottery, apparently of Romano-British ware; but on the 20th of December we again made an excavation on the eastern side of the mound, where it was partly constructed of loose stones, and there found the greatest part of the skeleton of an ox, accompanied by a few rats' bones, and some more pieces of the same kind of earthenware.

On the 7th of August we made a little further trial in the barrow at Slip Low, near Wetton (first opened 12th September, 1846), and in the south edge found the skeleton of a young person and a few pieces of flint, and near the surface a piece of urn.

On the 30th of August we opened a barrow near the turnpike road, a few hundred yards north of Newton Grange, composed of earth, measuring thirty-six yards diameter, and two feet high in the middle, where, sinking down, we came to a depression three feet wide, cut about a foot deep in the loose upper beds of rock. It was filled with ashes and charcoal, amongst which were hazel nuts, but no trace of interment, except some pieces of an urn and a slender arrow-point of burnt flint. A few more bits of flint were found in other places.

On the 12th of September we examined a small barrow at Calton, Staffordshire, without success, finding only animal teeth and a few bits of calcined human bone.

WETTON.

By referring to the 8th of June, 1849, it will be seen that we then opened a barrow at Longlow, near Wetton, situated amongst mine hillocks, from which circumstance we overlooked the singular structure of which that barrow forms the termination only. At the distance of 220 yards, S.S.W., is another bowl-shaped barrow, sixteen yards diameter, and between the two is an artificial ridge or vallum, running the whole distance and connecting them; its average height is about four feet, but in some parts it increases to six feet. It is constructed by a central wall, built of large stones nearly to the required height of the ridge, against which flat stones of all sizes have been inclined, so as to save material; finally, the whole has been covered with small stones and earth, so as to form a regular slope from each side to the summit, along which at present runs a high stone wall, which had long prevented us observing the true character of this very remarkable work. Many of the stones used in its construction appear to have been quarried, while others have, no doubt, been collected from the surface of the land. In several places opened at intervals along its course, we found very numerous fragments of human bone, skeletons of rats, weasels, &c., and a substance resembling old mortar, whilst on the undisturbed surface there was a good deal of charcoal which had not been burnt on the spot, but had been scattered about.

On the 27th of September we opened the barrow at the S.S.W. extremity, and found the interior arrangement of its centre to consist of a row of broad flat stones, set on end in the natural soil for the length of about eleven feet, in a line with the connecting ridge, and terminating at the N.N.E. end, in the middle of a wall built at right angles, three yards long and one high. In the western corner, formed by their junction, we found burnt bones scattered all the way down from the top, accompanied by no instrument, and by but few rats' bones.

On the 11th of October we examined the remains of a large barrow between Parwich and Pike Hall, Derbyshire, consisting of a segment about eight yards wide, crossed by a wall. The original circle was plainly discernible, measuring nearly thirty yards across. We found an imperfect human skull, a piece of flint, and some other bones, about two feet deep in the undisturbed part. When the mound was destroyed a few years before, several skeletons being found, it was considered by the natives as the burial place of those who had fallen in Oliver Cromwell's wars, the finder stating that one of the skulls had a slice cut " clean " off the side by the stroke of a sword, and that he found a brass plate from the hat of one of the soldiers. The latter was unfortunately lost before our visit.

LEEK.

On the 29th of December we proceeded to excavate the Cock Low barrow, close to the town of Leek, a large mound forty yards diameter and eighteen feet high, composed of sand, and raised above a natural surface of red sand, unmixed with any other tint. After cutting a square six yards each way down the centre to the depth of five feet, we came to a layer of ashes and charcoal, resting on a stratum of white sand. Among the former were some small pieces of an urn, a few pieces of calcined human bone, and a round-edged instrument of flint. Besides these we observed nothing; and it does not appear that any interment had ever been deposited on the natural level, in which respect the barrow resembles many other large mounds of earth in which an interment by cremation has been made at a high level or near the summit.

The following notice appeared in the *Derby Mercury* of January 7th, 1852 — "On Tuesday, some degree of excitement was caused in Leek by the circumstance that Mr. Bateman had sent an exploring party to open the Cock Low, a barrow standing on part of the property of Mrs. Watt. The party worked vigorously on Monday and Tuesday, and were so far successful in their search as to find the usual deposit of charcoal, &c. They found one instrument and a small piece or two of bone, which, however, pulverised on coming into contact with the air. The party began their cutting a few yards to the south of the centre, and continued to sink the opening until they arrived at the original surface, which is about six yards below the present surface of the tumulus, and was indicated by being of the same red sand as the surrounding surface of the field, and by its being unmixed with charcoal or any other extraneous substance. It appeared evident, from the appearances presented by the cutting, that when the tumulus, at its formation, had attained to within five feet of its present altitude, a large fire had been kindled upon it, as was manifested by the abundance of ashes and charcoal found at that elevation, amongst and nearly in the centre of which they found a few fragments of an earthen vase or urn, and one of those small rounded flints, for which conjecture has as yet assigned no certain use. Below and in contact with this layer of charcoal and ashes was a layer of white sand, and it was surmised that this lightness of colour might have been the effect of the fire; and in this idea Mr. Carrington coincided, or at least conceded to have been well founded. On and about these particular spots Mr. Carrington bestowed the most minute attention, as he believed that there the body had been calcined; and he was the more inclined to believe this opinion from the fact that there were no indications below of any kind to lead him to infer that any interment had ever taken place at a greater depth. With the exception of a very few tumuli, Mr. Bateman and Mr. Carrington have always found that, in all barrows composed entirely of soil, as in the present instance, nothing has been discovered except a deposit of calcined bones, charcoal, and a few flint instruments, arrow-heads, &c., accidentally dropped there during the ceremony, or brought casually in the earth of which the mound has been formed. The opening of the tumulus has led to this satisfactory result — that there no longer remains any doubt that this barrow has been a place of interment; and although it has added nothing to the museum of the gentleman who has been at the cost of the undertaking, he has had the satisfaction of imparting much gratification to many anxious observers; and we trust not without having added something to the fund of information he has amassed upon this subject."

BARROWS, MOSTLY IN STAFFORDSHIRE, OPENED BY MR. CARRINGTON IN 1852.

BITCHIN HILL.

On the 4th and 6th of June we re-opened a barrow at Bitchin Hill Harbour, which had been partially excavated on the 8th of July, 1845. The present operations were directed to the southeast side, where, at the depth of about a foot from the surface, we found the contracted skeleton of a young person, lying on its right side, and having a small vase, 6¼ inches high, simply ornamented, standing upright at the feet — a very unusual position in this part of the country, as the vessels are almost always placed near the upper part of the person. The vase was guarded by a flat stone, a foot square, set up by its side. A similar stone was set on edge by the skeleton, which was embedded in rats' bones, and was much decayed. About a handful of burnt bones' was found at no great distance from it. More to the east we found the skeleton of an adult, wanting the head, although the bones had not been disturbed; it lay in the usual contracted posture, with the shoulders towards the head of the other skeleton, and was accompanied by a boar's tusk of small size only. Amongst other animal remains observed in the barrow were bones of the polecat (*Mustela Putorius*, Linn.). It will be remarked that headless skeletons are not very unusual in tumuli in this part of England.

On the 5th of June we examined a mound on Bunster Hill, by Dovedale, which, from being raised on a natural prominence, is very conspicuous. Its actual diameter is twenty-five yards, the height two feet. A road has been cut through the north-east side, without, however, injuring the centre; yet we were unsuccessful in finding any interment, although we made five parallel trenches, each five yards long, through the principal part of the tumulus, without seeing more than a little charcoal about the middle.

On the 29th of July, a barrow near Blore, in a field adjoining the Ashbourne road, was opened. Its diameter was twenty-six yards, and its height two feet six inches in the middle, through which we made a section, eight yards long and five feet wide, finding the material to be earth, slightly mixed with charcoal. At the south end of the trench we found a few calcined bones, lying together, about a foot beneath the surface, with a fragment of firmly-baked pottery at no great distance. We next dug a parallel trench at the north-west side, but found nothing, the mound being there wholly of earth. The opposite side of the tumulus being chiefly of stone, we were induced to make a large excavation, which, after all, produced only a few flakes of flint, and a shred of the glazed coraline pottery known as "Samian ware."

THROWLEY.

On the 30th and 31st of July we re-opened the barrow on Arbor Hill, first investigated by us on the 20th of May, 1858, when we limited the search to the centre. On the present occasion we began by sinking through the north-east side, which being done to the depth of six feet without affording anything of interest, we then undercut the side nearest the middle of the barrow, where the stones were larger and more open, and soon discovered a skeleton, accompanied by a deposit of calcined bones, laid without protection about a yard below the turf. The skull shows the individual to have been young, and the following articles were placed on a flat stone near the skeleton — a barbed arrow-head with a serrated edge, and a prism-shaped instrument of burnt flint, the latter polished; a small flat piece of wrought bone, that may have been part of a larger implement; and the root end of a horn of the red deer, which has been obliquely broken, and measures about nine inches in length. We examined the contrary side on the 31st of July, and found in the earth a very compact mass of black ashes, having amongst them part of a coarse urn, in small pieces, accompanied by a few burnt bones and one flake of flint. Chippings of the same and pieces of firmly-baked pottery were found during the two days' excavation.

STANSHOPE.

On the 31st of August we opened a barrow near Stanshope, about 300 yards from Longlow, which covers a considerable surface, the boundary of which is ill-defined. We began by digging a wide trench from the south-west side, through earth mixed with stones, until we came to a well-built wall of flat stones, that presented so regular a front to the exterior of the mound that we at first mistook it for a cist. The excavation was continued straight forward for eight yards, and was then turned round so as to form another parallel trench. As far as we uncovered the level on which the barrow was raised there was no indication of interment, though a pavement of flat stones had been carefuly laid down, on which was reared the core or nucleus of the mound, composed of flat stones, placed on edge, with an inclination towards the centre. Above these the material, consisting of earth and stone, was heaped up without care. Amongst the latter, and occurring from the top to about half way down, we found numerous rats' bones, pieces of human skull, and other bones (some calcined); fragments of two or three urns, including one of very hard black ware, and another of red pottery; two small pieces of bronze, warped by heat; an iron awl, three inches long, which has been fixed in a wooden handle, like many others that we have found in the tumuli; and a piece of a very thick cup or bason of green glass, in an iridescent state, like the Saxon tumbler found at Cow Low in 1846 (Vestiges, p. 94), here reproduced.

Glass Cup.—Cowlow.

In addition to these we gathered some pieces of unglazed pottery, medieval in appearance, whence we conclude that the barrow was previously disturbed at what has now become an ancient period, perhaps by those in search of beads or stones to decorate objects of ecclesiastical display, as was frequently the case. An ivory diptych, of the eighth or ninth century, in the collection at Lomberdale, is surrounded by metal work of the thirteenth, enclosing several Roman gems, and a number of amethyst beads, precisely like a necklace engraved in Akerman's "Pagan Saxondom," page 5, which are most probably the plunder of a Saxon or Frankish barrow.

On the 10th of September we opened the gravehill of a Saxon lady, at Wyaston, Derbyshire, the diameter of which is thirteen yards and the central height four feet; it is entirely of earth, overlaid with a few pebbles on the surface. We began by cutting from the south side to the middle, where was no indication of interment, either upon or below the natural level; but it was seen that a grave had been made on the east side of our trench, where from the surface to the depth of two feet the earth was much darker than in other parts of the mound. By digging in the direction thus indicated, we had the good fortune to discover the remains of a human skeleton, consisting merely of the enamel crowns of the teeth, which, though themselves but scanty mementos of female loveliness, were accompanied by several articles indicating that the deceased was not unaccustomed to add the ornaments of dress to the charms of nature. These comprise a handsome necklace of twenty-seven beads, a silver finger ring, silver earrings, and a circular brooch or fibula. Five of the beads are of amber, carefully rounded into a globular shape, the largest an inch diameter; the remaining twenty-two (two of which are broken) are mostly small, and made of porcelain or opaque glass, very prettily variegated with blue, yellow, or red, on a white or red ground. The finger ring is made of thick silver wire, twisted into an ornamental knot at the junction of the ends. The earrings are too slight and fragmentary for description. The fibula is a circular ring, ribbed on the front, an inch and a half diameter, composed of a doubtful substance. The remains of the teeth show the person to have been rather youthful, and afford another instance of the extreme decay of the skeleton usual in Saxon deposits in this part of the country, whilst those which we have reason to reckon centuries more ancient are mostly well preserved.

A smaller barrow, at a short distance, was opened immediately after, affording nothing. It was composed of thin layers of differently coloured earth, amongst which dark brown, approaching to black, predominated.

BARROWS OPENED BY MR. CARRINGTON IN 1853.

CASTERN.

On the 17th of April we re-opened the barrow at Little Lea, Castern, which was first examined on the 20th July, 1848, when our excavation was confined to the centre. We now began to dig at the south side, and continued to do so in a direction concentric with the former cutting till we reached the eastern quarter of the barrow, where at the depth of half a yard we found a deposit of calcined human bones, which were partly contained in a funnel-shaped hole, near two feet deep and a foot wide at the top, into which the bones and the heated embers of the funeral pyre had been thrust, without any separation having been made. The deposit being mixed with a great deal of charcoal, both in masses and in powder, and with small stones reduced to lime, was so much increased in quantity as not merely to fill the hole made for its reception, but also to form a heap above and around it. The following articles had accompanied the corpse through its fiery preparation for the grave, and were deposited with its remains — a few shreds or broken pieces of an urn; a neat bone pin, upwards of four inches long; and about a dozen instruments of flint, mostly of neat manufacture, but nearly all destroyed by the fierceness of the fire to which they had been exposed: one, however, is perfect, and is a fine circular-ended implement, three inches long. We have here our attention arrested by the fact that *portions* of earthen vessels were sometimes burnt along with human bodies, as it is to be observed that the fragments found with this deposit have evidently been submitted to a great heat *since their fracture,* and also that, had anything like an entire vessel been interred, its fragments would doubtless have been discovered among the ashes. I have long surmised that this was a custom observed in some particular and perhaps exceptional cases, but have not paid sufficient attention to the state of fragments of pottery when newly discovered until of late. I find, however, a few well-marked examples of burnt fragments in the collection at Lomberdale, derived from deposits of calcined bone, as at Arbor Low in 1845, and in one instance from an incinerated interment *within an urn* (see barrow on Ballidon Moor, 30th July, 1849).

In illustration of this, we reprint the following from a letter communicated in 1845, by the Rev. Ferdinand Keller, President of the Society of Antiquaries of Zurich, to Sir Henry Ellis, explanatory of an obscure passage in Shakspere, *Hamlet*, Act V., Scene 1, wherein it is said that —" In almost all the accounts of the opening of Pagan sepulchres and tumuli, mention is made of the discovery of fragments of pottery strewn in the soil, which appear to be portions of vessels similar to such as are often found by the side of the human remains interred in these tombs, and consist of earthenware, not baked in a kiln, but imperfectly hardened by a fire. These potsherds are found in sepulchres where there are no urns, and are almost always fragments of different vessels. Archæologists have considered them to be the relics of the Lyke-wake held at the funeral. Kleeman observes that it was customary to bring the corpse to the place of interment clad in festive garments, and show it to the friends; a banquet then commenced, and a share was offered to the deceased. The revelry must have been of a very lively character (?) from the quantity of broken pottery found in these tombs. (See the "Handbook of German Antiquities," Dresden, 1836, p. 94.) Another remarkable circumstance in connection with Pagan places of burial is the discovery of flints, which are found in all parts of the tumulus, but chiefly over the skeleton, varying considerably in size. This fact has been noticed by antiquarians, who do not appear to have recognised the observance of a heathen custom, and have not ascertained whether it may be regarded as characteristic of the customs of Celtic or Germanic tribes. These traces of ancient usages appear to throw light on a passage in *Hamlet* hitherto unexplained. At the burial of Ophelia, Hamlet remarking that the usual rites were not observed, supposes that the deceased had perished by her own hand. Upon this, Laertes enquires with what rites the corpse is to be interred, and the priest replies that her death had been doubtful; that, but for the command that her obsequies should be otherwise ordered, the corpse should have rested in unconsecrated soil; and ' for charitable prayers *shards, flints,* and *pebbles* should be thrown on her.' Mr. Keller supposes that Shakspere had in view some ancient usage, retained possibly in some part of England, in accordance with which those who, like Pagans, had laid violent hands upon themselves, were buried with ceremonies peculiar to the heathens. Amongst such sepulchral usages that of scattering flints and potsherds over the corpse, as shown by the examination of tumuli in Switzerland and Southern Germany, appears to have been observed. Mr. Keller remarked, that if English archæologists succeed in determining to which of the two ancient races of their island the customs recorded in this passage of Shakspere may be ascribed, some light may thereby be thrown on the origin of those sepulchral remains on the Continent which had given rise to so much dispute."

As far as our experience has given an opportunity of coming to a decision, we should unhesitatingly say that the Celtic origin of the custom is demonstrated in the course of the present volume. The fragmentary pottery, the flints, and the pebbles, to which we would add the teeth of oxen, have been all but universally present in the earlier tumuli opened in the course of our researches.

On the 24th of May, 1858, an attempt was made to open a barrow on the eminence near the Compton Road, Ashbourne, by digging a circular pit in the centre. The natural soil appeared at the depth of three feet, and it was evident that the whole of the middle had been before disturbed, as pieces of decayed wood were mixed with the earth; still the interment must have escaped observation, no trace of bone or fire being visible, as would have been the case if its whereabouts had been discovered. The barrow, where undisturbed about the central excavation, exhibited a section of sandy earth, resting on a foundation of boulders. Violent rain, accompanied by a strong westerly wind, compelled us to abandon the search, after having found a few casual flints, one of which is a piece from the middle of a very superior celt, or other large weapon, that has been fractured by exposure to heat.

NOTICE OF DESULTORY EXCAVATIONS ON THE SITE OF A ROMANO-BRITISH VILLAGE, NEAR WETTON.

As far back as the year 1845, Mr. Carrington opened a very small barrow in a field in his occupation, called the Borough Hole. The mound was not more than nine feet across, or raised above one foot above the surrounding land, but contained a skeleton, extended at full length, accompanied by a spear and knife of iron. About the same time, he also found a small brass coin of Gallienus, with an antelope on the reverse; and a curious article made of two semi-circular bars of lead, each perforated at both ends, as if intended for a collar, meant to be tied together when round the neck. Stimulated by these discoveries, Mr. Carrington turned over a considerable part of the field in the beginning of August, 1848. The soil appeared to have been anciently disturbed to the depth of eighteen inches, and in some places were remains of pavements, of thin limestone slabs, which had undergone the action of fire; about them were many pieces of pottery, both of coarse and imperfectly-baked vessels, and of more highly-finished ware, exhibiting a Roman character. Numerous large pebbles of grit and ironstone, pieces of bone, both human and animal, and a few instruments of iron, amongst which were a slender fibula and a small knife, were found about the pavements.

In the beginning of September, a curious rectangular limestone was found at the bottom of the disturbed ground, about eighteen inches beneath the turf. It measures twelve inches long, eight wide, and two and a half thick; is of black limestone, the surface coated with a kind of porous shale, the result of decomposition; and on the face are numerous incised lines, crossing each other in different directions, and continued round the edge. Its use is uncertain.

On the 22nd July, 1849, was found a very beautiful bronze fibula, of the harp-shaped kind, with a lozengy pattern, enamelled yellow and red down the front.

In addition to the above short notices, the following account of all the discoveries made in the Borough Fields, from the first casual finding of the skeleton to the results of a systematic course of excavation begun in 1852, has been drawn up by Mr. Carrington, whose connected and lively narrative will be read with pleasure. A few particulars mentioned in the above are omitted in the narrative, so that we have decided to retain the former, at the risk of a very slight amount of repetition.

MR. CARRINGTON UPON A ROMANO-BRITISH SETTLEMENT, NEAR WETTON, STAFFORDSHIRE.

There are certain fields in the village of Wetton, known by the name of the Borough Hole, which name we may venture to say has for centuries conveyed no other idea to the occupiers thereof than that of a rabbit warren. Other etymologists trace the derivation of borough, or burrow, from the fact that the habitations of the ancient Britons, like those of the Ethiopian Troglodytes, were frequently placed underground. But neither pits nor caves have ever existed in these fields, and the Britons who located themselves here have burrowed no deeper than the surface of the rock, which is to be found at no great distance below the turf. The name of the fields is undoubtedly derived from the Saxon, *burh* being the name applied by that people to any place, great or small, town or village, that was fortified by walls or mounds of earth. The settlement in this case was apparently protected in the latter manner, for no traces of walls are to be found at the present day in the banks surrounding it. Attention was first directed to the place by observing small mounds and low banks in various parts of the fields, which, being dug into, disclosed soil of a darker colour than elsewhere, intermixed with loose stones, many of which were boulders of sandstone, ironstone, and other rocks foreign to the soil. Eventually the sites of many dwellings have been discovered, both along the ridges and also in other places where no outward irregularity was perceptible. The precise situation of each house was indicated by the pavement of rough limestone, which had formed the floor, remaining either entire or in part; or else by a sunken surface, covered with ashes or charcoal, broken pottery, the teeth, bones, and horns of animals that had been used as food; burnt stones, and other vestiges of human occupation. The discoveries yet made afford no evidence of the station having been occupied prior to the Roman conquest; neither have we yet met with any traces of the Saxon period, further than the name of the fields, as before stated. Still it was undoubtedly a settlement, which was inhabited for a considerable length of time; but when, and under what circumstances it was finally abandoned, we have no means of ascertaining. It is certain, however, that the removal was quiet and deliberate, for had it been otherwise we should have doubtless found a greater quantity of their household utensils in a more perfect state than has been the case, as the greater part of what we have found, such as earthenware, small millstones, &c., are such as have been cast aside after having been broken and rendered useless. Not only have the living had their abodes or burrows in these fields, but the dead have had their barrows. A small mound, which covered a human skeleton, accompanied by a spear-head and knife, both of iron, was broken up in the Spring of 1845; and two more interments have been found, in the same field, during the present year (1852).

Although they had evidently profited in some respects from contact with their Roman invaders, they were still Pagans, who buried their dead after the fashion of their more barbarous progenitors. The funeral pyre still blazed, haply to introduce the shades of their deceased friends with becoming honours into the presence of Baal, or some other grim and imaginary deity; or, perhaps, they sought by a more revolting sacrifice to propitiate his capricious wrath, or to bribe his exorable justice. The bones of various animals that had not undergone the action of fire, as well as fragments of other bones which had been nearly consumed, accompanied the remains of those who had been committed to the earth here, along with their weapons and ornaments. It was in the year 1848 that these fields were first conclusively ascertained to contain the site of a British town or settlement, and that the systematic excavations were attempted, which have still been followed up, at intervals, until the present year (1852), during which time the greater part of two of the fields, and a portion of the third, have been turned up by those most successful solvers of archæological problems, the pickaxe and shovel, by the operations of which so many floors of huts — in rows or streets, as well as standing detached — have been found as to constitute the locality the very Pompeii of North Staffordshire. It is likewise very probable that more of these pavements yet remain undiscovered, as their presence is not always indicated by any outward sign on the surface of the land. Many banks and irregularities are also visible in the neighbouring fields which have not been in any degree investigated. Our first labours were employed upon a mound at the lower part of the largest field, which is between the other two to which the diggings have at present been restricted. This mound, which in appearance is somewhat like a tumulus, is composed of earth of a deeper colour than that which prevails in the district, mingled with limestones and gritstone boulders, some of which were much burned. In some places, at the depth of eighteen inches from the surface, a pavement of rough limestones was discovered, which, from the intense heat of the fires that had been kindled upon it, was reduced to lime, so that the spade passed through it with facility. Heaps of charcoal and ashes were found here, especially in a place where a few large blocks of stone were lying on the floor, probably the fittings of the fireplace. Numerous bones of animals, such as teeth of the ox, horse, deer, and hog, with broken horns of the stag and cow, were scattered in all directions, as were also pieces of earthen vessels, of various degrees of refinement, some of which were no more artificially wrought than the sepulchral urns of the ancient Britons. Some again were firmly baked, though as coarse in quality as modern roof-tiles, whilst others were highly finished, and marked with the lozenge-pattern common upon funeral vessels of the Romano-British period. A small knife, a pike-head, and a plain fibula, all of iron; a beautiful bronze fibula, tastefully ornamented with yellow lozenges down the front; and part of a human skull, were likewise found upon this floor, which appears, from its superior extent, to have been that of a house of more lofty pretensions than the others. It appears also that the table of this habitation was better provided than usual, as more bones of animals, fit for food, were found upon and round the floor than elsewhere.

A broad low bank extending from the place just described was next examined, and turned over as low down as it appeared artificial. Near the place first examined we found occasional depressions in the floors, having a few stones ranged round them, which, from their containing ashes, charcoal, bits of calcined bone, fragments of pottery, &c., we at once concluded to be fire-places. Several holes, about a yard square, of greater depth than the fire-places, and almost filled with flat stones, set in edgeways, were observed. Further up the field, we found a rectangular piece of black limestone, lying upon the undisturbed surface, which was eighteen inches beneath the turf. It measures about twelve inches by eight, and is from two to three inches thick, and on one side is covered with numerous lines, some straight, others diagonal, which have been cut in rather deeply by a sharp instrument, for a purpose by no means evident, or, most probably, for no purpose at all, further than lack of more profitable employment by some *ennuyéed* aboriginal who was ignorant of politics or such like remedy for the destitute or vacant mind. How could these people exist without their stimulating Sunday paper? Higher still, at the depth of about a foot, we found a firm and undisturbed level surface or floor, of stiff earth, by the side of which was a space several yards in length, sunk to the further depth of nine or ten inches, the edge of which, adjoining the earthen floor, was perfectly straight and well defined, though the width of this depression could not be satisfactorily ascertained, owing to the further edge being more broken and irregular. It was filled with large stones, amongst which we observed scarcely any fragments either of bone or pottery. Another floor, paved with rough limestones, was uncovered at the upper end of the bank, upon which, at the depth of one foot from the surface of the ground, we discovered a small iron fork of two prongs, widely separated, whence it appears that the inhabitants of Wetton, in the remote ages, were not entirely unacquainted with those conveniences of life generally supposed to be of recent introduction. Near the south side of the before-mentioned bank, at the depth of eight inches from the surface, we encountered a large stone,

Romano-British Fork, Wetton.

nearly a yard square and about a foot thick, lying upon a stratum of ashes, and surrounded with a heap of other stones of various sizes. There was a natural hole quite through the centre of this stone, which, being turned over, disclosed a hole about two feet wide and one foot deep, which was filled with charcoal and stones that had been perfectly reduced to lime; a few pieces of pottery, bone, and lead ore were found among the ashes at the bottom of the hole. We then dug up an irregular mound of earth and stone in the adjoining field nearest to the present village, to the depth of three feet, when the natural rock was exposed to view, covered over with traces of fire. Here many fragments of earthen utensils and a small instrument of iron were picked up, as well as the bones and teeth of animals, including those of the rat. A small brass coin of the Emperor Gallienus (A.D. 253 to 268) — reverse a stag, with the legend, "DIANAE. CONS. (AVG.)" — was found in this place in 1845; and in the present year part of a very neat whetstone, perforated for suspension to the person, was discovered in the same place. In 1850, another bank, at the further side of the middle field, running in the same direction as that previously examined, was opened. Here we found, amongst the remains of animals and pottery, portions of at least two paved floors, around which abounded small limestones, and gritstone boulders that had been burnt. In this bank we observed a low wall, built of flat limestones, in which was inserted a hard slab of gritty slate, about an inch thick, that had evidently been used as a bake-stone, as it projected out from the wall so as to receive the heat of a fire kindled beneath it, the traces of which were obvious, both upon the stone itself and the ground beneath it, whereon there lay a collection of ashes and charcoal. On clearing this away, we found the surface of the floor to consist of clayey earth, burnt very red and hard by repeated fires. By breaking it up, we found a large table knife, 9½ inches long, of peculiar shape, still retaining its original handle of stag's horn, rubbed smooth, the preservation of which may be attributed to its having been embedded in the fire-hardened earth. (It is here engraved as a companion to the fork.) As in the other bank, so here also

Romano-British Knife, Wetton.

were holes nearly filled with flat stones, set around the centre on edge, so as to leave a small space in the middle, which we found to be filled with earth and a dark-coloured powder as fine as vegetable ashes. Three of these were observed; two of them being on one side of the bank, and the other on the opposite side, over against one of the others. They were between three and four yards asunder, and were respectively about a yard deep. We concluded that they had been prepared for the reception of strong posts or beams of wood, that formed the corners of the house, which had been inserted into the ground and then wedged in with flat stones, so as to stand firmly in the desired position. The remaining discoveries made in this part of the field consist of broken querns, including a rude kind of mortar made from a stone in shape like the frustrum of a cone, hollowed out at the top for the reception of the grain, which would be bruised by a rounded stone or muller; a portion of a stone ring, four inches diameter, of uncertain use, several other examples of which are in the collection at Lomberdale; a thin piece of bronze, perforated at each end; and part of the reeded handle of a vessel of green glass, of Roman manufacture. In digging at the end of this bank, in 1845, a leaden collar for the neck, formed of two pieces, perforated at the ends to fasten it together, was discovered. In the year 1851, the floors of four habitations were discovered, in the third field, which is furthest from the village. They were found along the line of a low ridge which forms part of a parallelogram, some faint traces of which are perceptible in an adjoining field, called the "Wether Pasture." One of the floors found within this enclosure was quite perfect. It was constructed of rough limestone slabs, the surfaces of which were in a state of disintegration; part of a thin millstone had also been introduced as a paving-stone amongst the others. The pavement was about five yards square, and was buried from one to two feet below the turf. At one corner we found a heap of ashes and charcoal, amongst which was an iron awl; the rest of the floor was quite free from any refuse whatever, in which respect it differed from the others that we have found, all of which have been more or less strewed with animal bones, &c. In this case the family dust-heap, containing as usual bones and potsherds, was found at the south-west side of the floor, probably just outside where the door was situated. Burnt bones, animal bones, and numerous pieces of Romano-British pottery, were found upon and around the other three floors; and broken handmills, together with stones and pebbles foreign to the soil, were found in the banks which covered them, as in other places in the fields.

During the year 1852 three or more pavements, similar to the others, were discovered in the middle field, where no external indications of their existence presented themselves. We also met with traces of occupation in other places where no flagged floors were found. One of the floors was small, and surrounded by the usual accompaniments: upon it was found an iron spike. The others were much larger; but, owing to their imperfect and damaged condition, we were unable to obtain their dimensions. A large bouldered stone, surrounded by ashes, lay in a hole in one of them. The ground for a considerable extent all round had been removed, down to the natural rock, which was in some places three feet beneath the surface of the clods we dug out. The earth throughout was intermixed with limestones, pebbles, broken earthenware, animal bones, stags' horns, ashes, and burnt wood. Amongst this accumulation of rubbish we found a stout bronze awl, like some we have found in tumuli, a small iron knife, half of a small pair of iron shears, and a coin of the small brass size, which seems to be a barbarous imitation of one of Claudius Gothicus or Tetricus. Here — as is not unfrequently the case in more serious and weighty matters — there was but a step between the living and the dead, for on the 10th of August, 1852, we found, by continuing the excavation along the surface of the rock, that we were gradually extending deeper and deeper as the rock inclined downwards; the earth also that we had to remove became darker in colour as we advanced, and was mixed with ashes and large loose stones. After we had removed some large blocks, a human skull appeared upon the rock, by which it was evident that we had unawares broken into a cist, which by careful examination was found to contain the skeleton of a female — the femur measuring seventeen inches, and the skull indicating a person of middle age — which lay on the right side, with the head towards the south and the feet to the north. The bones, with the exception of the legs, which were slightly bent back, were extended at length by the east side of the grave, which was formed by a wall built of flat stones, the uppermost of which were very large, and almost reached up to the surface of the land. A flat stone was set up edgeways at the head, as is not unusual in barrows of a much more remote antiquity; and close to it was a broken upper millstone. The bones were embedded in compact dark-coloured earth, intermixed with charcoal and burnt bones, and the body had been interred with three small beads, two of lilac-coloured and one of blue glass, and a plain bronze ring fibula, 1½ inches diameter, about the neck, as they were discovered upon removing the skull. An iron awl, several iron nails, and pieces of stags' horns and other animal bones, were found about the skeleton. Some of the horns have been sawn across, particularly a very large palmated one; a tine from another had been neatly sharpened for some purpose. Another strong iron awl was found beneath the uppermost stone of the wall guarding the east side of the grave, the other sides of which were fenced out by large stones, extending almost up to the surface, two feet six inches above the bottom of the grave. The surrounding ground, except on the north-west, had been cut down to the rock, about six inches lower, a circumstance which induced us to continue the search, in the hope of finding other interments, to a further distance of eight yards, finding throughout the whole extent abundance of ashes, boars' tusks and other bones, as well as a few articles of greater interest, comprising the skull of a stag, a neatly squared sharpening stone, between two and three inches square, and two coins in small brass, one of them of the Constantine family—reverse, "GLORIA. EXERCITVS," two soldiers holding standards; the other is one of the minute imitations of the currency of the Lower Empire, in such poor condition as to be quite illegible.

In the course of the autumn of 1852, it was observed that the ground, at one side of the place where the interment was found in 1845, was slightly raised; and that stones, bones of animals, broken vessels, &c., were plentifully intermixed with the soil to the extent of about twelve yards in length and eight in breadth. The whole was afterwards turned over, down to the undisturbed level, and the following discoveries made. A little from the centre of this area we found that the ground, for about three yards square, had been sunk deeper than elsewhere, having been disturbed to the depth of two feet from the surface, whilst in places contiguous it varied from a foot to half a yard only. It was here also filled up with stones larger than usual, amongst which were the broken remnants of at least three large stags' horns, and numerous fragments of others, some of which had been tooled, as in other instances. On the undisturbed level we found a slender bronze skewer, 12½ inches long, having the thicker end cleverly fashioned by the graver into the cloven foot either of a ruminant animal or a hog, from whence it is gradually attenuated to a point. Continuing our labours from the depression where the stags' horns were found, at a short distance we discovered a human skeleton that had been previously disturbed, and much broken in consequence. It lay about a foot below the turf, extended at length, with an iron knife, six inches long, and a smaller implement, probably the point of a javelin, near the head.

By turning over this part of the field, we found pieces of Roman tile, potsherds, and bones and tusks of rats and other animals, but no indication of further interments or pavements. The most curious object discovered here was a sort of drinking cup, made from the straight part of the leg bone of a large animal, closely resembling a modern drinking horn in shape and size, as it is rather more than three inches high, and is slightly decorated by a line cut in round the top, and two more round the bottom, with a single chevron running between. We also found in the same place one side of a pair of small iron shears.

Many sandstones, that have evidently been applied to a variety of uses, broken querns or handmills of different sizes and qualities, and numerous large boulders, are to be seen in the walls that enclose the Borough Fields, rendering it clear that the ruins of the settlement have long served as a quarry whence to obtain building materials with but little trouble. It is doubtless owing to this facility of supply that the existing remains are so inconsiderable, and that greater success has not attended our persevering efforts to exhume the buried city.

NOTICE OF BARROWS IN THE NORTH RIDING OF YORKSHIRE, OPENED BY MR. JAMES RUDDOCK; THE REMAINS FROM WHICH ARE PRESERVED AT LOMBERDALE.

1849.

On the 22nd of February we opened a tumulus at Crosscliff, of twenty yards circumference and four feet high, by cutting a trench through it from north to south. The upper part, chiefly consisting of stone, below which light-coloured sand predominated, except in the centre, where it was replaced by loose stones. No interment was found there, but near the northern edge of the mound we discovered a large cinerary urn, eleven inches high, containing burnt bones, and covered with a flat stone; and on the south side of the barrow was another urn, embedded in red sand, also containing calcined bones, amongst which were a rude arrow-point and a flake of flint. The first of the urns, exhumed in imperfect condition, is decorated by a broad border, having a pattern of vertical lines alternating with horizontal ones, produced by the impress of a twisted thong on the soft clay. The other is an extremely fine and perfect vessel, $13\frac{1}{2}$ inches high, having a border ornamented with a chevron pattern, deeply cut by the application of a slightly twisted cord. The whole of the tumulus was turned over without further success.

On the 28th of March a second barrow, near Crosscliff, thirty-four yards circumference and four feet six inches high, composed of loose stone, was excavated by a cutting from the north side, towards the centre, where, nothing being found, the trench was continued in the direction of the circumference of the mound for the distance of sixteen yards, until we ultimately found, at the south side, a mass of calcined bones, accompanied by a rude arrow-point and a good circular knife of flint: the latter appears to have been partially burnt.

On the 7th of August we examined a barrow, seven miles north of Pickering, twenty-four yards in circumference and four feet high, composed of sand and stones, by cutting from the north side to the centre, where we found a large urn, much decayed and broken, with the upper part ornamented by a lozenge or network pattern, containing burnt bones and a small vessel, 2¾ inches high, of the kind called incense cups, which is a beautiful example of its class, being ornamented with a diamond-pattern, terminating above and below in punctures. It has also two perforations at one side. When found it was filled with ashes. The remainder of the tumulus was strictly searched without result.

On the 14th of August we opened a barrow, six miles north of Pickering, twenty-seven yards round the base, and four feet six in central elevation, by digging as usual from the north to the middle. After clearing away a layer of sand, large stones appeared, their position indicating that they were intentionally placed to guard the interments which were discovered on removing them. These were the calcined remains of probably two persons, enclosed in two fine sepulchral urns, embedded in sand and covered by a flat stone, which was too short to extend over the mouths of both. The bones were accompanied by a neat lance-head of flint, near two inches long, and two circular-ended flints, which had been calcined. The urns are respectively ten and eleven inches high : the former has a border of diagonal lines, occasionally crossed by others in the contrary direction; the latter is bordered by a simple pattern of a single chevrony line, running between two horizontal ones. They are both of coarse material and workmanship.

On the 17th of October we examined a tumulus, eight miles north of Pickering, twenty-five yards circumference and four feet deep, composed of stones and sand. In digging from the north to the centre, at a short distance before gaining the latter, we discovered an urn, inverted upon the natural surface, and embedded in red sand. After its removal, calcined bones appeared and continued downwards to the depth of a foot below the level. With them was a rude arrow-head of flint. The vase is too small to have contained the bones, being but 5½ inches high; it is of thin earthenware, with a very neat chevrony border, and may have been a domestic vessel belonging to the deceased. At the distance of a yard further south were some fragments of another plain vessel of sandy clay.

On the 25th of October a tumulus was opened at Saintoft, near Cawthorn Camps, of the circumference of fifty yards; the original height reduced by agriculture. Commencing the section from the north, we found the barrow to consist of sand of different colours, overlaying a collection of stones resting on the natural soil, which was strewed with charcoal. In the centre was a large stone, upwards of a yard long by two feet six inches broad, covering a cist two feet square and two feet six inches deep, containing a deposit of calcined bones, from amongst which was taken a small incense cup, three inches diameter by $1\frac{1}{2}$ inch high, ornamented with punctured diagonal lines, rather irregularly disposed, and enclosing a broken bone pin. In searching other parts of the mound we found a splinter from a stone celt; and near the top were small fragments of earthenware, which appeared to have been dragged about by the plough.

On the 26th of November a large barrow was opened, near Cawthorn Camps, sixty-five yards in circumference, seven feet in elevation, composed of sand, burnt clay, and limestone rubble. We commenced on the north side with an excavation nine feet wide, which was increased to double the size at the centre, through the following strata — sand six feet, burnt clay, limestone rubble, and, lastly, burnt clay repeated, covering a grave sunk in the rock eleven feet below the natural level, the total depth from the crown of the barrow to the floor of the grave being eighteen feet. The grave was filled with the stones that had been quarried out of it, and after they were cleared we found its length to be fifteen feet and width seven feet. At the bottom were two skeletons lying at length, embedded in charcoal, with the heads pointing respectively east and west. At the right side of one lay a coarsely-made spear-head of flint, $2\frac{1}{4}$ inches long, and at the same side of the other was a bronze dagger, $4\frac{1}{2}$ inches long, of archaic type, which has been attached to a crescent-shaped handle by three rivets. It is in every respect the same as those previously described, from the Derbyshire and Staffordshire tumuli. The cranium of the latter interment is, unfortunately, very imperfect; it is that of a middle-aged man. Another very interesting barrow, situated in the same field, was next opened; its circumference at the base was sixty yards, the central height five feet, and it was composed of sandstones. By cutting from the north towards the centre, we uncovered some flat stones, set upright in the ground, which on further examination were found to be part of a complete circle, seven yards diameter, standing about two feet above the natural level, and enclosing a grave five feet long by four wide and three deep, filled with limestone, which, being emptied, disclosed a skeleton, necessarily contracted, with its head to the south. Close to the skull was a small vase, 4½ inches high, of well-baked thin earthenware, the upper part slightly moulded, and ornamented with four rows of large dots, above a single chevrony line scratched in the clay. It is in perfect preservation, and must be esteemed as a highly valuable specimen from having been discovered in connection with what would be called a "Druidical circle," were the upright stones exposed by the removal of the tumulus. It is probable that most of the smaller circles were altogether sepulchral, being nothing more than enclosures for the purpose of keeping sacred or tabooing the graves of chieftains.

On the 4th of December we examined a barrow situated near the Cawthorn Camps, forty-two yards circumference, diminished in height by farming operations. Between the north side and the middle we met with three places exhibiting traces of fire; and in the centre was a layer of charcoal, two feet square, amongst which were some pieces of an urn. After its removal, the excavation was continued about two yards beyond the centre in an eastern direction, when a change appeared at the natural surface, arising from a grave four feet deep, which was filled with stones and sand, containing at the bottom two skeletons, deposited with their heads to the south, the skull of one lying on the breast of the other. Near the head of each was a small vase, and beneath the skull of one was a well chipped flint javelin-point, two inches long;

whilst in a similar position with regard to the other were two round-ended flints. One of the vases is $4\frac{1}{4}$ inches high, superficially moulded, and decorated with a few vertical scratches only, altogether of coarse workmanship, contrasting very unfavourably with the other, which is an inch taller, and beautifully ornamented with a fine herring-bone pattern, interspersed with small dots. It has likewise four small perforated knobs, placed at regular intervals, in a hollow moulding below the border.

On the 10th of December, a tumulus on Allerstone Common, 32 yards round the base, and near five feet high, was opened, as usual from the north. The upper part consisted of variously coloured sand and stone, succeeded by white sand, which, being removed, disclosed some calcined bones, and part of a small globular vessel of reddish clay, rather more than three inches diameter, most elaborately ornamented with rows of herring-bone pattern, finely incised. After strictly examining this part of the barrow the cutting was taken south, and near that edge of the mound more burnt bones were found; after which we excavated the centre to the extent of twelve yards diameter, without meeting with any thing more.

On the 20th of December, a barrow upon Gindle Top, forty-six yards circumference, and five feet six inches high, composed of sand and stones, was opened by sinking down the centre. When we had penetrated to within a foot of the natural surface, a large flat stone appeared, which, on removal, exposed an unusually large and fine cinerary urn, containing burnt bones and embedded in tenacious clay. After it was taken up, we found two flints beneath where it had rested: one is a circular-ended instrument; the other is a small disk, three-quarters of an inch diameter, chipped all round. The urn is $15\frac{1}{4}$ inches high, finished by a projecting border, decorated by the impression of two cords, twisted in contrary directions, and repeated in parallel horizontal lines, so as to produce a kind of herring-bone pattern.

1850.

On the 23rd of January we opened a cairn, or stony tumulus, about a mile north of Pickering, which in its present imperfect state, caused by agriculture, measures forty-two yards round and four feet in height. After removing stone in the centre, from an area four yards square, to the depth of two feet, we came to a concretion of lime, charcoal, and calcined bones, firmly compacted together, covering the whole space. On breaking through it a skeleton was found, in a contracted posture, on its left side, with the head to the north, having near the skull a very curious drinking cup, 5¼ inches high, with a handle at the side sufficiently large to admit the finger, thus differing from the per-

Celtic Drinking Cup, with Handle. — Pickering.

forated knobs that are not unusual on the smaller vases from tumuli. It is the first instance in which we have seen a drinking cup furnished with such an appendage. The ornamentation of the vessel is also peculiar, consisting chiefly of angularly pointed cartouches, filled with a reticulated pattern, and having a band of the same encircling the upper part. A little to the south were several calcined instruments of flint, including a small javelin-point and four round-ended implements.

On the 6th of February we examined another barrow, one mile north of Pickering, forty-six yards in circumference and five feet in height. Having dug through an outer covering of sand a foot thick, loose stones succeeded, beneath which was a grave or cist, well constructed of four flagstones, and covered in by a fifth. Its interior dimensions were four feet three inches long, two feet wide, and eighteen inches deep. Within were two skeletons, the principal one laid on its left side, with the back bent in a semicircular form, the knees drawn up, and the head to the north; the other skeleton was that of an infant, much decayed, and lay behind the former. At the back of the skull of the adult skeleton was a very thick vessel of coarse clay, $5\frac{1}{4}$ inches high, roughly dotted all over, lying on its side, and having upon it a very neat flint spear-head near three inches long, which, together with the teeth and some of the bones, is encrusted with a calcareous deposit, resulting from the percolation of water through the limestone above, during the lapse of ages. Beneath the skeletons were remains of branches, whilst the presence of a hazel nut indicated at once their nature, and the autumnal season at which the funeral took place. A few other flints, two of them circular-sided, were found in other parts of the mound. The large skeleton was recovered in almost perfect condition, and is now articulated and placed with the bones of the child, and other objects found with it, in a glass case in the museum at Lomberdale. Though it may reasonably be supposed to be the skeleton of a female, there is certainly nothing feminine in its appearance: the head is of the Brachy-Kephalic type, the pelvis rather contracted, and the entire height about five feet four inches.

On the 7th of February a large cairn in the same field, constructed of stone, seventy yards round the base, and five feet and a half high in the middle, was opened by a cutting made from the east. Having proceeded about three yards, an urn was discovered about a foot below the surface; and a little to the south was a second urn placed about a yard above the natural level. After taking it up, the cutting was directed to the centre, where was a cist, six feet long, four wide, and a yard deep, filled up with limestone rubble, which, being emptied out, disclosed a skeleton resting at full length, with the head to the south, having near the skull a vase $5\frac{3}{4}$ inches high, with the upper part moulded and ornamented in the usual way. At the right hand were two neat lance-heads and a round-ended implement of flint. From the ambiguity of the original notes, it is uncertain which of the two urns to be described was first found; and it is equally so whether either of them contained burnt bones at the time of discovery. One is, however, evidently a cinerary urn, being almost fifteen inches high, of elegant shape, with a deep border, richly ornamented both within and without: below the border outside is a hollow moulding, also ornamented. It is one of the handsomest Celtic urns that we have seen, and resembles the fine one from a tumulus near Beverley now in the York Museum. The other is an equally fine specimen, though of more limited capacity, being only $6\frac{1}{2}$ inches high. It has a projecting border above a slight hollow, as the other, and is of sandy clay of a brick-red colour. The border is ornamented with a chevron, running through a ground of diagonal lines, and the hollow is punctured by large dots.

On the 13th of February, a barrow on the moors, six miles north of Pickering, was examined. Its circumference was twenty-four yards, its depth between four and five feet, and our cutting from the north side exposed a peculiarity in the structure not hitherto observed, the mound being covered with large flagstones, succeeded by limestone gravel, which continued to near the centre, where larger stone appeared. On cutting eastward, a mass of calcined bones, embedded in charcoal, was found. They were accompanied by a plain incense cup, $1\frac{3}{4}$ inches high, shaped as a truncated cone, placed on a base of less diameter, and a neatly-wrought bone pin about four inches long. One yard from this interment a change appeared on the natural surface, where, after removing limestone rubble to the depth of four feet and a half, we discovered a grave lined with freestone slabs, which, strange to say, did not contain any human remains.

On the 9th of March, we opened a long barrow near Cropton, five miles north of Pickering, measuring twenty-four yards in length by thirteen in breadth, and five feet in height, having the longest diameter north and south. The excavation was begun at the north first, through sand; afterwards through large stones, covering others somewhat carefully arranged, on which were some animal bones. On removing the latter stones we found that they were part of a cist containing two skeletons, with their legs drawn up close to the trunk, and the heads to the north. To the right of one was a finely chipped lance-head of grey flint, 1¾ inches long; and to the right of the other was a neat arrow-point and some inferior flints. By continuing the trench southwards, fragments of two urns—one of them having a neat net-work-pattern border—were found, and near the top of the barrow two simply-formed spear-heads and a knife of grey flint were picked up.

On the 3rd of April we opened a barrow near Newton-upon-Rawcliff, four miles north of Pickering, fifty-six yards in circumference and five feet high. Ground was broken on the north side by a cutting three yards wide, extending to the centre, which was covered with large stones, overlying sand mixed with charcoal for the depth of three feet, when ashes and pieces of urn appeared. The trench being continued southward, we found on the natural level a skeleton extended at length, with the head to the south, having a beautiful vase near the skull, and a fine javelin-point, 2¼ inches long, and three arrow-heads of flint, at the feet. The vessel, but little above four inches high, is completely covered with small ornaments of herring-bone design. It is also moulded, and furnished with five equi-distant knobs; and is, moreover, decorated at the bottom in a very singular manner by the intersection of two bands, each composed of three rows of punctures at right angles, so as to form a cross—a design I have never seen on any other specimen of primæval fictile art.

On the 4th of April we examined a tumulus, three miles from Pickering, six feet high, covering an area forty-eight yards in circumference, by making an opening in the centre four yards diameter, where we first found large stones, which, being removed, exposed the skeleton of a large dog, embedded in limestone gravel, which continued to the natural surface: here were fragments of three human skeletons, having near them some peculiarly-shaped stones. The original position of these bodies could not be ascertained. One of the stones is a shapeless lump, about five inches in its greatest diameter, which has been intentionally reduced in size by flakes having been struck from it; another stone, chipped in the same way round a natural hole in the block, was found near the outside of the barrow; the other curiously-shaped stones were altogether natural.

On the 16th of April a stony barrow, fifty-two yards in circumference, and between five and six feet high, situated two miles north of Pickering, was opened by a trench three yards wide, cut from the south to the middle. A little north of the latter we found a skeleton, with the head to the north; near it was a small iron knife, 3½ inches long, a canine tooth or tusk of some animal, and an egg-shaped article of baked clay, nearly two inches long. Still further north was a large sandstone, with a cup-shaped cavity, 2½ inches diameter, worked in it, other examples of which have been found in tumuli in various parts of the kingdom; but their use is as yet unknown.

On the 4th of May we examined a barrow, eight miles east from Pickering, sixty-four yards round and seven feet high, composed of sand of various colours. The opening commenced from the top, and continued over a space 27 yards in circumference, and led to the discovery of a bed of charcoal at the natural level, beneath which was an interment, consisting of a mass of calcined bones, having with them a rude flint spear, and near them some pieces of an urn, with a neatly-ornamented border.

On the 22nd of May a barrow was opened, on the moors, seven miles north of Pickering, fifty-six yards in circumference and eight feet high. An excavation six yards diameter was made in the middle, where, after removing large stones to the depth of four feet, some pieces of a kiln-baked vessel, partially covered with green glaze; two flat stones, rubbed into a circular shape, 1½ inch diameter; and some flints, including a lance-head and two round instruments, were found. The opening was then sunk down to the natural surface, without any other result than the discovery of large masses of charcoal at that point.

On the 19th of June a cairn, consisting of large stones, measuring thirty-eight yards round and four feet high, situated six miles east from Pickering, was examined by an opening three yards wide from the north side to the centre. Nothing being discovered by these means, the cutting was directed south, when a small and handsome vase, 5¼ inches high, was found inverted upon the natural soil, and near it was a fine calcined flint spear, three inches long. From the vagueness of the original notes, it is uncertain whether the human remains found with these articles were calcined or not. Other parts of the mound yielded a few more flint instruments of no special interest.

On the 9th of July a sandy barrow, forty-four yards round the base and two yards in height, situated fifteen miles north of Pickering, was opened by a large cutting in the middle. After digging out sand to the depth of a yard, considerable masses of charcoal occurred, below which sand was again found till the natural surface was reached, where a little to the east of the centre was a very rude urn, 8½ inches high, with a projecting border, quite unornamented, and tall in proportion to its diameter. Slightly further was a mass of burnt bones, accompanied by very small fragments of pottery, embedded in clay, a little below the natural level.

On the 10th of July a stony mound, four feet high, twenty-six yards circumference, situated thirteen miles east of Pickering, was examined by an opening from the south side to the centre, where were the remains of a skeleton, accompanied by a flint spear about three inches long. More north, we found some circular flints and a little animal bone.

On the 16th of July a tumulus, on the moors, eight miles north of Pickering, composed of limestone gravel, and measuring five feet high and thirty-eight yards round, was opened by a trench from the north side to the middle, where we found nothing; but proceeding southwards, we met with part of a large sepulchral urn, nine inches diameter, that had contained burnt bones, from among which was taken a pointed piece of unburnt animal bone, two inches long, that has probably been a javelin-head. The urn had been roughly ornamented with indentations by the thumb nail and other means.

On the 28th of August a barrow, on the moors, six miles east of Pickering, measuring forty-three yards round by 6½ feet high, was opened by an excavation from the north. The mound was covered with stones, beneath which sand prevailed as far as the centre, where a skeleton was found below the natural surface, with a vase, 5½ inches high and almost plain, at its head, and a small flint spear near the right hand. The cutting being then continued southward, shortly disclosed another skeleton, with a rude flint point under the head: inside the latter was a three-edged conical stone, probably the result of accident. Both skeletons lay with the skulls to the north, and the first had the legs drawn close up to the trunk.

On the 29th of August a stony barrow, eighty yards circumference, situated four miles in a northerly direction from Pickering, was opened by a large excavation in the middle, where, on arriving at the natural soil, we found fragments of a large urn, and a plain incense cup, of globular shape, three inches diameter. South of these, and a foot below the surface, we found a very plain urn with a border, seven inches high, and a flint spear, three inches long. No skeletons being mentioned in the original notes, it is presumed that both interments had been by incineration.

On the 14th of November, a barrow, eight miles north of Pickering, eighty-six yards circumference and ten feet high, was opened by a very large excavation from the top — firstly, through three feet of sand, when masses of charcoal, mingled with calcined bones, appeared on both the north and south sides of the cutting; beneath, through stones, down to the natural soil, where, at the south confine of the trench, was part of a human skeleton, accompanied by four instruments of flint, one of which is a spear. At the same level, on the west side, we found calcined bones, surrounded by much black earth, which concluded the discoveries in this large and unprofitable tumulus.

On the 19th of November we opened another barrow, near the last, forty-nine yards circumference and four feet high, wholly composed of sand, by digging down the middle. About a foot below the top, fragments of calcined bone were found over the whole extent of the cutting, which we thought might have been occasioned by the plough. No further discoveries were found till reaching the surface, where a large flat stone appeared, beneath which was a deposit of calcined bones, with two arrows of burnt flint, one of them very nicely chipped. North of this interment we cut through two strata of pure charcoal, but discovered nothing worthy of notice.

On the 26th of November another tumulus, a mile north of the two last, eight feet high, having a base circumference of seventy-eight yards, and composed of sand and stones, was examined by cutting from the summit, first through about two feet of sand, when exactly in the centre of the barrow we discovered a very fine urn, embedded in burnt bones, much taller in proportion to its diameter than similar vessels found in the adjoining counties, and at the same time more elegantly formed. It has a deep moulded border, ornamented both within and without, and the total height is eleven inches, four being devoted to the border. Below this interment stone appeared, and continued down to the natural surface, where was a large flagstone, computed to weigh two tons, which being too large for removal, was left undisturbed, we sinking down by its edge and finding it to cover the entrance of a natural cleft or cavern in the rock, fifteen feet long, four feet high, and four feet six wide, in the middle of which was a human skeleton, embedded in stiff red clay, with the head to the north, the calvarium of which has been preserved in an imperfect state. Near the right hand was a very fine instrument of flint, of unique form, that has first been carefully chipped into its present shape, and afterwards rubbed down: it is a kind of axe or tomahawk, with a very sharp angular cutting edge. Near the head was another good instrument, and on the breast had been placed five more instruments of flint. In another part of the mound a small piece of an urn was found, which bears a peculiar ornament, resulting from the impression of a six-toothed implement, applied vertically.

On the 3rd of December another barrow, near the last, fifty-six yards in circumference and five feet in height, was opened by an excavation from the apex. After passing through sand to the depth of four feet, a large bed of charcoal, and a calcined flint of oval shape, were found in the centre. Directly under, and in contact with the charcoal, we discovered stones forming a cist, containing calcined bones, and a plain globular incense cup of well-baked reddish clay, two inches high. The opening was afterwards much enlarged without success.

On the 4th of December a barrow, close to the last, composed of sand, and measuring twenty yards across, by four feet six in height, was opened, when we found, just beneath the summit, the remnants of an interment that had been disturbed by cultivation, consisting of burnt bones, a small portion of an urn, too much decomposed to show the pattern, and four pretty good calcined flints, one of which has served to point a spear. A great part of the mound was afterwards searched without success.

On the 7th of December a barrow, situated ten miles N.E. from Pickering, was explored. Its circumference at the base was fifty-two yards, and the central elevation six feet. By a large opening, carried from the summit to the natural surface through sand, we found the latter to have been burnt at that level; and digging about two feet lower, we found a plain urn, 6¾ inches high, with a projecting border, embedded in charcoal, which being cleared away exposed some loose stones, which were found to continue downwards for four feet. At that depth a skeleton was found, lying with the knees drawn up, the head towards the north, and having near the right hand a rude spear-head and two other flints. It appeared to have been placed in a grave five feet long, four wide, and seven deep.

On the 10th of December another mound, ten miles N.E. of Pickering, forty-eight yards circumference, seven feet high, composed of sand, was explored by a considerable cutting in the centre, by which a bed of charcoal was found on the natural face, whence were taken a few burnt bones, with a spear-head and two round flints, also calcined. Continuing the excavation a little further below the natural soil, we met with portions of a slender human skeleton, much decomposed.

On the 12th of December a large sandy tumulus, eighty-six yards round and eleven feet high, situated ten miles N.E. of Pickering, was excavated by a trench from the north side. After the removal of sand to the depth of four feet, a small vase, $4\frac{3}{4}$ inches high, tastefully decorated with a herring-bone pattern, was found standing with the mouth upwards, before reaching the centre. Farther south we discovered a cist-vaen, formed of four large stones placed on edge, and having a fifth as cap-stone. It, however, enclosed nothing more important than black earth and a rounded flint. The cutting was afterwards continued till the barrow was fully investigated, without producing more than a sprinkling of calcined bones and nine flints, most of which are of the circular shape.

On the 18th of December, a barrow, ten miles N.E. of Pickering, measuring sixty-eight yards round, and eight feet high, was investigated by a cutting from the south side, passing through differently coloured strata of sand, succeeded by stone, till the surface of the ground was reached. The latter was covered with a layer of charcoal, and no discovery occurring there, the earth was removed to the further depth of five feet, when we found an earthen vase, $5\frac{1}{4}$ inches high, with a minutely ornamented border, the pattern being made by the impression of a tightly-twisted cord, several times repeated, interspersed with rows of small round punctures, and having below a slight groove, in which are, at intervals, longitudinally perforated stops. No trace of bone or other relic was found with this vase. After returning to the surface, the trench was continued in a northward course, where the barrow was composed of stones only. Some of these being removed, led to the discovery of another vase, inverted, upon the natural level, over a neat lance-head and three other inferior instruments of calcined flint. This latter vessel is smaller than the first, being a quarter of an inch less in height, and much more confined in diameter: it has a moulded border, neatly impressed with a punctured design. At a little distance from it were fragments of human bone, lying on charcoal; and about two feet from these was a simple deposit of burnt bones, placed a little beneath the surface, which concluded the discoveries.

On the 21st of December, a tumulus, near the last, measuring forty-four yards in circumference, and five feet in height, was opened from the top without making any discovery till arriving near the natural surface, where we found three plots of burnt earth, disposed so as to form a triangle. After their removal a cist was found in the centre of the barrow, containing calcined bones, from the midst of which was taken a small misshapen vessel, of the usual fabric, 4½ inches high, with a deep border, ornamented with a lozenge pattern, the lines being impressions of string or twisted thongs.

In addition to opening the above-described barrows, Mr. Ruddock collected many articles from the sites of various dilapidated or removed barrows in the same district, as will be seen by the ensuing notice of some of the more curious objects thus discovered.

From a barrow near Cawthorn Camps, opened about the year 1840, a sepulchral urn, in an imperfect state, and a calcined pin, were recovered. The former has been about 9¼ inches diameter, of thinner and more firmly baked clay than usual, with two hollow mouldings round the upper part, ornamented by carefully arranged rows of dots alternating with twisted lines. The pin has the thicker end rounded, and, wanting a small piece of the point, measures 3½ inches long.

From the site of another tumulus, near Cawthorn Camps, in 1849, were obtained a finely chipped spear-head and a rude arrow-point of flint; and from the moor in the neighbourhood a bronze spear, 4¼ inches long, of very primitive form.

In the remains of a barrow, near Pickering, a calcined flint spear and a large jet bead, more than an inch diameter, were found in 1849.

On the site of another a flint spear and arrow were found; and from similar places fragments of seven urns, of various sizes, some beautifully ornamented, were procured in 1849 and 1850.

Amongst the archæological products of the primeval period found on the moors around Pickering, up to the end of the year 1850, Mr. Ruddock's collection contains three querns or hand-mills of gritstone; flat pieces of sandstone, with a hole through the centre, so as to resemble rude quoits; and flint weapons of various shapes and sizes, mostly rude, but occasionally very neatly formed, and in nearly every instance calcined.

By examining the remains of a tumulus in Goathland, in 1849, a few jet or coal ornaments were found, comprising three cylindrical beads, one flat bead with a large perforation, and a conical stud. A set of these ornaments, consisting of numerous pieces, had been previously taken from the mound.

Mr. Ruddock also obtained a full-socketed bronze celt, found along with the skull of a wolf, the fore-part of which is broken away, from the Wolds, near Scampstone, in 1850; and descending to a more recent age, we may mention some pieces of Romano-British pottery, and a conical object of sandstone, $1\frac{3}{4}$ inches high, found by quarrying for stone in 1849, close to the town of Pickering; also the upper stone of a Roman handmill, of Andernach lava, having the original iron rhind secured by lead; together with the lower stone of a pot quern, carved out of a block of limestone, with a hole for the discharge of the flour at the side, both found, with a large quantity of animal bones, near Old Malton, in 1849. The lower jaws of two wild boars, armed with formidable tusks, picked out from these bones as the most characteristic, are preserved in the collection.

1851.

The first barrow opened this year, on the 22nd of January, is situated about seven miles east from Pickering, and is four feet six high, covering an area fifty-four yards in circumference. We commenced by digging from the summit through the sand of which the hill was composed, till the level of the surrounding land was reached, where on the south side large flat stones were uncovered, beneath which small portions of charred wood and black earth continued to the depth of three feet below the natural surface, when we discovered a skeleton lying embedded in clay, with the head to the north, accompanied by a lance-head and a slender arrow-point of unburnt flint, placed close to the head.

On the 24th of January we opened a tumulus in the same locality, forty yards in base circumference and four feet in central elevation, composed of limestone rubble, by an incision from the north side, by which nothing was discovered till the centre was almost reached, where large stones made their appearance, the removal of which disclosed an urn, $6\frac{1}{4}$ inches tall, resting on its side, and enclosing a small incense cup of very dark coloured clay. The largest vessel has a moulded border, with stops decorated by the application of a twisted cord, relieved by two rows of impressed markings. The other is cylindrical, ornamented by V shaped lines of deeply punctured dots, and the composition is so much inferior to that of the larger vase as to convey the idea of greater antiquity, and to lead to the supposition of its having been a valued heirloom, which it was the intention to preserve more effectually by enclosure within the other, which does not appear to have contained bones. A little further south another large stone was found, and after its displacement a skeleton was discovered a little below the surface, lying in clay and limestone rubble with the head south, with a beautiful stone adze or celt, $3\frac{1}{2}$ inches long, wrought in green basalt, and a very elaborately chipped spear of flint, near four inches long, near its right hand. The latter weapon has been submitted to heat sufficient to vitrify the surface to a grey colour, the inside being pure white. It is also to be remarked, that at the head and feet of this interment were two more human skeletons, of very small size, which illustrate similar discoveries made in the Derbyshire and Staffordshire barrows.

On the 30th of January a barrow was opened, about seven miles east of Pickering, of the circumference of forty-eight yards, and five feet high, composed of sand, interspersed throughout with particles of calcined bone and charcoal to the natural level, which was reached by digging down from the top. At this point, in the centre of the barrow, limestone rubble succeeded the sand, and continued to the depth of four feet lower, where the body of a young adult had been interred, with the head to the north. At the right hand of the skeleton was a plain spear-head of grey flint, and near the skull were the remains of a small vase, very prettily ornamented with herring-bone work and part of the upper jaw of a sheep. Three round-ended flints were found in an indeterminate position on the natural surface.

About five miles north of Pickering is a barrow four feet high, measuring twelve yards across, composed of rubbly limestone, which was excavated on the 5th of February by a trench cut from its northern edge. The centre was passed without any discovery, and it was not until the trench had been carried into the south half of the tumulus that the interment was found, consisting of a skeleton, lying in a grave sunk about two feet below the surface of the ground, with the head to the north, accompanied by a very small celt or chisel of grey flint, smoothly rubbed and a plain spear-head of the same material.

On the next day we opened a tumulus about a mile nearer Pickering, thirty-two yards round, five feet high, and, like the last, composed of limestone rubble. After excavating from the north side to the middle, we observed some large stones, by the removal of which we found a cist, measuring five feet in length and four feet in width, filled with clay and rubble to the depth of six feet, having at the bottom a skeleton that had been interred with the head and knees bent together, accompanied by three neat flints placed at the right side, comprising a leaf-shaped lance, a barbed arrow, and a circular implement.

A tumulus, seven miles north of Pickering, forty-eight yards circumference and six feet high, composed of sand and stones, was opened on the 8th of February, by digging a large hole from the summit. After penetrating to the natural level, a large flat stone appeared exactly in the centre, the removal of which disclosed a quantity of calcined bones, from among which we took a small incense cup, 1¾ inches high, with a contracted mouth, and two indifferent instruments of burnt flint. No other interment had ever been deposited in the mound.

On the 11th of February there was opened a good-sized mound, six miles north of Pickering, rather more than twenty yards diameter, and two yards in actual height. Like several of the last, it was of small limestone, and was investigated from the north side. In cutting towards the centre, portions of a small vase, with a projecting herring-bone border, occurred near the surface; and after passing the centre, towards the south, a small cist of stones was found about a yard beneath the turf, enclosing a tall cinerary urn, nine inches high, with a prominent border, altogether unornamented, and filled with burnt bones. After the removal of these secondary interments, no other was found till we arrived at the natural level at the south side, where, beneath a large mass of burnt earth and charcoal, the upper part of a large cist-vaen of sandstone flags appeared, filled up with loose stone. When the latter were lifted out, we ascertained the length to be seven feet, the width four, and the depth five. At the bottom was the skeleton of a middle-aged man, deposited with the head to the north, having at the right hand a fine spear-head, a plain and a barbed arrow-point, and a lump of red flint, that had been used as a hammer for chipping other flints. The skull is rather elongated in form, and near it was the head of a goat, without horns.

On the 13th of February we opened a smaller tumulus, near the last, measuring forty-three yards round, and five feet high, also composed of limestone rubble. Our cutting was taken from the north side direct to the centre, where we found some calcined bones, with two spear-heads and a round-ended instrument of burnt flint, one of the former having been nicely chipped and rubbed, the other more boldly cut into shape, with less trouble. The excavation was continued to the south without success, but by exploring the west side of the mound, a little beneath the natural surface, fragments of human bones were found, having near them a sandstone ball, about four inches diameter, roughly chipped all over like one found on the 4th of April, 1850.

On the 18th of February, a stony barrow, four miles N.E. from Pickering, eleven yards across, and four feet high, was opened from the west side, nothing being discovered till the natural surface beneath the southern half of the mound was gained, when we met with a large bed of charcoal, covering the primary interment of burnt bones, accompanied by a small incense cup, 1¾ inches high, quite unornamented, and three flints, the last being a short spear-head. Much more of the tumulus was excavated without further discovery.

On the 28th of February, we opened a small barrow, near the last, eight yards in diameter, and four feet in height, composed of sand. The cutting was begun at the top, where we found a rectangular sandstone, eight inches long by six wide, having a shallow circular cavity worked in the middle of each side, the use of which we are not able to determine, although several of the same kind have been found in the barrows. No further discovery was made until coming to the natural soil; at the north side we found the greater part of a very rude upright urn, shaped like a flower-pot, some burnt bones, and a considerable quantity of charcoal. Rather more south we found part of a very fine flint dagger, and a small flint knife, both of which have undergone a degree of calcination sufficient to turn them grey. They were embedded in burnt earth and charred wood.

On the 20th of March, we examined a large stony cairn, near the last, sixty-eight yards in circumference, and three yards high, by an excavation commenced at the north, which afforded nothing but a few burnt bones, and particles of charcoal, until having passed the centre to the south side, we came to a fine cist, ten feet long, six feet broad, and seven feet deep, partly filled with limestone gravel, which being shovelled out, exposed a human skeleton, with its head in an eastern direction, and its feet towards the setting sun, embedded in strong clay at the bottom. A small carelessly ornamented urn, 4¾ inches high, with a moulded border, lay near the skeleton; and a small broken arrow-point, with a large rough instrument of flint, were placed at its right hand.

On the 25th of March a barrow, eleven miles east of Pickering, fifty-seven yards in circumference, and near six feet high, composed of sand and stones, engaged our attention. It was opened from the top; and after having dug about two feet down, we perceived a large flat stone, covering a large sepulchral urn, eight inches diameter at the mouth, with a deep border, decorated with vertical and horizontal lines, alternating at intervals of two or three inches, filled with calcined bones, but injured in the lower part by the burrowing of rabbits. The cutting was next taken east, where a cist, constructed of five large stones, containing a simple deposit of burnt bones, was found, which concluded the discoveries.

The site of a barrow near the last, that had long been removed by agricultural operations, was examined on the 3rd of April, when it was found, that, although the mound had been cleared away down to the natural surface, the original interment had escaped destruction, owing to it having been placed lower in the earth. A grave, nine feet long, five feet wide, and eight feet deep, had been dug for the reception of the body, and after the funeral, had been filled up with large stones. When we removed them, we found the skeleton lying at the bottom, with the head to the north, embedded in red gravel, which, we may observe, is frequently the case in the Yorkshire tumuli, and which may result from an instinctive unwillingness to place large and rough stones immediately in contact with the corpse at the time of burial. A similar precaution has been taken in many of the Derbyshire barrows, and it is remarkable how well the contemplated end has been secured by these simple means, the relics thus guarded being always in good condition. At the right hand of this skele-

P

leton was an assemblage of curious articles, the foremost of which is a fine bronze dagger, now upwards of six inches long, though more than an inch is broken off: it has been fastened to a handle with a V shaped termination by three rivets. It is much to be regretted that the investigation was not conducted with greater care, as there was a possibility of recovering the handle, which was formed of bone, but unfortunately the butt end of it only was preserved. This is made of three pieces of bone, riveted together by two bronze pins, and perforated with two holes for tying or pegging on the other part. It resembles the bone ornament discovered with the ancient British chief, in a tumulus near Gristhorpe, now in the Scarborough Museum. Next was a thick-backed cutting instrument of flint, three inches long, from which we may judge that this interment took place during the period of transition, when stone weapons were about to be superseded by bronze. Next were two small balls of stone, one and two inches diameter respectively; and a peculiarly shaped stone, much like a coprolite, probably valued by the deceased, and, consequently, interred with him. In addition to these there was a small tool, neatly cut from a cow's tooth, very suitable for impressing designs on the clay vessels of the period; and two remarkable little objects, like acorns both in size and shape, that have been charred. They are evidently a vegetable product, but of what kind I am unable to determine.

On the 9th of April, we resumed our labours in the same neighbourhood, by opening a large sandy tumulus, twenty-one yards across and five feet high, by a large cutting from the top. After digging through three feet of sand, we uncovered some large stones, which, being lifted away, exposed a perfectly uninjured cinerary urn, $7\frac{1}{4}$ inches high, with a moulded border, impressed with twisted cord in vertical and horizontal lines at alternate intervals. It was filled with calcined bones and black earth, and near it was part of another vase, and six flints of the usual sorts. The excavation being then continued to the surface, we observed two simple deposits of burnt bones, respectively north and south of the centre of the barrow. The mound had been reduced by cultivation, which had also caused the destruction of a later interment buried near the top, as on passing over it on the 11th of the preceding March, Mr. Ruddock found a very elegant axe-head, five inches long, of reddish basalt, beautifully wrought, with a slight moulding round the angles, and a perforation for the shaft; also part of a well-made clay vessel, 4½ inches diameter at the mouth, minutely decorated at the outside, both of which had been exposed by the plough.

On the 8th of April we opened a small tumulus, four miles N.W. of Pickering, measuring eight yards through and two feet high, composed of a mixture of sand and stones. Nothing was seen until, on arriving at the natural level, we met with large stones, which being removed disclosed a small grave filled with loose stones: upon the latter being cleared out, we ascertained the length to be three feet, the width two, and the depth four. At the bottom was a skeleton, much contracted to fit the confined space, having at the head three poor flints, one of red silex, and a very beautiful miniature vase, two inches high, carefully decorated all over with lines of deeply punctured dots, disposed with great regularity, the edge and bottom each exhibit a single line of herring-bone work. Had this vessel been deposited with a burnt body, it would have been called an incense cup, which it resembles in every respect; and were it not for the extreme accuracy of Mr. Ruddock's notes, I should feel disposed to think that the skeleton had undergone combustion, as the incense cup has uniformly been found with such.

The following discoveries were made upon the site of a long barrow, four miles N.W. from Pickering, which had been almost levelled to the ground by agriculture. The longest diameter was from east to west, and our excavation was begun at the former extremity, where, after the removal of earth and stone to the depth of a foot, portions of a human leg and arm-bone were discovered, quite black in colour. Beneath them loose stones continued downwards for five feet, when a skeleton was found, lying east and west, with a very delicately chipped leaf-shaped lance of grey flint, upwards of three inches long, at the right hand, but, strange to say, wanting the skull, which had evidently never been buried with it. Several instances of mutilated deposits found in the Derbyshire and Staffordshire barrows are recorded in the former part of this volume, and the subject is well worth further investigation.

Returning to the surface, the excavation was directed southwards, where we found more bones, presenting the singular black appearance of those first observed. After their removal, a grave four feet deep was found, which being cleared of the large stones, succeeded by rubble, with which it was filled, afforded another skeleton, placed with its head to the east, and accompanied by part of a fine and large dagger of grey flint, laid near the skull.

Again going back to the surface, the excavation was pursued westwards, uncovering in its course several depressions, from two feet to a yard deep, containing imperfect skeletons, that had, perhaps, suffered when the tumulus was levelled. On gaining the western boundary, large stones indicated another grave, the lower part being, like the former, filled with limestone gravel, covering a skeleton, with its head to the west, and a large rough spear of mottled yellow flint near the skull. The northern part of the area of this large barrow was not explored.

A pair of twin barrows, six miles N.W. of Pickering, previously opened by another person, were re-examined by Mr. Ruddock on the 28th of May, on account of a casual discovery of jet ornaments within them. The circumference of the first is forty-six yards, its height four feet, and it consists of sand. The trench, begun at the north side, had only advanced about two feet from the surface when a variety of jet beads was found, sufficient to compose a very pretty necklace, comprising a rectangular centre-piece, ornamented with a saltire made by small holes drilled a little way in; thirteen long beads, and nine cone-shaped studs. There are two lateral perforations through the centre-plate, so that the cylindrical beads are strung in a double link. After these cherished jewels of the stone period had been carefully gathered up, we diverted the cutting westwards, and found the skull of a child and other human bones, which had been before disturbed.

The companion barrow is rather larger, being fifty-two yards round and four feet high, and is also composed of sand. The excavation was commenced from the south, and its downward progress did not exceed a foot before we were rewarded by the discovery of a curious pendant ornament of coarse jet or Kimmeridge coal, about two inches long, shaped something like an heraldic shield, and ornamented by a saltire of plain lines proceeding from a round depression in the middle; together with a large ring, about 1½ inches diameter inside, cut from a flat piece of the same black shale, and fragments of another, very like it, both, probably, being a pair of child's bracelets. The trench was then continued northwards, yielding in its course the tusk of a wild boar; a thick instrument of grey flint, much rubbed; and a flat kidney-shaped stone, which, though merely a natural production, may have been valued by its ancient proprietor.

On the 10th of June we opened a barrow, four miles N.W. of Pickering, forty-eight yards round and five feet high, comprised of sand and stones. After sinking three feet from the summit, large stones were discovered lying over a human skeleton, laid with the head pointing south, having near the skull a small inelegant vase, 5½ inches high, with a border roughly ornamented by chevrons. On this vessel were laid a small spear head and knife of clear unburnt flint. These articles being taken up, the cutting was continued, and a little to the south of the human skeleton we found the bones of an ox in good preservation. Ultimately, the excavation was increased to a very considerable extent, but nothing was found more interesting than a few rude flints. The human bones appear to be the remains of an elderly person, whose vertebral column exhibit an abnormal feature, in seven or eight of the joints being firmly and immoveably connected by the formation a smooth ribbon of osseous matter upon their inner surface.

The next was an interment beneath the surface, without any mound having being raised over it. The locality was six miles N.E. of Pickering, and attention was first drawn to it by the appearance of a few large stones above the turf. The place was dug into on the 30th July, when we first removed the gravel, in which we found a rectangular stone, 6½ inches long, 4½ wide, with a shallow hole worked in the centre of each side, and a large square bone about the same size, from a whale or some very large fish, with two natural lateral perforations. No other object of interest was seen till we had sunk six feet down, when large flat stones appeared, leading to the discovery of the skeleton of a fine young man, embedded in coarse sand, with the head to the south and the feet to the north. Near the latter was a deposit of calcined bones, and a very curious collection of twenty-one flint implements or tools, of various shapes, evidently intended to serve a variety of purposes, which it is impossible to describe intelligibly. The best is a cutting instrument, with a very keen edge, like a celt, nicely polished. They have all been submitted to the action of fire, to a greater or less degree. There is also another irregularly shaped sandstone, near six inches long, with neatly-wrought round holes in it, marked as having been found in this sepulchre; but Mr. Ruddock's notes do not state further particulars. The opening was continued till a space fourteen yards in circumference, and eight feet deep, was cleared out, but no other discovery repaid the labour.

On the 28th of December we opened a very ancient tumulus, near Heslerton-on-the-Wolds, measuring about fifty-seven yards round the base, and six feet high, composed of chalk stones. We began the cutting at the west side, but did not observe any indications of interment till reaching the centre. At that point, however, there were no less than fifteen human skeletons, several of which lay one upon another, without much arrangement; still, as far as we could ascertain, the heads were mostly directed eastward. Inside one skull was a small and neat flint arrow, and by the skeleton of the same individual we found a small pointed bone, and half of an extremely rough bead of baked clay.

The crania from this barrow, that have been preserved, are all more or less mutilated; but about six remain sufficiently entire to indicate the prevailing conformation to be of the long or Kumbe-Kephalic type of Dr. Wilson ("Pre-Historic Annals of

Scotland," p. 180). They range from youth to old age, as in other cases where large numbers of skeletons have been found in the same barrow. The longest thigh bone measures $19\frac{1}{4}$ inches; another is $18\frac{1}{2}$ inches long.

Mr. Ruddock also collected many minor objects of antiquity, during the year 1851, from the moors and warrens about Pickering, including a numerous series of flint instruments of the usual forms, and several examples of stones, with artificially worked cavities in one or both of their sides; in one case, five such cavities are drilled into a single stone. There are also two stones from handmills, of very primitive construction; and the collection includes a few articles of the Romano-British period, the most important being a large harp-shaped bronze fibula, $4\frac{1}{4}$ inches long, still wearable and perfect, found near Rillington. The other things comprise black pottery, of coarse texture, from Coston; and red ware, of similar quality, from Knapton.

1852.

At various times in the year 1852, many sites, formerly occupied by tumuli destroyed in the course of agricultural improvements, were examined in the hope of gleaning some relics that might have escaped the general wreck, with the following results, some of which are interesting, although the objects discovered are of but little importance.

The first is a drinking cup, $7\frac{1}{2}$ inches high, ornamented with many parallel lines, encircling the upper part. Next is half of a very handsome hammer-head, of reddish coloured stone, neatly moulded round the angles, found near Robin Hood's Bay.

Part of a perforated quoit-shaped stone, four inches diameter, found on Daulby Warren.

Two curiously-marked stones; one divided into a number of small squares, as a draught-board, found in the barrow at Scambridge, in which a stone hammer and a bronze dagger were discovered in 1851.

A barrow near the last afforded two inferior flint spear-heads.

Another barrow, in the same locality, yielded three instruments of calcined flint; one of them fine, and four inches long.

A barrow, near Kinthorpe, produced five tolerable flint instruments; another, in the same neighbourhood, afforded a neatly-chipped pear-shaped spear, and two other implements of flint.

A barrow, near Ebberston, repaid our labour with a fine cutting instrument, an arrow-point, and two round-ended flints.

In the ruins of a mound, near Pickering, we found only two rude instruments of flint.

Three silicious implements were recovered from the remains of a tumulus near Middleton-by-Pickering.

A small block of flint, a knife, and two round-ended flints were found in a barrow near Newton-by-Pickering.

Mr. Ruddock also collected, during the year, 105 calcined flints, consisting of roughly-chipped spears, arrows, circular instruments, and flakes, many of the latter having doubtless been used as knives.

BARROWS OPENED IN THE YEAR 1853.

On the 17th of February we opened a barrow about two miles north of Pickering, which, being situated in land long cultivated, had become ploughed down to within a foot of the surface of the land. We began to search at the north side, but made no discovery until gaining the opposite side, where, at the depth of two feet from the surface, we found two urns embedded in ashes; one of extremely rude workmanship, and upright form; the other of better shape and finer material, but both imperfect from disintegration. After their removal, the other parts of the barrow were examined, but nothing was found but five inferior flints.

On the 23rd of February we opened another barrow, in the same field, which had been so much reduced by cultivation as to exhibit but a slight approximation to the tumular form; indeed, the sepulchral character of the spot was accidentally discovered by the plough coming in contact with several large stones, which, on removal, disclosed some calcined bones. By digging to the depth of four feet a grave was found, measuring six feet long, four wide, and five deep, which contained portions of an unburnt skeleton, accompanied by four silicious instruments, one of which is well adapted for the point of a large spear; another is of the round-edged shape.

On the 24th of February we examined a third tumulus in the same field, thirty-five yards circumference, and about four feet high. We commenced on the east side, where we found a deposit of burnt bones, having near them portions of an urn and two poor flints. No further discovery was made until we reached the south side, where, on the natural earth, was another deposit of calcined bones. A small jet ring, and a fine barbed arrow-head of flint, had been previously found in the barrow by the occupier of the land.

On the 5th of April we opened a barrow on Allerston Warren, fifty-six yards circumference and six feet high, by an excavation from the south. After passing through different coloured strata of sand, to the depth of three feet, we came to a mass of charcoal, having in the midst a very remarkable elliptical vase of thin clay, neatly ornamented, the mouth measuring six inches by 4¼. Near it lay five flints, of various shapes, one rather large. These articles having been removed, the search was continued, and at the east side of the mound we found a large quantity of black ashes, containing calcined bones and a round flint, placed on the natural soil.

On the 13th of April another sandy barrow, on Allerston Warren, twenty-eight yards round and four feet high, was investigated by an excavation from the south. After passing the centre, towards the north, a change appeared in the natural surface for the space of about three feet square. Here the first substance to be removed was limestone gravel, which continued to the depth of about two feet, when it was replaced by a bed of black ashes, beneath which was a deposit of calcined bones, covered by an extremely fine sepulchral urn, inverted over them. A slightly moulded incense cup, two inches high, was in the midst of the bones. The urn is thirteen inches high, with a wide ornamented border, marked inside with small punctures, and is of the tall and elegant shape occasionally found in the Yorkshire tumuli, but seldom met with in any other district. The remainder of the mound was afterwards searched, but yielded only a few flints.

On the 14th of April a third barrow, on Allerston Warren, eight yards across, by three feet high, was opened from the north side, when we found a sprinkling of burnt bones and pieces of earthenware. On gaining the centre we found an interment of burnt bones, mixed with charcoal, slightly below the natural surface, and with them an ornamented vase, six inches high, with a border, probably filled with food when deposited in the barrow. Five flints were disinterred from other parts of the mound, where they had most likely been thrown by the friends of the deceased as offerings to his spirit.

On the 15th of April the fourth barrow on Allerston Warren, composed of stones and sand, was opened by a trench from the north side, in which part of the mound we discovered an imperfect vase, $4\frac{1}{2}$ inches high, embedded in black earth. The cutting being carried forward to the opposite side, we found a deposit of burnt bones, containing a fine spear-head of flint, also calcined. About two feet from these was a curious vase of coarse clay, with a rudely ornamented border, altogether about four inches high, embedded in a mass of ashes. The remainder of the tumulus afforded six other flints.

On the 21st of April a barrow, fifty-eight yards circumference, and near four feet high, situated in cultivated land near Kingthorpe, was opened by an excavation from the north, which, being pursued to the depth of a little more than two feet, disclosed a large plot of burnt earth, continuing nearly to the surface of the land, whereon an interment, by combustion, had taken place. Amongst the calcined bones was an incense cup, two inches high, decorated round the outside with an incised diamond pattern, and with it was a flint knife: the cup contains wood ashes, as when discovered. We next directed our attention to the east side, where disconnected human bones appeared above a rude cist of stones, by removing which we found a richly ornamented vase, upwards of six inches high, with a moulded border divided by stops, accompanied by a spear-head of flint. The barrow was thoroughly examined without further success.

On the 20th of September a second barrow, at Kingthorpe, composed of stones and sand, and measuring forty-six yards round by five feet high, was examined from the south side. We soon discovered some calcined bones, and an imperfect vase, with a moulded border, measuring altogether seven inches in height. A broken ring of jet and two flints were also casually found. An interment of the Saxon age had been deposited near the apex of the tumulus, but had been disturbed. We found, however, some of the bones, including the jaws; a cruciform bronze fibula, slightly broken, $3\frac{1}{2}$ inches long; a boar's tusk, and a piece of the edge of a vessel of dark-coloured earthenware. This is but the second instance of an interment of the Teutonic, or iron period, that has occurred in the course of Mr. Ruddock's extensive operations.

On the 23rd of September we examined a tumulus, three miles north of Pickering, forty-four yards in circumference and two yards high, by an excavation begun at the north side, which yielded in its progress a variety of flints, a small perforated stone, apparently part of a pendant sharpening-stone, and a small piece of jet. The primary interment was not discovered until we were past the centre, shortly beyond which was a cist, constructed of large stones, enclosing a mass of calcined bones and charcoal, accompanied by a vase of well-baked clay, $5\frac{1}{4}$ inches high, with a decorated border, and a neatly-chipped silicious spear, so completely vitrified by the heat of the funeral pile as to present a surface closely resembling white porcelain. Nothing else was found in any part of the barrow.

1854.

On the 16th of February, 1854, we opened the fifth tumulus on Allerston Warren, a sandy mound, five feet high and twenty-six yards circumference, by cutting from the east to the centre, where a large flat stone was placed on the natural soil, so as to cover the principal interment, consisting of calcined bones, accompanied by a plain incense cup, shaped like a flattened sphere, an inch and three-quarters high and four inches diameter, filled with ashes. After the removal of this deposit, the cutting was directed to the south side, where another interment by combustion had taken place. Amongst the latter remains we found a very neatly chipped arrow-head of light-coloured flint.

In addition to the foregoing discoveries, Mr. Ruddock obtained, during the year 1853, the following miscellaneous articles from the sites of desecrated tumuli, and other scenes of ancient occupation —

A spherical stone, perhaps intended to be tied up in a piece of leather and used as a mace, like the "slung-shot" of the United States; and a flint arrow, found among the debris of a barrow at Daulby.

A neat arrow, found upon the barrow near Tweesdale in which the axe-hammer was discovered in March, 1851.

Five chipped flints, from a mound near Pickering.

Six flints, from the mound near Pickering in which the drinking cup, with a handle, was found in January, 1850.

Eight flints, from a barrow near Crosscliff.

Four flints and a small piece of perforated earthenware, from a barrow at Newton.

Five flints, including a large barbed arrow, from two other barrows near the last.

Seven flints, from a barrow near Pickering.

A collection of 211 flints found on warrens round Pickering, where many tumuli have formerly stood. They are mostly calcined, and may be classed into —

Thirty-nine flints for spears, thirty-eight arrow-points, twenty chipping-blocks or instruments used in the fabrication of other instruments of flint, thirty-six of the mysterious circular-edged implements, and fifty-eight flakes or knives.

Two rude stones, about 3½ inches across; one partly, the other entirely pierced, from Daulby warren.

Half of a beautiful axe-hammer, of red-coloured basaltic stone, found in a field, in which there is a barrow, two miles north of Pickering.

Two Celtic coins, in billon or mixed metal, of the peculiar rough type apparently characteristic of, and confined to, the coinage of the Brigantes, found by quarrymen engaged in baring the rock near Pickering.

A well-preserved skull, apparently of a female, found with others, and iron weapons, in preparing to cut the Boardhill tunnel of the Malton and Driffield Railway. It is most probably of the Saxon period.

Since the foregoing was written, Mr. Ruddock's death has taken place, so unexpectedly that he was unable to prepare any notes of his later discoveries, the proceeds of which, in accordance with his last wishes, have been added to his former collections in the author's possession. The ensuing list furnishes the requisite description of the articles themselves, and the localities where found are indicated in a small memorandum-book; but, unfortunately, the objects found in each tumulus cannot be identified.

From barrows in the neighbourhood of Pickering, opened in 1854 and 1855, were derived —

1. A tall cinerary urn, sixteen inches high, and eleven diameter at the mouth, with a deep border, ornamented by repeated impressions from a crenated tool of coarse clay, mixed with angular gravel, and pretty well baked.

2. Part of another large cinerary urn, upwards of a foot diameter, with the border ornamented by circular dots.

3. A small cinerary urn, nine inches high, 6¼ diameter, with a border decorated with vertical lines, the part immediately beneath with rows of small star-like punctures.

4. Vase or cinerary urn (?) of reddish clay, nine inches high, with oval mouth, having a border very carefully ornamented with triangles of twisted impressions, made by oblique lines of cordage

disposed in opposite directions; below, the vessel is encircled by three horizontal rows of deeply indented chevrons. It is one of the most elegant and well-finished productions of the ceramic art amongst the ancient Britons that we have ever seen.

5. Is an incense cup of light-coloured clay, somewhat in the form of a depressed sphere, 2½ inches high and three in diameter, which, from bearing the same ornament of oblique lines disposed in triangles, may probably have been found with the last.

6. Is another very unusual incense cup, of similar shape and size, decorated above with vertical lines, alternating with others in a horizontal direction, beneath which are eight perforations arranged at equal distances around the cup: below the latter are four concentric circles of round punctures covering the bottom. The ornamentation bears an analogy to that of the urn No. 3.

7. Is another incense cup of altogether novel form, being shaped like a cylinder mounted on four small feet. It is 2⅛ inches high, and is ornamented with vertical impressions of a twisted cord.

It was found in November, 1854, in a barrow about a mile from Pickering, near that opened on the 23rd January, 1850, whence the eared drinking cup was obtained.

8. A small roughly-ornamented food vase, of gritty clay, six inches high.

9. A small moulded food vase, 4½ inches high, entirely covered with deeply-indented chevrons.

10. A vase with narrow border, of dark-coloured ware, quite devoid of ornament, 7¼ inches high.

11. Another unornamented vase, of light-coloured clay, with a similar narrow border, six inches high.

12. A porringer-shaped vessel, four inches high, very rudely modelled in sandy clay, but rather firmly baked.

Besides these fictilia, the greater part of which have accompanied interments by cremation, we find, in this part of the collection, a considerable quantity of oak charcoal; part of a fine jet necklace, consisting of a conical stud, two cylindrical beads, and two flat dividing plates, each ornamented with a saltire in punctures; two sandstones, with cavities worked in them; and a large collection of white flints, some of which present the glazed surface before alluded to in this volume. The most interesting of these are —

Fifteen barbed arrow-heads, fifteen leaf-shaped arrows, twenty spear-points, twenty-eight circular-ended instruments, nine chipping blocks; two pounded or abraded pieces, one of them spherical; a rectangular piece, apparently chipped from the splinter of a polished celt of grey flint; and numerous flakes and other indeterminate implements. Some of the barbed arrows are extremely beautiful.

In 1856, Mr. Ruddock removed from Pickering to Whitby, and his final discoveries were made in the neighbourhood of the latter town in 1857 and 1858. They consist entirely of incinerated remains, often accompanied by instruments of flint excessively burnt, and incense cups. From some of the urns having come into my possession in the state in which they were exhumed, I am enabled to say that they were embedded in charcoal, in an upright position, at an inconsiderable depth below the surface; and that after the bones were put in the urn, an incense cup was placed upon the deposit, and that then the pieces of the flint weapons, fractured by the heat of the funeral pyre, were thrown in, sand being lastly heaped over them.

Before proceeding to an enumeration of the urns, I copy the following notice of the tumuli where they were found —

"There are several tumuli on Sleights Moor. The one nearest Whitby has been partly opened. The part unexplored is worthy of examination. Circumference of base sixty-eight yards, depth near six feet; the base enclosed with large stones.

No. 2. Resembling No. 1 in formation. On the south side an excavation has been made for the purpose of erecting a place of shelter for sportsmen in pursuit of grouse. Circumference of base sixty-four yards, depth near six feet.

No. 3. Composed of sand. It appears to have been strictly searched. Circumference of base 46 yards, depth near 6 feet.

No. 4. Composed of sand, partly open in the centre. Circumference of base thirty yards, depth three feet.

No. 5. Appears not to have been in any part explored. Circumference of base near seventy yards, depth nine feet. Base enclosed with large stones.

No. 6. Composed of sand. The east side has been partly mutilated by excavating for whinstone. Circumference of base fifty yards, depth six feet. Enclosed with large stones, well worthy of examination.

No. 7. Composed of sand, partly opened in the centre. Circumference of base thirty-two yards, depth near four feet.

Two other barrows near Egton, each about thirty-four yards circumference, and four feet deep; and

A barrow at Silhow, about the same size, but a little higher, are likewise entered in the memorandum book without further particulars.

The Whitby urns are —

1. A large plain cinerary urn, with border, fourteen inches high, and near a foot diameter at the mouth, containing calcined bones and part of a flint spear.

2. Cinerary urn, 12¾ inches high, the border ornamented with diagonal lines of cordage, containing a very clean deposit of burnt bones.

3. A tall-shaped cinerary urn, thirteen inches high, the border ornamented with vertical lines, filled with burnt bones mixed with sand, and accompanied by fragments of flint weapons.

4. Small cinerary urn of red clay, only seven inches high, with a border, contains burnt bones; above them a barrel-shaped incense cup and flint fragments.

5. Plain barrel-shaped cup, found inside the last, 2¼ inches high, 2¾ diameter, of red clay. When taken out of the urn, the roots of the heath had taken an exact cast of the inside.

6. A still smaller cinerary urn of red clay, very much like No. 4, but only 5½ inches high, containing burnt bones.

7. Remains of two others of the same kind and colour, with borders, each containing a few bones.

8. Remains of a course and rather large urn, of deep red pottery, with a border ornamented by the impression of twisted thongs, containing burnt bones and sand.

9. Remains of a large cinerary urn, of dark-coloured clay, with a deep border, decorated by twelve parallel lines, impressed by a twisted cord, containing its original deposit.

10. Remains of another large cinerary urn, with burnt bones attached to the pieces by the induration of the sand.

11. Small and rather funnel-shaped cup, of plain red ware, 3¾ inches high, containing roots and a few bones.

12. Portions of two incense cups, of red clay, much decomposed, but evidently barrel-shaped, liked No. 5.

14. Plain vase, with a very deep border, six inches high: when found it contained sand only, and was probably a food vase.

A broken celt, of fine-grained green stone, was with this part of Mr. Ruddock's collection, but it probably had no connection with the tumuli.

APPENDIX.

MISCELLANEOUS DISCOVERIES.

In April, 1847, men employed in getting stone under an accumulation of loose limestone, at the bottom of a low hill close to the river Lathkill, at Conksbury Bridge, near Youlgrave, found a considerable number of bones, both human and animal. The former comprised skeletons of four young persons and one infant, none having reached maturity; the latter consist chiefly of the skeletons of two horses. Amongst them were found a short piece of the leg bone of some animal, artificially perforated with six holes, and a plain bronze fibula, of the common Roman type, with the acus still remaining. All the articles (except the perforated bone) were added to the collection at Lomberdale, by the kindness of Thomas Masters, Esq., of Bakewell.

In illustration of this discovery, we may mention that a tall and singularly slender skeleton was found under limestone gravel, in a similar situation at the foot of a hill at Dowell, near Sterndale, in November, 1850; but being unaccompanied by any manufactured object, we are unable to fix any approximate date to the time of its interment.

Another skeleton was found under precisely similar circumstances, in October, 1859, by men digging for gravel in Glutton Dale, a very short distance from Sterndale. The bones were much broken by the workmen, but sufficient remains to show that they were those of a tall and muscular young man. A few broken animal bones accompanied the interment, but no manufactured article was found.

In February, 1848, during the formation of the Rowsley and Ambergate Railway, a sepulchral deposit was found in a field by the side of the river Derwent, immediately north of Matlock Bridge, consisting of a large urn, about half full of calcined bones, enclosing a smaller vessel of the kind usually known as the "incense cup," which was placed upon the bones. The largest urn was covered by a thin flat limestone, and was further protected from the pressure of the earth by a kind of cist, formed of two stones, each about three feet long by eighteen inches broad, placed on edge, one on each side, with a third laid transversely above. An empty vase was also found close by the other. I am indebted to Mr. Adam, the geologist, for the above information; and to Mr. Campbell, the engineer, for his kindness in placing the incense cup in the collection at Lomberdale. The large urn was broken to pieces by the excavators. The accompanying woodcut (lent by Mr. Pike, of Derby) will render this notice more intelligible.

Urn and Incense Cup — Matlock.

On the 10th of February, 1849, a person engaged in levelling about an old stone quarry in land near Monyash, called High Low, met with numerous bones, both of men and animals, as usually found in tumuli that have been disturbed; a circumstance here recorded for the purpose of establishing the fact of a barrow having existed at High Low, as the name would indicate.

BARROW AT WATERHOUSES, STAFFORDSHIRE, OPENED BY MR. HALL, OF THAT PLACE.

In the autumn of the year 1849, a small barrow was opened by Mr. Hall, in which he discovered a skeleton, which he pronounced to be that of a female, laid in a natural depression in the rock, beneath the centre. No instrument or pottery was found either with it or in any other part of the mound.

BARROW NEAR WARSLOW, OPENED BY MR. HERBERT MANCLARKE.

On the 18th of April, 1850, a barrow at Brownlow, near Warslow, was opened in the presence of numerous spectators, by Mr. Manclarke. It consisted mostly of earth, and was examined by digging a pit down the middle to the depth of five feet, when the undisturbed soil appeared strewed with charcoal, mixed with burnt bones, from among which were taken two pieces of flint, wherewith the discovery terminated.

On the 27th of November, 1851, a barrow near Warslow, called Lid-Low, was opened by Sir John Harpur Crewe, Bart., and Sir Gardner Wilkinson, in which they found a skeleton, accompanied by a fine bronze dagger, $7\frac{1}{2}$ inches long, with two rivets attached to it, and two others separate, all lying near the head, besides two well-formed spear-heads of flint, the largest of which measures $2\frac{3}{4}$ inches in length.

ASHBOURNE.

Sometime in 1852, some agricultural labourers engaged in levelling a tumulus composed of earth, at a place called Tinker's Inn, near Ashbourne, discovered a grave, sunk a foot lower than the surface of the land, under the central part of the mound, which was five feet high, in which was a skeleton, accompanied by a small metal article, which, not having seen, we are unable to describe: it was, however, most probably a bronze dagger.

BUXTON.

On the 24th of November, 1854, some persons engaged in levelling in front of the cavern near Buxton, called Pool's Hole, found, when about four feet from the surface, a number of human and other bones, comprising the remains of three individuals, accompanied by stags' horns and numerous pieces of corroded iron, consisting of buckles, staples, clench bolts, 1¾ inches long, nails (one with a globular head, three inches long), and a slender sheath or ferule, four inches long, exhibiting traces of gilding, all of which are preserved at Lomberdale.

In January, 1856, a bronze dagger or skean, 9¾ inches long, was found about two feet beneath the surface, in cutting drains in land in Buxton called "The Rake." There are two holes at the broad end, by which it has most probably been tied to the handle, no rivets being present. It is very similar to those commonly found in Ireland, but rarely seen in the midland counties of England, and on this account is mentioned, although unconnected with barrow-digging or human remains.

LEEK.

"In November, 1859, the workmen employed in irrigating the Birchall Meadows, near Leek, into which the sewage of the southern district of the town flows, broke ground on a very slightly elevated barrow, and found therein a cairn of stones, and a cinerary urn, ornamented with the herring-bone pattern, and containing a soft moist matter."—*Stafford Papers*.

WILSON'S M.S.

The following is extracted from an interesting unpublished manuscript in the autograph of John Wilson, Esq., of Broomhead Hall, near Penistone, Yorkshire, a zealous antiquary of the last century (born 1719, died 1783), of whom a portrait and notice will be found by referring to "Hunter's History of Hallamshire," p. 275. The M.S., on 25 pages 4to, records many curious discoveries of Celtic, Roman, and Medieval Antiquities, in the counties of Derby and York (of which we have selected such as come within the scope of this work); and bears the title of

"A COLLECTION OF MEMORANDUMS RELATING TO ANTIQUITY."

Upon the East Moor, near Grindleford Bridge (Derbyshire), in some large heaps of stones, called "Robin Hood's Pricks," which were led away to repair the turnpike leading to Sheffield, was found some urns. Most of them were broken by the carelessness of the workmen; one whole one, in the common shape of Roman urns, however, was preserved. It contains about three gallons of water, and was found with the mouth downwards, and nothing in it. It is now in the possession of Richard Bagshaw, Esq., of Wormhill and Oaks.

An urn was found in a large heap of stones, upon Eyam Moor (Derbyshire), called the "Round Hillock," near the road from Grindleford Bridge to a hill called "Sir William," in the Tideswell Turnpike, which were led away for the said turnpike in June, 1759. It was in this shape —

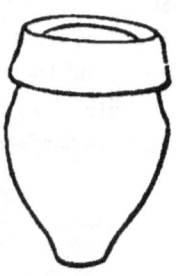

Urn — Eyam Moor.

of red earth, and so large it would contain about two pecks of corn, Winchester measure. In it was found some burnt bones. It was about ten inches and a half over the top, more than eighteen inches deep, and ran tapering to a bottom of about two inches and a half, and a hollow broad ledge hanging over the top. In it was found burnt bones, and a small round earthen vessel, about five inches diameter and two inches high, of a common brown clay colour, which had nine round holes in the sides; and in it were several beads, of about two inches long and half an inch diameter in the middle: they were of a brown, or rather amber colour, and, notwithstanding their antiquity, retained a strong aromatic smell. It was purchased of the workmen for me, by Mr. Jonathan Oxley, of Leam; but the workmen, instead of carrying it to his house, carried the pot and beads to the Rev. Mr. Seward, of Eyam, and the urn was found broken near the place some time after. It is said the pot and beads were sent to the Royal Society. Mr. Longston, of Eyam, says the beads he saw were of an amber colour, of the length of a barley-corn, and about the thickness of a fork at the bottom of the grains. The pot was of a light colour, and quite sound. Mr. Seward showed it him.

In making the turnpike through the hill called "Sir William," was found two small copper pieces — one of Constantine the Great, the other of Maxentius — which I have.

Upon Eyam Moor are many Druidical monuments, or burial places. The first of these is a circle of stones, like an old wall

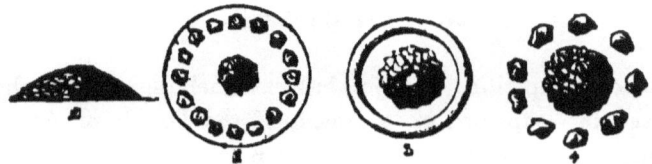

Circles and Tumuli — Eyam Moor.

bottom, the inside of which circle, close to it, is about forty yards long, and thirty-five broad from stone to stone on the inside the circle. Close to it stand sixteen stones of the large sort, set on the end, eleven or twelve of which are now standing, and the other lie near where they stood. In the middle appears to have been a small heap of stones, now even with the ground. Exactly in the middle, on one side the circle, is a huge heap of stones (see Figure 2). Figure the 3rd is a small circle on another part of the common, much like that described, but smaller, the inside of which is dished or hollow, and from the hollow rises a heap of stones, exactly on the top of which, in the centre, is a round cavity, about the bigness of a large pot: there are two or three of this kind. Figure 4 — A heap of stones, with a circular row of large stones on the outside: there are many of this sort on the moor.

Some of the above places have been made use of as places of burial, by some urns of coarse earth, badly baked, almost in the shape of flower-pots, found in them, with bones and pieces of skulls, not burnt, but pressed into them; as one, in my possession also, had, besides the bones, part of a small pot therein, in which it is supposed the heart was deposited, of the same kind of earth, in the form of a small gallipot. In searching into the place where the great heap of stones lay, called the "Round Hillock," was found a large pendant drop (in my possession), with a hole in it, in this shape —

Jet Pendant — Eyam Moor.

of a black composition, like jet, but extremely light, with a hole near the top, supposed an ornament of the Druids or Ancient Britons, to hang at the ears, neck, or nose. A large perforated bead was found by John Wadsworth, Mr. Oxley's man, of Leam, in digging into one of the smaller lows or heaps, now in my possession, which is of the same black colour and disposition, and supposed to be worn with others as a necklace.

William Wagstaff, of Tideswell, in the county of Derby, labourer, in July in the year 1749, in getting a stone for a gate to hang or clap to, for Mr. Hardy, of the same town, at the side of the common at the lower end of the town, leading to the river Wye, on the hill-side there near the mill, in removing a stone for that purpose found an earthen pot, and in it the handle of a large cup of pure gold, which he showed to Mr. John Hough, an attorney-at-law, and several other people of the town; but upon Mrs. Stainder demanding it, who rents the waifs and strays, and other tolls and perquisites of Mr. Archer, lord of the manor, he sold it to a jeweller at Manchester for £18; but Mr. Hough aforesaid, and other persons who had seen it, thought it of much more value. Mr. Archer brought an action against him for treasure trove. It is supposed that there was money and other things of value found with it, as it hardly would be put into a pot by itself. The pot contained about a gill, and upon taking up fell to pieces. The start or handle of the cup weighed near six ounces. This account I had from Mr. Hough himself.

In the year 1780, upon the 29th day of February, in getting stone out of a large low or heap of stones in Law Field, belonging to the Abbey, in Woodland, two of the Rev. Mr. Hall's sons found a hollow stone, or part of a very small trough, and several bones, like ribs and skulls, supposed to be human, and buried there.

A British celt or axe, of brass, or rather mixed metal such as the Roman coins now in my possession, was found in the Spring of 1778, in improving a brow or hill-side above Parkin Field, in Derbyshire, by John Yellott, a farmer there.

Joseph Platt, a mason at Edale, in Derbyshire, in riving up a stone at Nether Tor, near Grimesbrook-in-Edale, the latter end of April, 1778, found about forty adder-beads, or Druid's amulets, underneath it. They were of various colours and sizes — green, blue, others striped and variegated; some were so very large that one might have put one's thumb into the hole. They were given to the Rev. Mr. Lingard, Curate of Edale. I got three or four of the smaller sort; the rest were sent to one ————, a friend of his and antiquarian. The stone they were found under was near the top of the Tor, very large and flat.

[Although the following extract may appear out of place in a volume devoted to primeval antiquities, it is valuable as recording an earlier desecration of the grave of the popular hero, Little John, than any yet published. It will, therefore, be read with interest by all admirers of our old ballad poetry, who

> "———— of Robin Hood have heard, and Little John;
> Of Scarlock, George á Green, and Much the Miller's son;
> Of Tuck the merry Friar, which many a sermon made
> In praise of Robin Hood, his outlaws, and their trade."
> DRAYTON.]

Little John's grave, in Hathersedge Churchyard, at the back of the clerk's house, is distinguished by two small stones set up at each end, and is four yards ten inches long, betwixt stone and stone: he is said to be Robin Hood's man. Dr. Moor, of Wakefield, who frequently came here to attend Mr. Ashton, of Hathersedge Hall, in his illness, about the year 1728, caused it to be dug up. Nothing was found except bones of very great size, much larger than what is now found in graves, and, having satisfied his curiosity, had it filled up again — *Ex informatione Jonathani Oxley, de Leam, Gent.*

Mr. Allott, Rector of Kirkheaton, says — At a place called Killam, near Bridlington or Burlington Bay, was a battle fought, and that there are many tumuli or graves; and asking some persons who were stubbing whins or gorse, they told him there was one under the whins, and several round about him. He says further, that many are sunk level with the ground, but by what remains he supposes there were twenty thousand slain. There are axe-heads, spears'-heads, &c., constantly dug up in opening them. A stone is set up on high, as a steeple, which no engines now used could raise. It is supposed to be set up by the Danes, in a line between the field of battle and Burlington Hill, where their camp is yet to be seen, very perfect. This is not mentioned in any author I have read.

There is said to be a Roman Station, at a small village in Derbyshire, near Hope, called Brough; and in a hilly field near the water, where the station was, are frequently ploughed up bricks with letters upon them, and Roman pavements composed of brick and lime; and in 1847 was found, near the beck or river side, two Roman urns, with inscriptions on them, very legible. Mr. Seward, Rector of Eyam, bought them both of Robert Marshall, of Brough, who found them. There is a military way goes from hence to Buxton, called Bathom Gate. I have some of the bricks, pavement, and part of a rim of a broken urn, with part of an inscription upon it. This stone was found in ploughing a field at Brough, about thirty years ago (1747), in a field belonging to ———— Morewood, Esq., of Alfreton, and was fixed in a wall opposite to a public-house door here. It is two feet high, and one foot six inches broad. It is now taken away by a gentleman who bought it. This seems to have been cut since Christianity was introduced in the place of Paganism.

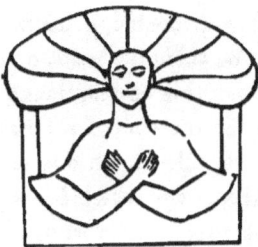

Stone Figure — Brough.

July the 5th, 1775, one of the workmen upon the turnpike road found, upon the edge of Agden, a little beyond the Bardike, a small British celt, of brass, or rather of mixed metal: one of them broke it, to see what metal it was, as is often the case with those ignorant persons. It was found amongst loose stones, near the surface; the workmanship is very rude. I got it pieced, and have it now in my possession.

Mr. Hodgkinson, of Wormhill, in Derbyshire, has an urn taken out of "Robin Hood's Pricks," on the East Moor, found with the mouth downwards, full of red ashes.

Upon Strynd's Moor, at the upper edge, is a large flat stone, supposed Druidical, so equally poised on a point it may be moved with the finger, though some tons weight. There is another very large one at Rowtor, near Bakewell, in Derbyshire.

APPENDIX. 253

On the right hand of the turnpike road going from Hathersedge to Sheffield, about a mile below the Cupelo, at Callow, is an old encampment, called "Carleswark." At the west end is a breastwork yet remaining, walled with stones as large as strong gate stoops, some a ton apiece, and twenty or thirty yards long; the north side a steep perpendicular rock, and the south side and east end defended with large stones, evidently laid to defend the passage up the hill. No engines now in being could move such great stones. On the top of the rock, on the north side, is a large stone reared up, with a ridge of stones under it: probably this was Druidical. This encampment, I think, was made by Carasius, the British Emperor, who set up against Constantine the Great [Maximianus], and by corruption called Carleswark, or work; and what makes it more probable, coins have been found at "Sir William," in making the turnpike road, of both Emperors.

A little distance from this encampment, but nearer the turnpike road, seem to be the remains of a Druid's temple — stones of ten ton weight, or more, piled upon one another like a wall; and a kind of square entrance, over which lies a prodigious large logan or Druidical rocking-stone, as it is said, though I did not try it. Such stones could not be removed and laid on each other by any engines now in being; indeed both these places are wonderful, and as well worth seeing as any piece of antiquity in the country.

The latter end of June, 1780, some persons getting stone for Mr. Greaves, of Rowley, in Woodland, to wall in a piece of common to his land, called Handcocks, in digging into a low or heap of stones called Bole Low or Bone Low, upon the edge of Darwen Moor, above a place called Bamforth House, found three or four pots of earth, badly baked, and scored on the outside, full of human bones, very fresh, in this form —

Urn — Woodlands.

with rings about, scored with three scores: the pots they broke. I have part of a side and bottom, and other pieces, and some of the bones. They were small, and covered with a common flat gritstone, about sixteen or eighteen inches each way, which on the under side had eight or ten holes picked in it about one inch deep, like the holes an old gate-pike wears. Amongst the bones was found a piece of copper, near two inches long, and above a quarter of an inch in breadth, which appears to be of the same kind as the British weapons were made of, and covered with aerugo, now in my possession, flat and rather curved. There was found, besides the bones in the pots, a large trench, above a yard wide, on the east end of the low, quite filled with human bones, but so decayed they would scarce bear touching. The workmen say there was a cart-load, they were sure, but could not think of disturbing them. I wish they had had the same tender regard to the pots.

This year (1780)—in ploughing a field at Brough, in Derbyshire, found a piece of a bridle-bit, as supposed, with a large brass top, cast with figures; in my possession. He also gave me a British arrow-head, made of flint, found in the bank-side facing his house. It was very perfect when found, but they were so silly as to deface the point and grains a little by breaking small pieces off.

In the year 1780, the Rev. Mr. Hall's son, at Abbey, in Woodland, in digging at the east end of the low, or heap of stones, in Low Field, belonging the same place, found several bones, supposed to be human, laid in ashes, and a piece of a hollow stone, like a piece of a small trough, now in my custody. I have also a small piece of brass, found in it some years ago, of the ancient metal, about two inches long, and edged on each side, as if part of a sword. I have also a small flint arrow-head, found near it. Mrs. Hall says they once found a flint arrow-head five times as large, but knows not what became of it.

17—, Thomas Marsden, of Cock Bridge, in Woodland, in digging in a heap of stones on the side of Winhill, in Derbyshire, found an urn, which he broke some pieces from, of which he gave me: it was badly baked, of rude workmanship, and nearly in this shape—

Urn from Winhill.

The top edge was half an inch thick, sloping inwards, with three or four small circles, the sides scratched in horizontal lines, backwards and forwards: it contained pieces of human bones. The tradition, that Winhill, near Hope, and Losehill, by Castleton, took their names from a battle fought here, but at what time is quite uncertain.

Mr. Longworth, Curate of Eyam, had in 174— a brass sword, found four yards deep in a peat moss, I think in Lancashire. It was about two feet six inches long, two-edged, and thickest and broadest in the middle; in this shape—

Celtic Sword—Lancashire.

Mr. Yates, of Denby, steward to Sir John Kay, says there was an axe, the shape and bigness of my brass celt, of flint, but sharp ground, found in a clay-hole at Womersley, which Dr. Drake, who wrote the "History of York," saw, and took to be Roman, and by it was found some fir trees; but I think it was British.

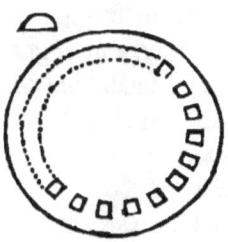

Circle—Leam Moor.

The form of a Druid's Circle, on the East Moor, near Leam. There are yet eleven stones standing, which all lean inwards, and are five yards and a half asunder. At the figure **A** is a heap of stones. There are several small circles of stones on these moors, about three yards broad, and about half a yard high.

The rest of the manuscript is principally taken up with notices of discoveries of Roman and English coins in various parts of Yorkshire, which it has been considered needless to print. The foregoing extracts are sufficiently circumstantial to require no comments further than the statement, that we are not responsible for the worthy writer's inferences, with some of which we do not agree — as, for instance, his attribution of the "Carleswark" to the Emperor Carasius.

A DESCRIPTIVE LIST

OF

SKELETONS, SKULLS, AND SEPARATE BONES,

EXHUMED FROM TUMULI, CHIEFLY OF THE CELTIC PERIOD,

IN

DERBYSHIRE, STAFFORDSHIRE, AND YORKSHIRE.

LIST P.

1 W — Fine SKULL, found in Kenslow Knoll Barrow, 1821.

    Oval, and rather platy-cephalic, with very prominent occiput and large wormian bones; the foramen magnum three inches from the occipital protuberance; the parietal tubers full, the orbits square, nasal bones projecting, prognathous mouth, lower jaw thick and pointed, the angles wide apart, the teeth perfect but worn. Probably a Saxon.

2 W — Teeth, from a Barrow near Arbor Low, July, 1824.

3 W — Teeth, from Cronkstone Hill, May, 1825.

4 W — Teeth, anchylosed Vertebræ, and Stag's Horn, from Cross Flatts, December, 1827.

5 W — Human Teeth, and a few Bones of animals, found in the chink of a rock at Rusden Low, 1828.

6 W — Lower Jaw of a young person, turned black from tannin, found in the Row Lows, near Middleton, 8th November, 1831.

1843.

7 T — Teeth, from Bee Low, June.

8 T — SKULL, from Lean Low, June.

    Medium form, with prominent parietes and rather narrow forehead, thus giving considerable breadth to the posterior part of the calvarium; the chin rather pointed in contour, though squared at the front; tooth sound and unworn.

9 T — Child's SKULL, from End Low, June.

10 T — Upper Maxillary and Teeth, from the centre of Galley Low, June.
   From an Anglo-Saxon interment; the teeth rather squarely arranged and unworn.

11 T — SKULL of aged female.
   Short and regular in form; the chin pointed, the teeth imperfect, and much worn down.

12 T — SKULL and Femur of a tall man.
   Short and elevated, the superciliary ridges very prominent, the chin rounded and the teeth rather worn, but very sound. Femur 19¼ inches long.

13 T — Child's SKULL.

14 to 16 T — Parts of the Skulls of three other children.
   10 to 16 discovered in different parts of the same Barrow.

17 T — Lower Jaw, from a Cist in the large Barrow, Minning Low, 5th July.

18 to 21 T — Jaws and Teeth, from a Barrow near the Railway, Minning Low, 12th July.

22 to 23 T — Fine SKULL, Pelvis, and other bones of principal interment, and portions of another Skeleton, from Liff's Low, 14th July.
   Shape long oval, with prominent parietals and narrow forehead, wide across the malar bones, mouth rather prognathous, teeth sound, and rather squarely arranged in the upper jaw. Femur 18¼ inches long.

24 T — Teeth, from Green Low, Brassington Moor, 19th July.

25 to 26 T — Imperfect SKULL and Jaws of another, from Elk Low, 5th August.
   25 (1st interment). Short, with prominent occiput and superciliary ridges, the sutures obliterated, contracted palate, with very regular teeth, rather worn.
   26. Very imperfect, with lower jaw pointed, and both filled with large teeth of the most perfect form, slightly worn.

27 to 28 T — Teeth of a great number of persons, from two Cists at Stony Low, Brassington Moor, 8th August.

29 to 30 T — Portions of the Skulls of two children, from Wolfscote Hill, 23rd August.

31 to 32 T — Parts of two Skulls and other Bones, from Cists at Bole Hill, Bakewell Moor, 24th August.
   Of narrow boat-like form; see a typical specimen of this variety of cranium figured at page 69 of "Wilson's Pre-Historic Annals of Scotland," 8vo, 1851.

33 T — Lower Teeth, from Borther Low, near Middleton, 4th September.

34 to 40 **T**—SKULLS of seven individuals, from a Barrow near Cross Low, opened 9th September.

> No. 36 was the principal interment.
>
> 34 (1st interment). Short round skull, elevated at the vertex, having the frontal suture and prominent superciliary ridges; teeth small and sound. From wanting the dentes sapientiæ, probably young.
>
> 35 ( ). Short, very prominent parietal tubers; the forehead narrow. Probably a young female.
>
> 37 ( ). Rather short, with prominent occiput and parietal tubers, the forehead elevated and capacious, the chin acutely pointed, the teeth fine and not much worn. Age circ. 25.
>
> 39 ( ). Oval, with full parietal tubers, prominent superciliary ridges, the mouth large and wide, the teeth worn level.
>
> 40 ( ). Long oval, with protuberant occiput and wormian bones; an elevated ridge runs along the sagittal suture to a frontal suture which divides the narrow forehead; wide across the palate, the teeth a little worn.

1844.

41 **T**—Imperfect Skull and Leg Bones of a young person, from Moot Low, Grange Mill, 6th May.

> Medium shape, with protuberant occiput, and a full set of good teeth.

42 to 43 **T**—Remains of about four individuals, from Sliper Low, Brassington Moor, 8th May.

44 to 45 **T**—Parts of two Skulls and other bones, found by reopening Galley Low, 10th May.

> 44. Brachy-cephalic, with elevated vertex; lower jaw square in front, with unworn teeth, indicating a young adult.

46 **T**—Fragments of two interments, from Elton Moor, 10th June.

47 **T**—Fragments of about six individuals, from a Barrow at Cales, 31st July.

48 to 50 **T**—Two fine SKULLS, and others not so good, from Rolley Low, 6th August.

> 48. Short and elevated, wide behind, the forehead narrow, mouth prominent, with sound teeth, worn level; the lower jaw inclining to the pointed form, but with square corners. Femur 18¼ inches long.
>
> 49. Brachy-cephalic type, with parietal tubers, broad forehead, with traces of frontal suture, and full superciliary ridges; the orbits small, the malar bones vertically narrow; the mouth large, and the teeth much worn and split by forcibly biting hard substances, perhaps in warlike frenzy as the Bersekirs. Femur 19¾ inches long.

51 **T**—Remains of about six skeletons, from Upper Haddon Moor, 7th August.

52 **T**—Remains of an individual, from a Barrow in a plantation near Cross Low, 13th August.

1845.

53 **T** — Fine characteristic HEAD and other bones, found with some beautiful flints in Green Low, Alsop Moor, 25th April.

<small>Brachy-cephalic and rather elevated, with a peculiar flatness from the top of the occipital bone to the vertex; prominent parietals, and superciliary ridges; very sound teeth, large and strongly marked face; internal capacity 110.15 cubic inches, or 88 ounces. Femur 19¼ inches long. Selected for the "Crania Britannica."</small>

54 **T** — Bones, from a Barrow near Sheldon, 6th May.

55 **T** — Part of a Cranium, and a large Humerus, from Brier Low, 12th May.

56 **T** — Bones of five individuals, mostly infants, from the first barrow opened at Hindlow, 15th May.

<small>One skull, of long and narrow shape, has a supplementary bone between the parietes at their junction with the frontal bone.</small>

57 **T** — Part of a Skull, from the second Barrow at Hindlow.

58 **T** — Bones from two individuals, from the third Barrow at Hindlow.

59 to 60 **T** — Parts of Skull, and long Bones, from two skeletons found in Carder Low, 21st May.

<small>The femur of No. 60, which was a secondary interment, measures 20¾ inches in length.</small>

61 **T** — Bones from Taylor's Low, Wetton, 28th May.

62 **T** — SKULL, in good condition, found with bronze dagger in a Barrow at New Inns, 28th May.

<small>Very short, with protuberant parietes and broad forehead; the round mouth filled with regular teeth indicates a young man. The femur measures 18 inches.</small>

63 **T** — A few Bones of an athletic Anglo-Saxon, found with the iron umbo of a shield in a grave-hill called The Low, near Alsop-in-the-Dale, 30th May.

<small>Femur 19¾ inches long.</small>

64 **T** — Fragments of Skulls, from Painstor Barrow, near the last.

65 to 66 **T** — Remains of two person, from Moot Low, near Dove Dale, 2nd June.

67 **T** — Part of a Skull, from Netlow, found with coal ornaments, 4th June.

<small>A short skull, with prominent parietal tubers, the frontal bone posthumously contorted, so as to project at the left side; the alveolar process of the lower jaw partially absorbed.</small>

68 to 70 **T** — Three SKULLS, two of them in good condition, from Three Lows, Wetton, 7th June; also remains of infants.

 68. Oval, the hinder part elevated, the forehead retreating, with full superciliary ridges; orbits small, and wide apart; the teeth worn, and covered with tartar; the lower jaw and chin square and prominent.

 69. A female skull of the short form, with prominent parietal tubers, wide across the malar bones, rather large round mouth, with abraded teeth.

 70. Very long cranium, with protuberant occiput and superciliary ridges; an obscure ridge up the frontal bone, the sutures obliterated; the teeth irregular, much worn, and coated with tartar; a bony excrescence inside the right side of the lower jaw. The left ulna fractured. Femur 18½ inches long. An aged man.

71 to 72 **T** — Two SKULLS, one very fine, from Bostorn, Dove Dale, 9th June.

 71. Skull of a young person, with prominent parietes, and frontal suture.

 72 (2nd interment). Oval shape, much elevated, with prominent nasal bones; the teeth regular, and not much worn; the chin squared, the skull very thin, and probably of a person circ. 30 years old. Femur 17 inches long.

 A headless skeleton was also found, the femur of which is very slender, and only 16½ inches long. It was evidently a female.

73 to 75 **T** — Portions of three Skulls, from Castern, 14th June; also pieces of others, found in a disjointed state.

 73 (1st interment). Rather short, with prominent parietal tubers and superciliary ridges; the nasal bones projecting, the teeth regular and level, the chin square and prominent. The femur 19½ inches long.

76 **T** — Teeth of a Saxon female, from Stand Low, near Dove Dale, 19th June, found with glass beads, &c.

77 **T** — Imperfect Skulls and other Bones, from Gratton Hill, near Alstonfield, 21st June.

 77. A large round cranium of the platy-cephalic form, very wide behind, with a low forehead, wide across the malar bones, the mouth large and projecting, the teeth not much worn, the lower jaw very deep, the chin rounded; altogether a very large face.

78 to 79 **T** — Similar Skulls, from Gratton Hill, near Wetton, 28th June.

 78. Rather short and platy-cephalic, with a full forehead, the orbits large, the teeth worn level, the chin rounded; a skull of small internal capacity, but having large facial bones.

80 **T** — Portions of a Skull, and other Bones, from Ilam Moor, 2nd July.

81 **T** — Human Bones, together with those of the ox, partially burnt, found in a Barrow on Ilam Moor, 12th July.
   Probably a sacrificial deposit.

82 T — Part of a very thick cranium, from a grave on Ilam Moor, 16th July.

Of short form, with prominent superciliary ridges; the teeth worn down, and exhibiting signs of caries; the chin square.

83 T — Part of a Skull, from a Barrow on Wetton Hill, 28th July.

1846.

84 to 85 T — Two SKULLS, from a Barrow near Castern, 29th July; one found with an elaborately ornamented drinking cup.

84 (1st interment). Short and wide behind, with prominent parietal tubers and superciliary ridges; the forehead narrow, from which is a ridge along the sagittal suture; the orbits large, the teeth very level and good, the chin prominent and square.

85. (2nd interment). Medium shape, with broad frontal region, which gives a square appearance to the head; a prominent ridge along the vertex, teeth considerably worn. Femur, 19¼ inches.

86 T — Remains of a female Skeleton, found with jet beads; also some other human fragments, from Windle Hill, 12th August.

Skull rather long, with protuberant occiput; the lower jaw delicate in form, with pointed chin; the teeth small and regular, indicate an age of about 25.

87 T — Skull, found with a bronze dagger in a Mound near the last, 15th August.

Extremely short and wide at the back, with prominent parietal tubers, narrow forehead, and full superciliary ridges.

88 T — Portions of two Skeletons, from a dilapidated Barrow near the the last, 19th August.

One of them a female, having a short round skull of thin substance, with prominent parietal tubers.

89 T — Remains of about twelve persons, the crania of about three presenting examples of the narrow boat-shaped form, from the galleries in the Tumulus on Five Wells Hill, 25th August.

One very long cranium, with a protuberant occiput overhanging the foramen magnum for three inches, is distinguished by the peculiarity of having no sagittal suture, of which there is no trace, although the head being that of a young person fully grown, the other sutures are very distinct. There is also a singular depression just behind the parietal sutures, as if effected by constriction. The frontal bone is prominent in the middle of the forehead; the teeth are arranged rather squarely.

90 T — Remains of about eight individuals, from the interesting Barrow at Cow Low, 29th August.

One is short and posteriorly widened, with full parietes diminishing to a narrow forehead.

Another is rather long, with parietal tubers, the forehead narrow and prominent.

APPENDIX. 263

<blockquote>The latest interment, accompanied with jewellery, presented very slight remains of a young Saxon lady, whose wisdom-teeth had not made their appearance; the chin pointed.</blockquote>

91 **T** — Fragments of two human beings, from Withery Low, 1st September.

92 **T** — Portions of two more, one with bronze dagger, from Dow Low, 5th September.

93 **T** — Part of the Skull of a young person and the Beak of a Hawk, from Sliper Low, Wetton, 12th September.

<blockquote>Of short and elevated form, but much contorted by posthumous pressure; the age probably from 12 to 14.</blockquote>

94 to 95 **T** — Two imperfect Skulls, from two Barrows at Callenge Low, opened 30th November.

96 **T** — Fragments of two human Skulls, and many Bones of animals, found in the Fleets, Moot Low, near Middleton, 7th December.

1847.

97 **T** — Head of a young person, found with a vase on reopening Lean Low, 23rd February.

<blockquote>Very much crushed and posthumously contorted, but naturally very long and narrow, with wormian bones, as is often the case in this variety of skull. The teeth indicate the age of about 16.</blockquote>

98 **T** — Skull of an aged man, and other Bones, still retaining their solidity, though the heads of the joints are worn away by the percolation of water, from a Cist-Vaen in the chambered Tumulus at Ringham Low, near Monyash, 17th March.

<blockquote>Popular tradition states that a bell in the neighbouring church was found in this tumulus, whence its name, Ringham Low; a clumsy way of accounting for its derivation.</blockquote>

99 to 100 **T** — Two imperfect Skulls, found in a Barrow at Gotham, 1st April and 23rd August.

<blockquote>100. Has a very protuberant occiput, but is otherwise Brachy-cephalic; the frontal bone retreating, with prominent superciliary ridges; the facial bones large, the teeth sound; the upper maxillary advanced, so as to overhang the lower jaw, which is massive and square. The foramen magnum is larger than usual, and the femur measures 18¼ inches.</blockquote>

101 **T** — Remains from three interments, from Pilsbury, 30th August.

1848.

101* **T** — Fragments of Skull, found on reopening Kenslow, February.
<blockquote>Femur 18¼ inches.</blockquote>

102 T — Fine SKULL, from a Rock Grave at Parcelly Hay, 6th March; also pieces of another, from a secondary interment.

Engraved in "Crania Britannica," by Davis and Thurnam, where it is described as evenly rounded with full parietal protuberances, giving to the vertical region a slight roof-like aspect; the occipital bone prominent in the middle, the forehead moderately arched and broad, the superciliary ridges projecting, the upper jaw overhanging, the angles of the lower widely averted. Internal capacity 72½ ounces, length of femur 18.3 inches, age about 55.

103 T — Beautiful female SKULL, and other Bones; also portion of a child's Head, from a Barrow near Gibb Hill, Middleton, 15th March.

Medium shape, with protuberant occiput and parietes; the vertex slightly elevated, the forehead well formed, nasal bones prominent, the orbits large, the teeth beautifully regular and worn level, the palate deeply arched, the chin elegantly formed and rather angular. Age about 40, internal capacity 66 ounces, the femur 15½ inches long. This unusually handsome skull is selected by the authors of the "Crania Britannica" as a typical example of the ancient British female. Several hundred coal beads were found about the neck of this skeleton.

104 T — Two imperfect Skulls and a Cow's horn, from Sharp Low, Tissington, 27th March.

A very large platy-cephalic skull of a young adult, with prominent occiput and parietes; the lower jaw massive. Femur 18 inches long.

105 T — Fragments of two interments, from a Barrow near the last, 30th March.

106 T — SKULL, and part of another, from a Barrow at Bostorn, 3rd April.

A short elevated cranium, with parietal tubers and prominent superciliary ridges; the teeth much worn, and the femur 17 inches long.

107 T — Small piece of a child's Head, unburnt; found with calcined bones in a Barrow at the Comp, Wetton, 6th May.

108 T — SKULL and Thigh Bones, the latter stained green from contact with bronze weapons, found in the Barrow at Shuttlestone, 3rd June.

Rather short and platy-cephalic, with a tendency to squareness; the sutures quite obliterated, the teeth very regular and worn level. The femur 18¾ inches.

109 T — Portions of a Skeleton, from Crake Low, 6th July.

Femur 19 inches.

110 T — SKULL, of the principal interment, from End Low, near Heathcote, 13th July, accompanied by a bronze dagger.

Engraved in the "Crania Britannica," and described as the skull of a man near 40 years of age, of good form, having the vault of the calvarium equable, but not large, presenting very clearly the conformation of the true ancient British cranium. The face is narrow, and the prominence of the upper alveoli produces a slightly prognathous character. Length of femur near 19 inches.

111 T — Three imperfect skulls, rather small, from an extremely ancient Tumulus at Moneystones, near Hartington, 15th July.
>One very short and round.
>Another of a young adult, with the teeth arranged squarely in the upper jaw.
>Another has the teeth rather worn.

112 T — SKULL of a young female, and remains of about six other interments, from a Barrow called Blake Low, on Longstone Edge, 24th July.
>A very thin skull, of oval shape, with prominent parietal tubers, projecting nasal bones, full mouth, and large teeth, wanting the dentes sapientiæ; the chin pointed, the femur 16½ inches long. The skull presented some indications of fracture, inflicted either during life or shortly after death.

113 T — Fragmentary remains of several persons, from the second Barrow on Longstone Edge, 24th July.

114 C — Portions of two interments, from Arbor Hill, 20th May.

115 C — Parts of six Skulls, from Mare Hill, 25th May.
>One of a young female, about 16 years of age, is a thin skull of the short round shape, with elevated vertex, prominent parietes, and narrow forehead; the teeth unworn, and wanting the wisdom teeth.
>Another of the brachy-cephalic form, with parietal tubers, has a broad and high frontal region. The teeth are a regular set, rather worn.

116 C — Imperfect Cranium, found with a bronze dagger near Grindon, 19th June.
>A narrow, flat-sided skull, with protuberant occiput and elevated vertex, the superciliary ridges large, and the teeth not much abraded.

117 C — Very large SKULL, with frontal suture, found with a collection of beautiful flint weapons at Mouse Low, 21st June.
>An example of the platy-cephalic variety, rather square in outline, with protuberant occiput, accompanied by wormian bones, the superciliary ridges strongly developed, the orbits small and widely separated, the mouth large and wide, and filled with perfect teeth, not much worn; the lower jaw wide between the angles.

118 C — Remains of two young Skeletons, from Green Field, Castern, 24th June.

119 C — Human remains, partially calcined, from Musdin Low, 5th July.

120 C — Imperfect Skull, found near the surface in Thorncliff Low, 10th July.
>Of a young person; of the short form, wide at the back, with prominent parietal tubers, diminishing to a narrow forehead.

121 C — Portion of a Skeleton, from Musdin Hill, 18th July.
>Of a young person of full stature, with an oval cranium, having a protuberant occiput; probably Saxon.

122 C — Parts of two bodies, from Castern Valley, 20th July.

123 C — Part of a Skull, found on the floor of an ancient dwelling, in the Borough, Wetton, August.

124 C — Skull of the primary interment from Thorncliff Low, found with a bronze dagger, 30th August.

125 C — Beautiful SKULL, and part of another not so good, found with iron weapons upon Readon Hill, 4th September.

<small>Of oval shape, with protuberant occiput and well-developed superciliary ridges, wide across the malar bones, the upper jaw overhanging the lower, the teeth perfect and not much worn, the front of the chin squared.</small>

126 C — Bones, from a Barrow near the last, 5th September.

127 T — Bones of two bodies, from the third Barrow on Longstone Edge, 29th August.

128 T — Damaged Skull of a female, and two others still worse, from Rusden Low, Middleton, 10th November.

<small>Very short, with a flattened surface from the upper part of the occipital protuberance to the vertex, which is elevated, the parietal tubers prominent. Apparently aged about 25.</small>

129 C — Portions of two interments, from Over Low, Stanton, Staffordshire, 20th December.

130 C — Parts of two more, from Ribden Low, 29th December.

1849.

131 C — Parts of Crania, from a Barrow near Calton, 12th and 20th January.

132 T — Part of a Cranium, from Borther Low, 5th February.

133 P — A few Bones, from a destroyed Mound at High Low, near Moneyash, 12th February.

134 C — CHILD'S SKULL, in beautiful preservation, and part of the Head of an Ox, from Cop's Low, near Stanton, Staffordshire, 3rd February.

<small>Short and very round, with prominent parietes and full mouth; evidently of a girl aged about 9.</small>

135 C — Part of a Skull, from Stonesteads, 7th April.

136 C — Part of a Skull, from Lomberlow, 7th April.

137 C — Parts of Skulls, and some animals' Ribs, upon which a human Skeleton was placed, from Far Low, 21st April.

138 **T** — Three SKULLS, found with coal beads in Grindlow, near Upper Haddon, 30th April.

One is long and narrow, with a protuberant occiput, and is very much contorted by posthumous pressure upon the left side of the frontal bone.

Another is similarly deformed by pressure in front.

Another, of shorter form, has a round chin inclining to the pointed form; the teeth in all cases are worn, and a perfect femur belonging to one of the skeletons measures 18 inches.

139 **T** — Portions of Jaws, from the second Barrow at Grindlow, May.

140 **T** — Four imperfect Skulls, from Vincent Knoll, 24th May.

One of these persons, with an oval and elevated head, the teeth worn level and coated with tartar, and thick lower jaw, has a portion of the pelvis attached to the head of the right femur by anchylosis.

Another, most likely of a female, is a very thin skull; the teeth are regular and not much worn, the chin pointed.

Another very short and full behind, with prominent parietal tubers, pointed chin, and teeth but little worn; is probably of a person about 20 years old.

Another short elevated skull, broad at the back, with prominent parietes sloping off to a narrow forehead, from the full mouth and unworn teeth wanting the dentes sapientiæ to complete the set; appears to be aged about 18. Two femurs measure 17¾ and 19 inches.

141 **C** — Five Skulls, rather imperfect, and Bones of the Wild Boar and other animals, from Top Low, Swinscoe, May.

141 (No. 1 interment). An oval, regularly formed, smooth skull, of a young person, probably of a female, with a very handsome set of large teeth, a little worn, and pointed chin.

2nd interment. A short cranium, very wide behind, with protuberant parietes, long mastoid and styloid processes, the teeth large and unworn; probably of a male aged circ. 25; posthumously contorted.

3rd interment. Short and elevated, the teeth worn, and chin rounded; contorted.

6th interment. Oval, with protuberant occiput, the sutures obliterated, teeth worn, and square chin.

12th interment. A very long head, curiously bent by posthumous pressure; the teeth much worn, the lower jaw square in front.

142 **C** — Remarkably fine and characteristic SKULL of an aged man, found with a beautiful vase in Wetton Hill Barrow, 24th May.

Engraved in the "Crania Britannica," and described by the learned writer as the skull of a man of about 60 years of age, with the distinguishing characteristic of a low broad forehead, rising rather suddenly into an extended and flat vertical region; the occiput is protuberant, the teeth are very much worn down, the nasal bones eminently prominent, and the internal capacity 80 ounces. The length of the femur is rather more than 18 inches.

142* **C** — Another fine SKULL, of elevated shape, found as a secondary interment in the same Barrow.

 A very singular skull, selected for illustration in the "Crania Britannica." It is unusually short in the diameter between the frontal and occipital bones, and much elevated; the posterior part is wide, and there is a flat surface between the occipital protuberance and the vertex; the retreating forehead appears based on prominent frontal sinuses, the nasal bones project, the teeth are regular and a little worn, and the chin is pointed.

143 **C** — Portions of two Skulls, from the large Barrow at Stanshope, 1st and 5th June.

144 **C** Cranium, from a Barrow upon Bunster, 6th June.

145 **C** — SKULLS, and other Bones, from about thirteen individuals; also Bones of animals, from the stone chamber in the Long Low Barrow, near Wetton, 8th June.

 Among the most perfect of these remains are three skulls — of a man, a female, and, apparently, a girl — all exhibiting, in excess, the peculiar boat shape before noticed in this list; by some considered as the type of an ancient race, by others as merely a tribal or family variation.

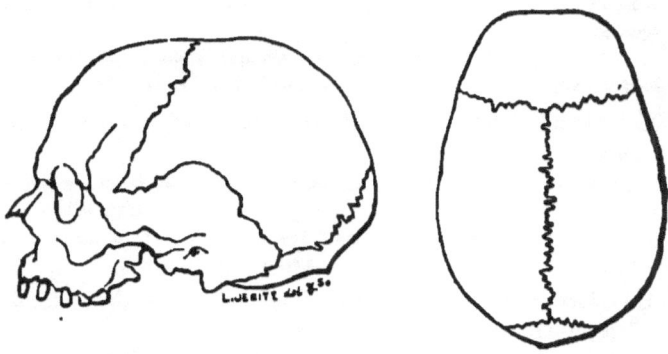

Longlow Skull.

 The male skull is further distinguished by its perfectly flattened sides and ridged vertex; the nasal bones are prominent, the chin pointed, and the teeth worn. Internal capacity 84½ ounces; femur 18½ inches. Engraved in "Crania Britannica."

 The female's has the same long shape, with a more prominent occiput, and parietal tubers; the sutures are solidified, and the skull is thick, dense, and smooth.

 The girl's cranium has all the peculiarities of the male skull in excess: the occipital protuberance projects 2¾ inches beyond the foramen magnum, there are wormian bones, and the face is singularly narrow, terminating in a pointed chin. A femur measures 17¼ inches.

146 C — Portions of two Skulls, from Hang Bank, reopened 11th and 12th June.

147 C — Parts of three Skulls, from the fourth Barrow opened on Musden, 16th June.

148 C — Parts of three Skulls, from a Barrow between Bitchinhill and Throwley, opened 18th and 19th July; one with a jet stud for the girdle, and instruments of flint.

> That with the stud is of oval shape, vertically elevated, having no wisdom-teeth. The individual was probably young.

149 C — Skull, from a Barrow at Deep Dale, reopened 4th August.

150 C — Teeth, &c., from a Barrow on Throwley Moor, 29th Sept.

151 C — Remains of five individuals, three of them young, from a Barrow at Ramscroft, Stanshope, 17th and 24th November.

> The interment found on the 24th of November was the skeleton of a tall young man, with a bronze dagger, whose femur measures 19¾ inches. The skull is of medium form, with protuberant occiput, parietes, and superciliary ridges; the sutures are almost obliterated, although the teeth do not exhibit much abrasion; the lower jaw is strong, and inclines to the pointed form, but is slightly squared at the chin.
>
> Another is a thin contorted skull of a young individual, whose wisdom-teeth have not appeared; it is long and narrow, and has a pointed chin.

152 C — Cranium, from a small Barrow at Three Lows, Wetton, 8th December.

> Very long, with protuberant occiput and extensive wormian bones, a ridge along the vertex, extending down the frontal bone, which is divided by a suture; the superciliary ridges very prominent, the orbits wide apart, the teeth excessively worn down, some wanting, and the alveoli absorbed.

153 C — Two ancient Crania, and fragments of a third, from the Cops, near Warslow, 24th December.

> Both very much alike, being of the medium form, with broad foreheads, sound and unworn teeth, pointed chins, and both posthumously contorted.

154 T — Skull and some other Bones of an Anglo-Saxon, from a Tumulus near Chelmorton, 23rd June.

> The skull oval, with protuberant occiput; the parietal sutures obliterated, the frontal bone narrow, and projecting to the left from posthumous compression. Inside, the brain, while in a fluid state, has left a mark about half-way across, showing that the corpse was deposited on the back. The molars exhibit incipient caries, and the chin is rather delicately formed for a male, as this certainly was. One of the thigh bones had been fractured and reunited.

155 T — Skulls and Bones of four persons of the flint period, from a Mound near the last, called Nether Low, 5th July.

One is a squarely formed head, approaching the platy-cephalic type; wide between the mastoids, having a broad forehead. The teeth are worn level, and the chin is rather pointed. [With flint dagger.]

Another is a very pretty skull of a young person, without the wisdom-teeth; of short and round form, with a broad forehead; the mouth rather prominent. The right side of the calvarium much gnawed by rats. [With beads.]

156 T — Remains of a Saxon female, from a Grave-hill at the top of the Hurst, near Hurdlow, 7th July.

157 T — Similar remains, from another small Barrow near the last, 10th July.

The femur, though only 17 inches in length, is very strong.

158 T — Ancient SKULL, found by reopening Cronkstone Hill, 21st July.

Of short form, with protuberant occiput and parietes; the vertex elevated, with a flatness from thence to the centre of the occiput; the forehead very narrow from the orbits inclining to the zygomatic arches; the teeth but little worn, the skull posthumously contorted, and the heads of both femurs singularly deformed.

159 T — Remarkably fine SKULL, and remains of others, from a Tumulus on Ballidon Moor, 30th July.

Engraved in Davis and Thurnam's "Crania Britannica," as a typical example of the aboriginal British cranium, and since reproduced in various cranioscopic works. It is described as a tolerably regular oval, with a rather full occipital protuberance, a forehead inclined to recede, projecting superciliary ridges, prominent nose, which has been fractured during life, the chin hollowed, and the bones of the face rugged, being impressed with strong muscular action. Internal capacity 74½ ounces, length of femur 18.6 inches. Apparently a man of about 45.

160 T — Bones, from several individuals, discovered in a Mound near Ryestone Grange, 30th August.

161 D — SKULL, found in a Barrow near Parwich. Presented by N. B. Twigge, Esq.

An oval skull, with elevated vertex; the orbits small, the malar bones vertically deep, the teeth not much worn, rather a small skull.

1850.

162 C — Remains of six SKULLS, from a Barrow on Ecton Hill, 9th May.

One short, very thick, sutures solidified, and teeth much worn down.

Another short, with very prominent parietal tubers, and a full set of teeth, quite unworn.

163 C — Parts of the SKULLS of two adults and an infant, found by re-examining the first Castern Barrow, June.

APPENDIX. 271

164 **T** — Imperfect SKULL, and other Bones, from the Skeleton of a Saxon, found in a Mound near Hasling House, 3rd June.

An elongated oval, with prominent occiput and wormian bones; the calvarium of thin substance, and smooth at the outside; the teeth rather worn, the lower jaw rather small; the femur 19⅜ inches long. Presumed age circ. 35.

165 **T** — Part of a SKULL, found with coal beads in a Barrow on Hill Head, near the last, 5th June.

The jaws wide, the teeth sound, and not much worn.

166 **T** — SKULL, and Bones of two other individuals, from a Barrow on Staker Hill, 5th June.

A thin skull, of short and elevated form; the frontal bone prominent in the middle, and having large superciliary ridges; the teeth closely packed, and worn down.

167 **T** — Two SKULLS of the flint period, from a Barrow opposite to Vincent Knoll, on the other side of the road, 25th June.

One of a young person about 18 years of age, is long and narrow.

The other is shorter, with a wide jaw and unworn teeth, and may have belonged to a person about 20 years old.

168 **C** — Perfectly preserved SKULL, probably of a young female, from a Barrow on Bailey Hill, Hanson, 3rd August.

A short cranium, with prominent occiput and wormian bones, the vertex elevated, the orbits large and square, the nasal bones projecting, and the palate rather square.

169 **C** — Imperfect SKULL, and portion of another, from the second Barrow opened at Elkstone, 31st August.

A large skull of medium shape, with protuberant occiput, from whence it is flat to the vertex, which is elevated; the frontal region broad and high; the mouth very large, rather prominent, and filled with sound teeth, worn level; the lower jaw massive, and chin slightly squared, so as to show two sharp corners in front.

170 **P** — Remains of two individuals, from the destroyed Mound at Crake Low, Tissington, October.

One had a thick oval skull, of rather small size; the obliterated sutures and considerably worn teeth indicate a person of or past the middle age.

171 **R** — Imperfect SKULL, found with a bronze dagger in a Cist eighteen feet deep, in a Barrow near Cawthorn Camps, Yorkshire, 29th November, 1849.

A long oval cranium, with prominent occiput and narrow forehead.

172 **R** — ARTICULATED SKELETON, in fine preservation, accompanied by the Bones of a child, a small vase of coarse clay, a flint spear, and remains of the branches of trees, found in a

square Cist-Vaen of flagstones, in a Barrow near Pickering, 6th February, 1850.

> Placed at full length in a glass case. This skeleton measures only five feet three inches, and has a very contracted pelvis; the skull is rather large, short, and full behind, inclining to the platy-cephalic form; the orbits are large, and much drawn down at the lower outer angle; the teeth are perfect, and are coated with calcareous matter from the drip of water into the cist; the chin is rather square.

173 **R** — Parts of two human SKULLS, and the skeleton of a dog, found in a Tumulus near Pickering, 4th April.

1851.

174 **T** — Teeth, from a Barrow near Taddington, called Sliper Low, 22nd April.

175 **T** — Pieces of Bone from about three individuals, found in a Mound upon Crakendale Pasture, near Bakewell, 23rd April.

176 **C** — SKULL of one individual, and fragments of two others, from a Barrow at Broad Low Ash, 1st March.

> A short and elevated skull, very smooth and round except above the occipital bone, where it is flattened; there is a large inter-parietal bone, and the sutures are generally closed; the teeth good and a little worn.

177 **T** — SKULL of a young person, found with a pretty drinking cup in Beo Low Tumulus, 3rd May.

> Apparently a female; the cranium of medium form, with protuberant occiput; the nasal bones prominent, the teeth perfect, the wisdom-teeth just making their appearance.

178 **T** — Short round-shaped Skull, found in a rectangular Cist-Vaen of flat limestones, in the same Mound.

> From the arrangement of the other bones, and the position in which this cranium was found, it was abundantly evident that the skeleton had been denuded of its flesh previous to interment; a custom occasionally practised by many nations both in ancient and modern times, but supposed to be most prevalent among the Patagonians.
>
> Unusually short, and extremely wide just above the mastoid processes, giving great broadth to the posterior part of the head; the parietal tubers prominent, and the vertex elevated to a roof-like ridge; the sutures partly solid, the superciliary ridges large, the teeth much worn and coated with tartar, the lower jaw square and massive. Age about 60; the lower part of the skull round, the foramen *broken away before interment*.

179 **T** — Skull, accompanied by bronze pins, found near the surface of the same Tumulus.

> A very thick oval skull, with wormian bones, prominent parietes, and superciliary ridges; the teeth considerably worn, and the lower jaw much pointed.

APPENDIX. 273

180 **T** — Four imperfect Skulls, found in a Barrow near Monsal Dale, 16th and 23rd May.

> One, a small oval smooth cranium, with wormian bones; the mouth large, and teeth unworn. Probably about 20 years of age.

181 **T** — Two rather small CRANIA, without the lower jaws, found detached from any other bones, though perfectly undisturbed, in the same Barrow.

> One extremely short, with prominent parietal tubers, which give great breadth to the hinder part; the occiput flattened, as if by artificial means during life; the sutures obscure, the orbits small, the teeth arranged rather squarely, and not much worn.
>
> The other (found with a flint) is more oval, with protuberant occiput and elevated vertex; the mouth round, and the absence of the dentes sapientiæ indicating youth. Exceedingly contorted.

182 **T** — SKULL of an aged person, found with a large bone pin and vase in the same Barrow.

> A short and well-marked platy-cephalic cranium, with wormian bones; the centre of the frontal bone and its sinuses prominent, the teeth irregularly disposed and worn down, the mouth rather prognathous, and the lower jaw pointed. The femur 18 inches long.

183 **T** — FINE SKULL, found in a Cist-Vaen not far from the two crania No. 181, in the same Mound.

> A platy-cephalic cranium of square form, with the frontal bone well elevated, the sutures obscure, the superciliary ridges prominent, the orbits small and drawn down at the lower outer angle, the teeth large and worn. The femur 18¾ inches long.

184 **T** — Imperfect SKELETON of a child, found with a beautiful vase in a small square Cist in the same Barrow, 24th May.

> Now articulated, and placed in a glass case.

185 **T** — Fragments of four individuals, found in a place that had been previously disturbed, in a Barrow by the Wardlow road side, 16th May.

186 **T** — Imperfect SKULL of a female, and four infants, found in a square Cist-Vaen, in a Barrow near Monsal Dale, 29th May.

> A short round cranium, with very prominent parietal tubers and occiput, giving considerable breadth to the back, which decreases to a narrow forehead; the teeth regular and worn, the lower jaw rounded. The femur 17¾ inches long.

187 **T** — MALE SKULL, found immediately beneath the last.

> A short and rather platy-cephalic head, of thin substance, slightly contorted; the parietes and superciliary ridges prominent, the teeth not much worn. The femur 18¾ inches long.

s

188 T — Pieces of a child's SKULL, and jaws of a Hog, from another part of the same Mound.

The former short and wide behind.

189 T — Fragments of a human SKULL, and the teeth and jaws of a canine animal, from the same Barrow.

190 T — CRANIUM from a skeleton found on the east side of the same Tumulus, 3rd June.

A short and platy-cephalic skull, somewhat contorted, having prominent parietal tubers and superciliary ridges, the orbits widely separated, the teeth not much worn, and angles of the lower jaw wide apart. The femur 17¾ inches.

191 T — Lower jaws and patella, from the first Barrow opened at Wardlow on the 27th of June.

192 T — FEMALE SKULL, green at the ears from contact with a small piece of bronze, found in a rock grave in a Barrow near Staker Hill, 2nd July.

Very short, with parietal tubers, and a flattened space from the upper part of the occiput to the vertex; apparently of a young person of about 20. The femur 18 inches long.

193 T — Skull, found with two bone lance-heads higher up in the same Mound.

Of well-formed oval shape, rather wide behind, with elevated vertex and a ridge down the frontal bone; the superciliary ridges prominent, the teeth worn level, square chin, and long styloid processes.

194 T — Parts of two others from the same Barrow.

Thin skulls, approaching the platy-cephalic form; the teeth not much worn, and the chin squared in front.

195 T — A few human Bones, and part of a Boar's tusk, from a mutilated Barrow on Anthony Hill, near Buxton, 4th July.

196 R — Imperfect Skull, found in a cavern beneath a Mound seven miles north of Pickering, 26th November, 1850.

Of medium shape, wide between the mastoid processes, a ridge on the occiput; full parietes, with elevated vertex, and narrow forehead; wide between the orbits, teeth sound and rather worn, the chin square; age about 35.

197 R — Lower Jaw, and portions of human Bone, from a Barrow ten miles north-east of Pickering, 10th December, 1850.

The former strong and massive, with sound teeth.

198 R — Portions of the Skulls of two individuals, and some bones of the Hog, from a Barrow seven miles east of Pickering, 30th January, 1851.

APPENDIX. 275

199 R — Imperfect human Skull, and cranium of a Goat, found in a Cist-Vaen in a Barrow six miles north of Pickering, 11th Feb.

> The former a long oval, with protuberant occiput and prominent superciliary ridges; the teeth worn, the chin square, and the angles of the lower jaw wide apart.

200 R — Imperfect Skull of a child, found with jet beads in a Barrow six miles north-west of Pickering, 28th May.

> Having the frontal suture.

201 R — Bones of an individual, who, from an osseous deposition on the inside of the vertebral column, must have had a stiff back; from a Barrow four miles north-west of Pickering, 18th June.

202 R — Bones of a small Ox, found with the last.

203 R — Imperfect SKELETON of a tall young man, found with a numerous series of flint implements, and the bone of a large fish, in a Barrow six miles north-east of Pickering, 30th July.

204 C — Part of a Skull, from a Barrow between Parwich and Pike Hall, 11th October.

205 D — A few pieces of human Bone, found upon the large Mound upon Longstone Edge, by T. N. Brushfield, Esq., October.

206 C — Parts of the Skulls of a full-grown person and a child, found on reopening Slip Low, Wetton, August.

1852.

207 T — SKULL and long Bones, from the primary interment at Waggon Low, Cronkstone, found 28th June.

> Of medium shape, and elevated, especially the anterior part, with prominent superciliary ridges; the face large, being wide across the malar bones, and having a very wide mouth; the teeth little worn, and chin round. The femur 18 inches long.

208 T — BEAUTIFUL SKELETON, of rather slender proportions, accompanied by a small bronze awl, an instrument of flint, and the leg bone of an animal like a dog, which formed a secondary interment in the same Barrow, found on the 25th June.

> Now articulated, and placed at full length in a glass case. The skull rather short, and posteriorly wide; the vertex elevated, and having a ridge extending to the frontal bone; rather wide in diameter between the zygomatic arches, the teeth very regular and perfect, the chin rather square. The present stature 5 feet 5½ inches.

APPENDIX.

209 T — Skull of a still later interment, which was accompanied by two iron knives and bits of Stag's horn, from the same Mound.

<blockquote>An aged and contorted skull, of medium outline, and rather platy-cephalic; the forehead retreating, many of the teeth wanting, and the alveoli absorbed, those remaining very much worn.</blockquote>

210 T — Fragments of the Skull of an infant, from the same Barrow.

211 C — Skull of a young person, and piece of Stag's horn, found on reopening Arbor Hill, 30th July.

<blockquote>An elevated cranium, with frontal suture, much contorted.</blockquote>

212 C — Imperfect Skull, found with porcelain beads, in the Boroughs, Wetton, 7th August.

<blockquote>Short, with protuberant occiput and retreating forehead, now much contorted; the teeth wide apart, and chin pointed. Probably of the Romano-British period.</blockquote>

213 C — Crowns of the Teeth of a female, most probably Saxon, who had been interred with the amber beads and ornaments, List H. 124, found in a Tumulus near Wyaston, 10th September.

214 C — Jaw of a Skeleton, found with an iron knife, &c., in the Boroughs, Wetton, 29th September.

215 to 223 R — Imperfect Crania of nine persons of various ages, chiefly of the elongated configuration; also two specimens of the sacrum, and two thigh bones, measuring respectively $19\frac{1}{4}$ and $18\frac{1}{4}$ inches in length, found in a very ancient Long Barrow, near Heslerton-on-the-Wolds, 28th December, 1851.

<blockquote>
215 (   ). Long and narrow, the occipital protuberance extending $2\frac{1}{2}$ inches beyond the foramen magnum, the parietal tubers prominent. Contorted.

216 (4th interment). Long and narrow, and vertically elevated. Contorted.

217 (3rd interment). A small skull, long and narrow, with prominent occiput and parietes.

218 (2nd interment). Very large and long, with protuberant occiput; sutures partly obliterated.

219 (1st interment). Long and narrow, with wormian bones. Much like 217.
</blockquote>

224 T — Interesting and characteristic SKULL of the primary interment, in a very ancient Barrow at Bole Hill, opened 29th Sept., 1854.

<blockquote>A narrow skull, much elevated and laterally compressed; the forehead narrow and retreating, with very prominent superciliary ridges; the nasal bones prominent, the orbits square, the malars receding to the sides, the mouth round and large.</blockquote>

APPENDIX.

1855.

225 T — Portions of the Skulls and Jaws of twelve persons, found with flint weapons in a large Stone Cist at Ringham Low, near Monyash, on the 7th of June.

<small>Including a good specimen of the long boat-shaped type, with protuberant occiput and wormian bones, narrow forehead, and prominent mouth, with good teeth, worn level.</small>

226 T — Similar remains of four other individuals, found in another Cist in the same Tumular Cemetery on the 9th of June.

227 T — Jaws of two persons from another Cist at Ringham Low, 21st June.

228 T — Piece of an extremely thick Cranium, from a mutilated Barrow near Ricklow Dale, 21st June.

229 T — Imperfect Lower Jaw, from another Cist at Ringham Low, 5th July.

1856.

230 T — Imperfect Bones and Crania of two individuals of the iron age, found in Miss Worsley's garden, Winster, 13th and 15th October.

1857.

231 T — Skull and long Bones of a young female about 19 or 20 years of age, found with instruments of flint in a Barrow upon Smerrill Moor, near Middleton by Youlgrave, 3rd June.

<small>Extremely short and elevated, with full parietals, the mouth rather prominent, the teeth perfect and chin rounded; a small and beautiful cranium, notwithstanding its excessive shortness. The femur measures 16¼ inches.</small>

232 T — Lower Jaws and fragments from twelve other Skeletons, including both infants and aged persons, found in a disturbed state in the same Mound.

233 T — Imperfect Skull and long Bones from the Skeleton of a young man, found with a drinking cup and instruments of flint in a second Barrow on Smerrill Moor, 13th June.

<small>The skull is exceedingly contorted, but is evidently of the long form, with a ridge along the vertex; the teeth are good and unworn, indicating the age to have been about 25. The femur measured 19½ inches.</small>

234 T — Skull and long Bones from a Skeleton, found in a contracted posture in a third Barrow on Smerrill Moor, 15th of June.

<small>The form is short and rather square, with broad forehead; the orbits are large, the teeth good, and the chin pointed. The femur measures 17¼ inches.</small>

1859.

235 **T** — Skull, Femur, and Tibia of a female, found in a Stone Cist in the ruined Tumulus at Bole Hill, Bakewell Moor, 25th May, 1859.

<blockquote>The skull is rather lengthy, but the parietal swellings render this peculiarity not so obvious as in other crania from the same barrow. The forehead is moderately high; the sutures are almost obliterated, and the skull is altogether smooth; the teeth are worn, and the chin is pointed; probable age upwards of 50. Femur 16¼, tibia 13 inches long.</blockquote>

236 **T** — Portion of the Skull, Humerus, and Ulna, from the Skeleton of a tall but slender Saxon, found with iron knives in a small Grave-Hill near Chelmorton Thorn, Derbyshire, 9th September, 1859.

237 **D** — Remains of the Skeleton of a young man, something above the middle height, found by men digging gravel in Glutton Dale, near Longnor, Staffordshire, in October, 1859.

<blockquote>Accompanied by a few animal bones.</blockquote>

OBSERVATIONS ON CELTIC POTTERY.

Our experience in barrow-digging will justify the statement, that all the vessels exhumed from Celtic Tumuli may be arranged in one of four classes, which are —

- I. Cinerary or Sepulchral Urns — such as have either contained, or been inverted over, calcined human bones, and which alone are correctly styled *Urns*.
- II. Incense Cups — so called, though their real purpose is doubtful. Diminutive vessels, only found with calcined bones, and frequently enclosed in urns of the first class.
- III. Small Vases — probably intended to contain an offering of food; usually found with unburnt bodies but not unfrequently with burnt bones, though never containing them.
- IV. Drinking Cups — tall and highly-ornamented vessels, constricted in the middle, and no doubt named in accordance with their use, by Sir R. C. Hoare.

Most of the woodcuts here introduced have been used in the former volume, but it is hoped that the repetition will be excused on the ground of the assistance they afford for clearly understanding the varieties, which it would be difficult to describe by words alone, without the help of diagrams.

Cinerary urns, being found in tumuli both of the earlier and later Celtic period, exhibit considerable variation in size, paste, and ornamentation. Those presumed, from their containing silicious weapons, to be the most ancient, are generally large, from ten to sixteen inches high, with a deep border, more or less decorated by impressions of twisted thongs, and incised patterns in which the chevron or herring-bone constantly recurs in various combinations, occasionally relieved by circular punctures, or assuming a reticulated appearance. We believe that no piece of Celtic pottery hitherto discovered, shows the slightest indication of an attempt to imitate any natural form, though the contrary is the case in the fictilia of most other savage nations. The paste of the older vessels consists of clay, mixed with pebbles or angular pieces of gravel; and being wholly wrought by hand, without the assistance of the wheel, is in large vessels necessarily thick, and from the imperfect method of firing has often been described as merely "sun-dried"—a mistake very evident to all practically acquainted with the readiness with which clay so hardened imbibes moisture and returns to its original unctuous state. These urns are mostly of a brown or burnt umber colour outside, though occasionally of a lighter tint: inside they are always black, and often show marks indicating that their contents were deposited in a glowing state. The fracture shows the dark colour to extend through the paste very nearly to the outside. It is only in rare instances that instruments of bronze have been found with the more ancient urns. The example chosen as a type of this variety was found near Middleton by Youlgrave, in 1846; it measures fourteen inches in height.

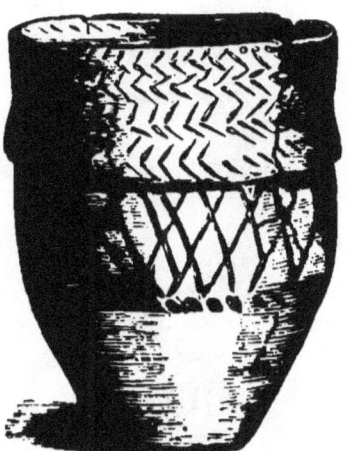

Urn from Flax Dale Barrow, Middleton.

Cinerary urns from the Yorkshire barrows are, in some instances, more elegant in shape, taller in proportion to the diameter, and have the inside of the border ornamented, a feature never found in any of the older Derbyshire or Staffordshire urns. It would appear that a considerable interval elapsed, in which burial by inhumation was in vogue, before a return to combustion rendered cinerary urns again requisite, and in the meantime some improvement had taken place in the ceramic art. We find the urns much smaller, from five and a half to nine inches high, still with the overhanging border which seems characteristic of cinerary urns. A reticulated pattern seems almost to have supplanted the chevron; the clay is mixed with coarse sand instead of pebbles, to prevent its cracking; the substance is thinner, and being more firmly baked, shows a lighter colour, varying from a red to a yellow brown outside; the paste and inside dark grey. It will be evident that the bones must have been more perfectly burnt than before, to enable them to be enclosed in such small vessels. The illustration, in which the lower figure represents an incense cup, is from an urn $5\frac{1}{4}$ inches high, found on Stanton Moor, Derbyshire, in 1799.

Urn and Incense Cup, from Stanton Moor.

Urns of a still later period, occasionally found as secondary deposits in some of our barrows, are palpable imitations of the common globular urn of the Romano-British period, both in form and material. There are two varieties. One of clumsy shape, modelled by hand from clay containing an unusual quantity of sand, and pretty well baked, often presents, besides the narrowed mouth distinctive of late pottery, and never seen in the archaic, another peculiarity in having occasionally a couple of perforations about an inch apart at the side. This form merges, by insensible gradations, into that of the Teutonic pottery sometimes found in considerable quantity in the cemeteries of Nottinghamshire and Lincolnshire. The other variety is a close and well-made imitation of the Roman urn, in clay mixed with angular fragments of quartz, turned on the wheel, and firmly baked to what may literally be denominated pot metal. The outer surface is rather rough, owing to the angular fragments of stone; its colour a bluish grey, the inside more or less red, and the paste mostly grey. Coins of the Lower Empire, chiefly of the family of Constantine the Great, have been found in connection with these urns.

The second class includes all varieties of the small vessels called incense cups, the use of which is not satisfactorily decided. They differ greatly in shape, but agree in being very small, seldom three inches high, more usually one and a half or two. They are found with calcined bones only, most frequently within larger urns, though occasionally with bones that have not been inurned, and are much more plentiful in Yorkshire than in other counties. There is reason to suppose that they do not accompany the earliest interments. From their small size, they are generally found in good condition. The oldest resemble the urns in their style of ornament, which is generally incised, and not pressed in by twisted cords. They have also, in many cases, two perforations at the side; rarely, two at opposite sides, as if for suspension. A later variety, generally very firmly baked, is quite plain, with the upper edge turned in towards the mouth, presenting a depressed outline often resembling a flattened sphere. The paste is generally less mixed with pebbles or sand than that of the larger vessels, as there was not so much risk of their cracking whilst being fired. They are also lighter in colour, from being more perfectly baked. The woodcut represents a cup found inside a cinerary urn on Baslow Moor, Derbyshire, about 1830.

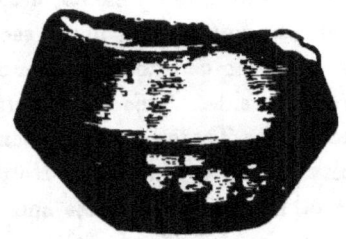

Incense Cup, Baslow Moor.

The third division, comprising the vases for food, includes vessels of every style of ornament, from the rudest to the most elaborate, but nearly alike in size, and more difficult to assign to a determinate period than any other, from the fact of a coarse and a well-finished one having several times been found in company. They occur both with skeletons and burnt bones; perhaps more frequently with the former, where they are often found near the head. Where two have been found, it has generally been with burnt bones, and probably indicates the combustion of two bodies. The woodcuts show two found in the barrow on the circle at Arbor Low, in 1845, with a ground plan of the cist indicating their position.

Vases -- Arbor Low.

284 APPENDIX.

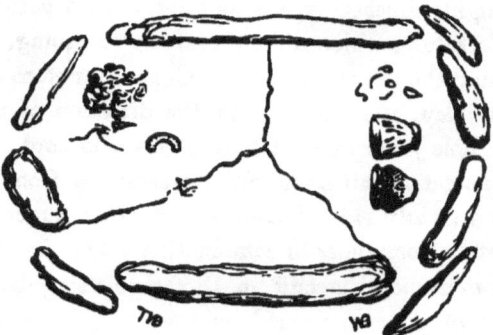

Ground Plan of Cist, at Arbor Low.

They vary from 4½ to 5½ inches in height, and have generally a wide mouth and a small bottom. They are composed of clay very similar to that used in the cinerary urns, and are pretty much of the same colour, though on the whole a shade lighter. The plainer specimens are ornamented by incised lines, disposed herring-bone fashion round the upper part, which is generally moulded with a simple hollow, the decoration extending to the edge; sometimes the whole of the outside is marked by the end of the finger. A good average specimen of the plain variety is represented in the cut; it was found at Crosslow, Derbyshire, in 1843.

Vase from Crosslow.

A more highly-finished type is constantly found both in Derbyshire and Yorkshire, which differs from the foregoing, in having a groove round the upper part, in which are four stops or projecting pieces of clay, often pierced in the direction of the groove with a small hole just sufficient to receive a thin cord. They are carefully ornamented all over with impressions from a toothed instrument, a tightly twisted cord, and circular punctures, sometimes separately, sometimes in combination. One found in Yorkshire, at Newton-upon-Rawcliff, in 1850, has a singular ornament in the shape of a cross, formed by rows of punctures carefully impressed outside the bottom; and an example altogether unique in shape and decoration, found on Wetton Hill, Staffordshire, in 1849, has the stops developed into small handles or ears. The last class is devoted to a series of vessels, happily denominated Drinking Cups, by Sir R. C. Hoare, who discovered several fine specimens in the course of his extensive researches in Wiltshire. They have been plentifully found in Derbyshire and Staffordshire, but only at rare intervals in Yorkshire. We have always found them associated with skeletons accompanied by flint weapons of a superior description, when they occupy a situation behind the shoulders. In one or two instances a very small bronze awl has been found, but there is sufficient evidence to show that they belong to a period when metal was almost unknown. They are from $6\frac{1}{2}$ to 9 inches high, of a tall shape, contracted in the middle, globular below, and expanding at the mouth: they are carefully formed by hand, of fine clay, tempered with sharp sand, and well-baked; the walls are thin, averaging about $\frac{3}{8}$th's of an inch, light red-brown outside, and grey within. The exterior is almost always covered with an elaborate pattern, produced by a toothed instrument: in two instances only we have seen it confined to a number of parallel lines encircling the upper part. The cut presents a fair example of this vessel, which does not vary so much as the other classes: it was found at Green Low, on Alsop Moor, Derbyshire, in 1845.

Two aberrant varieties have been observed, a single specimen of each having occurred. One, furnished with a handle or loop

286　　　　　　　　APPENDIX.

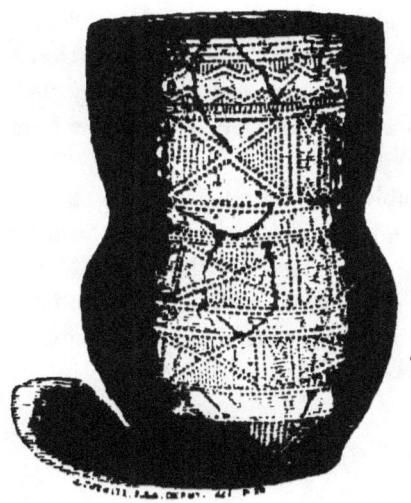

Drinking Cup, from Green Low, Alsop Moor.

at the side, found near Pickering, in January, 1850, is described in a former part of this volume; and another, of very small size, and peculiarly elegant shape, here represented —

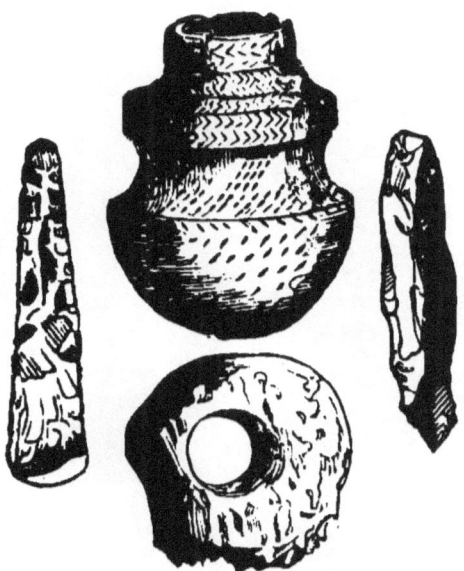

Small Drinking Cup — Liff's Low, Biggen.

was found with an assemblage of beautiful flint weapons, behind the shoulders of a skeleton, near Biggen, Derbyshire, in 1843. It is only from the circumstances of discovery that we are enabled to identify it as a Drinking Cup, as it differs from all others that we have seen.

It is remarkable that the usual shape of these vessels is analogous to that of a series of larger vases of the earliest Greek drab-coloured ware, to be seen in the Vase-Room at the British Museum: the geometrical ornament, too, offers many points of resemblance, although produced by brown pigment on the Greek, and incised upon the Celtic earthenware.

LIST OF BARROWS

IN THE

COUNTIES OF DERBY AND STAFFORD,

DISTINGUISHED BY THE WORD "LOW" SUBJOINED

TO THE NAME, OR OTHERWISE INDICATED BY THE ETYMOLOGY OF THE PREFIX.

"BEORH — BEORGAS. 1. A Hill. 2. A Rampart or Fortification. 3. A Heap, Burrow, or Barrow; a Heap of Stones; a Place of Burial.

"HLŒW — HLAW — what covers; a Grave, Heap, Barrow; a Small Hill; a tract of ground gently rising; a Low." BOSWORTH, *Anglo Saxon Dictionary*.

A.

BARROWS.	WHER
Abbot Low	Hopton.
Abney ,,	Abney.
Arbor Hill	Throwley. S.
Arbor Low	Middleton by Youlgrave.
At ,,	Hognaston.

.*. Perhaps A'd Low, equivalent to the Funeral. Pile or place of burning.—*Kemble*.

B.

Back Low	Swinscoe. S.
Bailey Hill	Hanson.
Bargoes, The	Middleton by Youlgrave.

.*. Saxon Byrgels, a Sepulchre.

Bar Low	Chesterfield.
Barrow Sedge	Hartington.
Barrow-upon-Trent	
Bas Low	Chatsworth.
Bee ,,	Youlgrave.
Birk ,,	Hathersage.
Blake ,,	Bonsal.
,, ,,	Etwall.
,, ,,	Hassop.
,, ,,	Warslow. S.
Blind,	Hartington.
,, ,,	Chelmorton.

T

BARROWS.	WHERE NEAR.	
Boar Low	Tissington.	
Bole Hill	Bakewell.	
,, ,,	Wirksworth.	
,, Low	Bamford.	
Booth ,,	Longnor.	S.
,, ,,	Sheldon.	
Boroughs The, or Burrows	Middleton by Youlgrave.	
Boroughs The	Wetton.	S.
Borther Low	Middleton by Youlgrave.	
Bottes ,,		S.
Brier ,,	Buxton.	
Broad ,,	Ashbourn.	
,, ,,	Tideswell.	
Brown ,,	Hartington.	
Browns ,,	Castern.	S.
Brund The	Sheen.	S.
Brund Cliff	Hartington.	

Bryne or Brand signifies the combustion or the burning, and indicates the Heathen rite of interment by Cremation.—*Kemble*.

Bullock Low	Hartington.	
Burnet ,,	Grindon.	

.*. A modern prenomen.

C.

Cal Low	Hathersage.	
,, ,,	Hopton.	
,, ,,	Mappleton.	S.
,, ,,	Mayfield.	S.
Caldon Low	Caldon.	S.
Calling ,,	Youlgrave.	
Calver ,,	Calver.	
Carder ,,	Hartington.	

.*. Carden Hloew occurs in Codex Diplomaticus twice, 427 and 1198.

Carter Low		
Cas ,,	Mayfield.	
Casking ,,	Hartington.	
Cast ,,		
Chelmorton Low	Chelmorton.	
Cock ,,	Leek.	S.
Cop ,,	Calton.	S.
Cop ,,	Great Hucklow.	

.*. The head, the top, the Apex.—*Bosworth*.

Cow Low	Buxton	
,, ,,	Chapel-en-le-Frith.	
,, ,,	Hartington.	
,, ,,	Holme End.	S.

BARROWS.	WHERE NEAR.	
Cow Low	Middleton by Youlgrave.	
Crake ,,	Parwich.	
,, ,,	Sheen.	S.
Cronkstone Low	Hartington.	
Cross ,,	Parwich.	
Culverd's ,,		S.

D.

Darby Low	Fairfield.	
Dars ,,	Monyash.	
Dirt ,,	Ashford.	
Dow ,,	Church Sterndale.	
Drake ,,		

E.

Elk or Ellock Low	Hartington.	
End ,,	do.	

∴ Enter Hlœo—Law of the Giants. Cod. Dipl.: 758—1156.—*Kemble.*

F.

Fairfield Low	Buxton.	
Far ,,	Cauldon.	
Far ,,	Tideswell.	
Fin Cop	Ashford.	

∴ The Funeral pile at the top.

Find Low	Chelmorton.	
Foo ,,	Eyam.	
Fowse ,,	Hopton.	
Fox ,,	Buxton.	

G.

Galley Low	Brassington.	
Gib ,,	Middleton by Youlgrave.	
Great ,,	Chelmorton.	
,, ,,	Hartington.	
,, ,,	Tideswell.	
Green ,,	Alsop Moor.	
,, ,,	Brassington.	
,, ,,	Mayfield.	S.
,, ,,	New Inns	
,, ,,	Wheston.	
Grind ,,	Eyam.	
,, ,,	Over Haddon.	
Gris ,,	Calver.	
Grub ,,	Waterhouses.	S.

H.

BARROWS.	WHERE NEAR.	
Hal Low	Pleasley.	
Har ,,	Mayfield.	S.
,, ,,	Bradborne.	
Hare ,,	Bamford.	
,, ,,	Tideswell.	
Harefoot Low	Hartington.	
Hawkes ,,	Parwich.	
Hay Cop	Monsal Dale.	
Heathy Low	Tideswell.	
Hern's ,,	Eyam.	
High ,,	Atlow.	
,, ,,	Hathersage.	
,, ,,	Monyash.	
Hind ,,	Church Sterndale.	
Hoar ,,	Hartington.	
Hob Hurst's House	Baslow Moor.	
Hoo Low or Woo Low	Fairfield.	
Horning Low	Burton-upon-Trent	S.
Huck Low, Great		
,, ,, Little		
Hurd ,,	Hartington.	
Hurst ,,	Grindon.	S.

K.

Kens Low	Middleton by Youlgrave.	
Kirk ,,	Tideswell.	
Knock ,,	Milnhouse Dale.	
Knot ,,	Flagg.	

L.

Ladmans Low	Buxton.	
Lady ,,	Blore	S.
Lady ,,	Chapel-en-le-Frith.	
Lapwing Hill	Crossbrook.	
Larks Low	Middleton by Youlgrave.	
Lean ,,	Hartington.	
Lidd ,,	Thorpe.	
Liffs ,,	Biggen.	
Little ,,	Parwich.	
Lomber,,	Waterhouses.	S.
Long ,,	Hartington.	
,, ,,	Wetton.	S.
Low The	Alsop Moor.	
,, Bent	Longnor.	S.
,, Close	Eckington.	
,, Field	Middleton by Youlgrave.	

APPENDIX.

BARROWS.	WHERE NEAR.	
Low Field	Uttoxeter.	S.
,, ,,	Woodlands.	
,, Moor	Parwich.	
,, Top	Ashbourne.	
Lower Low	Wheston.	
Lousy ,,	Holme End.	S.

M.

Mare Hill	Throwley.	S.
Masson Low	Matlock.	
Mayfield ,,	Mayfield.	S.
Mick ,,	Edale.	
Mining ,,	Brassington.	
Moot ,, or Mutts Low	Calton.	S.
,, ,,	Hanson.	
,, ,,	Grange Mill.	
,, ,,	Youlgrave.	
Mosey ,,	Pilsbury.	
Mouse ,,	Glossop.	
,, ,,		S.
Musden ,,	Thorpe.	S.

N.

Nay Low	Tideswell.	
Needham Low	Wheston.	

⁎ Probably a modern prefix.

Net ,,	Alsop Moor.	
,, ,,	Blore.	S.
,, ,,	Swinscoe.	S.
Nether ,,	Chelmorton.	
North ,, Field	Wednesfield.	S.

O.

Off Low		S.
Over ,,	Hartington.	
Over ,,	Stanton.	S.
Ox ,,	Peak Forest.	

P.

Painstor Low	Alsop.	
Pars ,,	Drayton.	S.
Peas ,,	Chapel-en-le-Frith.	
Peg ,,	Wheston.	
Penny ,,	Hartington.	
Pigtor ,,	Buxton.	
Pike ,,	Waterhouses.	S.
Pinch ,,	Hartington.	
Priestcliff ,,	Taddington.	

APPENDIX.

Q.

BARROWS.	WHERE NEAR.
Queen Low...	

R.

Barrows		Where Near	
Rains Low ...	...	Elton.	
Ravens ,, ...	...		
Ribden ,, ...	...	Cotton.	S.
Rick ,, ...	...	Monyash.	
Ringham Low	...	Middleton by Youlgrave.	
Ringham ,,	...	Monyash.	
Ringing ,,	...	Brampton.	
Risborrow ...	...	Etwall.	
Rocky Low...	...	Wheston.	
Rolley ,, ...	...	Mayfield.	S.
,, ,, ...	...	Wardlow.	

.•. Regale Sepulchrum.—Dr. Plot, "*History of Staffordshire.*"

Round Low...	...	Hopton.	
,, ,, ...	...		S.
Row ,, ...	...	Youlgrave.	
Rusden ,, ...	...	Middleton by Youlgrave.	

S.

Saint Low ...	Parwich.

.•. Modern Prefix.

Barrows		Where Near	
Sandpit ,, ...	...	Bradborne.	
Scrip ,, ...	...	Stanton.	S.
Soen ,, ...	...	Hartington.	
Senni ,, ...	...	,,	
Shack ,, ...	...	Bakewell.	
,, ,, ...	...	Sheldon.	
Shal ,, ...	...	Flagg.	
Shar ,, ...	...	Bradborne.	
Shard ,, ...	...	Derby.	
Sharp ,, ...	...	Dovedale.	
Sheen ,, ...	...	Sheen.	S.
Shutling,, ...	...		S.
Sinfin ,, ...	...	Repton.	
Sitter ,, ...	...	Parwich.	
Sitting ,, ...	...	Chapel-en-le-Frith.	

.•. Yttinges Hlœw. Cod. Dipl. 1141.

Barrows		Where Near	
Slip Low ...	...	Wotton.	S.
Sliper ,, ...	...	Brassington.	
Slipper ,, ...	...	Taddington.	
Smeet ,, ...	...	Holme End.	S.
South ,, ...	...	Walnesfield.	S.
Staden,, ...	...	Buxton.	

APPENDIX.

BARROWS.		WHERE NEAR.	
Stadmore Low	...	Wolfstanton.	S.
Stan Low Moor	...	Great Hucklow.	
Stand ,,	...	Dove Dale.	
Stannage Low	...	Biggon.	
Steep ,,	...	Alstonefield.	S.
Stone ,,	...	Baslow.	
,, ,,	...	Hartington.	
Stoney ,,	...	Brassington.	
,, ,,	...	Cold Eaton.	
,, ,,	...	Hartington.	
Swains ,,	...		
Swans ,,	...	Buttorton.	S.
Swarkeston Low	...	Swarkeston.	

T.

Taylor's Low	...	Wetton.	S.

.*. Modern appellation.

Thirkel Low	...	Buxton.	
Thoo ,,	...	Mappleton.	S.
Thorncliffe Low	...	Calton.	S.
Three ,,	...	Cotton	S.
,, ,,	...	Wetton.	S.
Tids ,,	...	Tideswell.	
Top ,,	...	Swinscoe.	S.
Totman's ,,	...		S.
Turning ,,	...	Hartington.	

U.

Under Low...	...	Heathcote.	
,, ,, ...	...	Chelmorton.	
Upper ,, ...	...	,,	

W.

Waggon Low	...	Cronkstone.	
Ward ,,	...		
Warry ,,	...		
Wars ,,	...		S.
Waterfall ,,	...		S.
West ,,	...	Litton.	
White ,,	...	Ible.	
,, ,,	...	Winster.	
Wigbarrow Low	...	Bradborne.	
Will ,,	...	Parwich.	
Wind ,,	...	Wormhill.	
Withery ,,	...	,,	
Wool ,, (Hoo Low)	...	Buxton.	

Y.

BARROWS.	WHERE NEAR.
Yarns Low	Eyam.

This List might be indefinitely extended were it possible to ascertain the names given to separate fields by those born in the neighbourhood, whose associations have from the earliest times rendered such a nomenclature indispensable, but it is obvious, that we can only become acquainted with them from the lips of the peasantry, or from the manuscript terriers of landed property, which are for the most part inaccessible to the inquirer.

It is probable, that although many of the names were given in Saxon times, the Barrows do retain, to an appreciable extent, the cognomen of individuals of an earlier race interred within them.

As a SUPPLEMENT to the LIST OF BARROWS, the following Patronymical Names of Places in Derbyshire (some of which occur in connection with Tumuli) are extracted from *Kemble's* "SAXONS IN ENGLAND," 1849, a few being added which do not appear in that most valuable work.

SAXON.	MODERN NAME.
Ballingas ...	Ballidon
Beonotleage ...	Bentley.
Bressingas ...	Brassington.
Brightholmsfield ...	Brushfield.
Brimingas ...	Brimington.
Callingas ...	Callenge Low.
Cardan ...	Carder ,,
Cersington ...	Carsington.
Cyllingas ...	Chellaston.
Dintingas ...	Dinting.
Durningas ...	Turning Low.
Eogingas ...	Eckington—Egginton.
Grendel ...	Grindleford.

.*. Though not properly a patronymic; the name occurs in the Teutonic Mythological Cycle.

Hæsling ...	Hasling Houses
Heortingas ...	Hartington.
Holingas ...	Hollington
Horningas ...	Horning Low.
Hwita ...	White Low.
Lullingas ...	Lullington.
Pœccingas ...	Packington.

SAXON.	MODERN NAME.
Ridingas	Riddings.
Scearthingas	Scarthen Nick.
Scythinga	Shutling Low, Shuttlestone.
Toedingas	Taddington.
Tissingas	Tissington.
Wossingas	Wessington.
Willingas	Willington.
Wittingas	Whittington.
Yttingas	Sitting Low.

ANIMAL REMAINS

FOUND IN THE

TUMULI ASSOCIATED WITH WORKS OF HUMAN ART.

Insectivoræ.

Common Mole	*Talpa Europœa.*

Carnivora.

Common Wolf	*Lupus Vulgaris.*
Domestic Dog	(Several species).
Common Fox?	*Vulpis Vulgaris.*

Mustelidæ.

Polecat	*Mustela Putorius.*
Stoat	*Mustela Erminea.*
Weasel	*Mustela Vulgaris.*

Arctogolidæ.

Badger?	*Meles Taxus.*

Cetacea.

Common Whale	*Balœna Borealis.*

Pachydermata.

Wild Hog	*Sus Scropha* (very large).
Domestic Hog?	

Equidæ.

Horse	*Equus Caballus.*

.*. Rarely, if ever, of large size.

Ruminantia.

Fallow Deer	*Dama Vulgaris.*
Elk?	*Cervus Megaceros.*

.*. A portion of a large palmated horn, found with Romano-British remains near Wetton, at least double the size of the antler of the fallow deer, may possibly be assigned to the Elk; but it is proper to state, that it does not reach the magnitude of a large horn from the extinct Irish Elk, in the collection at Lomberdale, though it resembles it in form so far as its fragmentary condition admits of comparison.*

Red Deer	*Cervus Elaphas.*
Roebuck?	*Cervus Capreolus.*

*Since the above Note has been in type, the horn has been ascertained to be that of the German Elk.

Capridæ.

Common Goat.
Black-faced Sheep?

Bovidæ.

Bos Urus?
Bos Longifrons?
Domestic Cow.

∴ Remains usually too imperfect to admit of the assertion of three species, but we think, that at least two may be recognized.

Rodentia.

Brown or Field Vole ... ... *Arvicola Agrestis.*

AVES.

Falconidæ.

Two species, unrecognizable from the remains, but one rather large.
Eggs of the Domestic Fowl.

Pisces.

Common Trout ... ... *Salmo Fario.*

Gasteropoda.

Helix Nemoralis.
Helix Arbustorum.
Helix Lapicida.

INSECTA.

Coleoptera.

Geotrupes Sylvatica.

Diptera.

Larvæ or Pupæ of Flesh Flies ... ... *Musca Sarcophaga.*

VEGETABLE SUBSTANCES

OF WHICH

TRACES HAVE BEEN FOUND IN THE BARROWS.

Linaceæ.

Common Flax	*Linum Usitatissimum.*

Leguminosæ.

Common Furze	*Ulex Europæus.*

Oleaceæ.

Common Ash	*Fraxinus Excelsior.*

Cupuliferæ.

Common Oak	*Quercus Robur.*
Common Hazel	*Corylus Avellana.*

Gramineæ.

Meadow Grass	*Poa.*

And other species not recognizable.

Polypodiaceæ.

Male Fern	*Lastrea Filix Mas.*
Common Bracken	*Pteris Aquilina.*

Muscæ.

Marsh Bryum	*Bryum Palustre.*

Fungi.

Puff Ball	*Lycoperdon.*

Compressed and preserved with moss, insects, &c., in a mound at Newton Grange, opened 1845.

MINERALS AND ROCKS

USED BY THE

OCCUPANTS OF THE TUMULI,

WITH THE LOCALITIES WHENCE DERIVED.

Silicides.

Quartz in Pebbles...	Derbyshire.
Flint...	Yorkshire.
Chert or Petrosilex	Derbyshire.
Hornstone.	
Jasper.	
Garnet	Imported by Saxons.
Serpentine.	

Carbonides.

Jet ...	Yorkshire.
Amber	Imported by Saxons.
Limestone, Black, Compact	Derbyshire.
Magnesian Limestone	Yorkshire.
Clay Iron Ore	Derbyshire.

Sulphurides.

Hepatic Iron Pyrites.	
Lead...	Derbyshire.

Leucolytes.

Tin, used as alloy with Copper ...	Cornwall.
Silver	Imported by Saxons.

Chroicolites.

Red Hæmatite	Derbyshire.
Red Ochre, Ruddle	Derbyshire.
Clay Ironstone	Derbyshire.
Copper.	
Gold	Imported by Saxons.
Electrum	Imported by Saxons.

Rocks.

Granito	Westmoreland ?
Syenite.	
Serpentine.	
Trap.	
Basalt.	
Wacke or Toadstone	Derbyshire.
Porphyry.	
Lava	Andernach, on the Rhine.
Argillaceous Schist	Westmoreland.
Novaculite, Hone Slate	Westmoreland.
Bituminous Shale, Kimmeridge Coal.	
Granular Quartz.	
Sandstone, Coarse or Millstone Grit ...	Derbyshire.
Sandstone, Fine-grained, Compact ...	Derbyshire.
Limestones, Compact, Black	Derbyshire.
Clay of various qualities	Derbyshire

INDEX.

A.

Armilla bronze, 167
Awls, bronze, 72, 85, 130, 130, 155
Axes, stone, 24, 155, 237
——— flint, 216
Arrow head, iron, 126
Arborlow, 17, 25, 42, 285
Arbor hill, Throwley, 112, 186
Animal remains found in tumuli, 298
Anglo-Saxon leathern drinking cup, 29
——————— enamelled ornaments, 29
——————— helmet, 31, 45
——————— chainwork, 32
——————— antiquities from Newhaven Low, 45
——————— Over Haddon, 48
——————— "Top o' the Hurst," 53
——————— sword from Brushfield, 69
Allerstone common, 208, 233, 335
Ashborne, 192
——————— tinker's inn, 245
Anthony hill, 81
Andle Stone, 84
Alstonfield, 121, 125, 138
Archford, 154
Agden, 252

B.

Brownedge, 38
Burial in sitting posture, 23
Benty Grange barrow, 28
Booth low, 35
Blake low, 40
Borther low, 45
Bronze dagger, 35, 39
Beads of jet, 25, 35, 47, 52, 66, 76, 152, 220, 228, 229, 230
——— amber, 189
——— glass, 75, 91, 260
Burnett's low, 115, 229, 232
Bronze box, 46, 53
——— vessel, 173
——— bowl, 48
——— awl, 201
——— skewer, 203
——— spear, 219

Brassington, 55
Baslow, Hob Hurst's House, 37
Barrows excavated by T. Bateman in
    1848, 17
    ——————————————— 1849, 45
    ——————————————— 1850, 64
    ——————————————— 1851, 71
    ——————————————— 1852, 84
    ——————————————— 1853, 86
    ——————————————— 1854, 89
    ——————————————— 1855, 92
    ——————————————— 1856, 97
    ——————————————— 1857, 101
    ——————————————— 1859, 104
    ——————————————— 1860, 106
Bone mesh rule, 103, 107, 116, 127, 135
Boar's tusk, 131, 147, 169, 172
Bone, perforated, 243
Ballidon moor, 57, 60
——— urn, 59
Bank top, 86
Bincliff, 117
Buxton, 65, 70, 246
Belvoir Castle, 109
Brushfield barrow, 68
Bole Hill, 90, 104
Bakewell, Crakendale Pasture, 71
——— Bole Hill, 90, 104
Bee low, 71
"Buries, The," 93
Barrows opened by Mr. Carrington in
    1848, 111
    ——————————————— 1849, 128
    ——————————————— 1850, 162
    ——————————————— 1851, 174
    ——————————————— 1852, 185
    ——————————————— 1853, 189
Barrows in Yorkshire, opened by Mr. Ruddock, 204
Barrows, list of, in Derbyshire and Staffordshire, 289
——— patronymical names, 296
——— animal remains found in, 298
——— vegetable substances found in, 300

Barrows, list of, minerals and rocks used in, 302
Bridle-bit, 254
Blore, 142, 150, 156, 163, 186
Back of the low, 124
Bunster, 143, 186
Bitchin hill, 152, 165, 185
Blake low, 162
Bailey hill, 168
Bostorn, 169
Broad low ash, 174
Back low close, 177
Brand, 177
Bone draughts from New Inns, 180
Bone low, 253
Borough Hole, Wetton, 193
Boardhill, 237
Brownlow, 245
Birchall Meadows, 246
Brough, 251, 254
Bole low, 253
Bones, descriptive list of, 257
Bathone Gate, 252

C.

Cist Gib Hill, 19
—— Middleton moor, 25
—— Ringham low, 94, 97
—— Minning low, 82
—— Hob Hurst's House, 88
—— Top low, 137
—— Long low, 145
—— Arbor low, 145
Celts, bronze, 34, 220, 250
Celts, stone, 22, 116, 206, 221, 222, 227, 231, 241
Combs, Saxon, 43, 179
Celtic pottery, observations on, 279
Cawthorn camps, 206, 219
Cross flats barrow, 22
Crake low, 37
Comp, The, 34
Casking low, 40
Celtic Antiquities from Gib Hill, 20
—————————————— Kenslow, 21
—————————————— Cross Flats, 22
Celtic coins, 237
Cross cliff, 204, 236
Carlswark, 253
Callow, 155
Church Sterndale, Dowel, 38
—————— barrows, 52, 64
Conksbury barrow, 44, 243
Cow low, 188
Chelmorton, 50, 105
Cock low, 188
—— Bridge, 254
Cronkestone Hill, 56
Compton, Ashborne, 192
Calton, 64, 118, 128
—— Moor House, 125, 151, 176
Cropton, 211
Chatsworth, 64
"Cop," 129
"Cops," 161
Cresbrook, 68, 74
Cauldon, 127

Cauldon, lows, 132, 150
—— hills, 153
Crakendale pasture, 71
Cotton, 127, 153, 157, 158
Calver low, 107
Castern, 116, 120, 152, 166, 168, 182
Cow Close Lea, 120
Cold Eaton, 179
Coins, Celtic, 237
Coins, Roman, 43, 55, 82, 122, 126, 201, 202

D.

Daggers, bronze, 21, 24, 35, 39, 57, 91, 113, 115, 119, 148, 160, 163, 204, 206, 228, 231, 245, 246
Drinking cups, 38, 41, 44, 72, 76, 80, 103, 106, 116, 136, 159, 209, 215, 218, 231, 234
—————— observations on, 229
Daggers, flint, 52, 167
Dove Dale, barrows near, 27, 143
Dowel or dower, barrow, 38
Deep Dale, 114, 115, 154
Derbyshire barrows, list of, 289
—————— patronymical names, 296
Dale, 125
Dam gate, 173
Draughts, bone, 180
Draught board, 231
Danby warren, 231, 236
Dowell, 243
Descriptive list of skeletons, skulls, and bones from barrows, 257

E.

Ecton, barrow, 34, 111, 147, 164
End low, 38
Enamels, 48
Elton, 55
Eastmoor, 255
Eldon hole, 97
—— hill, barrow, 97
Eyam, 107, 247
Ell meadows, 133
Eaves barrow, 154
Elkstone, 171
Ebberstone, 232
Edale, 250

F.

Fork, horn, 198
Food vases, 19, 27, 37, 42, 75, 78, 85, 98, 114, 133, 139, 149, 161, 169, 172, 175, 185, 207, 211, 238
Fern leaves, 35
Fish bone, 20
Fibulæ, 77, 100, 116, 148, 193, 196, 231, 235, 243
Flax Dale barrow, 62
Foggy low, 64
Fox low, 66
Foremark, 92
"Ferns," 92
Far low, 132

G.

Gib hill barrow, 17
Grindlow, 47
Greatlow, 50
Gospel hillock, 70
Grindon, 115, 117, 133, 147
Green low, 116
Gateham, 141
Grub low, 147
Glass cup, 188
Gindle top, 208
Goathland, 220
Glutton Dale, 243
Grindleford Bridge, 247

H.

Handmills, 100, 203, 220, 231
Hawk's bill, 80
Hair, 28, 34, 51
Helmet, Saxon, 31
Hak pen, 17
Hartington, Parcelly Hay, 22
——— End low, 38
——— Moneystones, 40
——— Cotes field, 67
——— Bank top, 86
Harborough, round low, 37
Hurdlow, 52, 58
Hasling houses, 65
Hill head, 66
Haytop, 74
Heslerton-on-the-Wolds, 230
Hollins clough, 81
Hope, 251
High Needham, 84
High low, 89, 244
Hob Hursts House, 87
Haddon field, 106
Hanging bank, 111, 164
Hurst low, 117, 126
Hazleton hill, 140
Holme end, 150
Hathersage, 251

I.

Introduction, i
Ingleby, 83
Ilam, 140
Inklywood, 140
Iron knife, 201
——— shears, 201
Incense cups, 84, 130, 142, 211, 223, 224, 227, 233, 238, 241
——— observations on, 279

K.

Kenslow barrow, 20, 64
King Sterndale, 89
Knowl hills, 92
Kingthorpe, 232, 235
Knives, iron, 22, 26, 43, 51, 54, 62, 105, 108, 123, 129, 193, 195, 199
Knapton, 231

L.

List of barrows in Derbyshire and Staffordshire, 230
Longnor, Booth low, 35
——— low bent, 36
Low bent, 36
Lathkill, 243
Longstone edge, 40, 79
Lowmoor barrows, 49
Leam moor, 255
Lapwing hill, 68
Lark's low, 83
Ladmanlow wharf, 81
Long low, 121, 131, 144, 182
List of skeletons, skulls, &c., 257
Lumber low, 131
Lousy low, 150
Lady low, 150, 156, 163
Leek, 183, 216
Little Tea, 189
Lid low, 245
Little John's grave, 251

M.

Middleton-by-Youlgrave, Gib hill, 17
——— Kenslow, 20, 64
——— Cross flats, 22
——— moor, 25
——— Rusden low, 43
——— Borther low, 45
——— Flax Dale barrow, 67
——— Ringham low, 64
——— Lark's low, 83
——— Minning low, 54, 57, 61, 82, 83
——— Smerrill moor, 102
Minerals and rocks, used by the occupants of Tumuli, 302
Miscellaneous discoveries, 246
Maggots, 123, 160
Monyash, Benty Grange, 28
——— Ringham low, 64, 93
——— High low, 244
Moneystones, 40
Minninglow, 54, 57, 61, 82, 83
Morridge, 165
Moot low, 57
Musden hill, 118, 119, 138, 148
Monsal Dale, barrow, 74, 189
Matlock bridge, 244
Mare hill, 112
Mouse low, 115
Martin's low, 117
Mayfield low, 152
Mappleton, 155
Millstones, Saxon, 29

N.

Necklace of jet, Middleton moor, 25
——— Grindlow, 47
Newhaven low, 45
Nether low, 51
Nettles (Net lows), 142, 179

Near hill, Wetton, 139
——— Swinscoe, 151
Newton Grange, 178, 181
New Inns, 179
Newton on Rawcliff, 212
——— by Pickering, 232

O.

Over Haddon, Grindlow, 47.
Observations on Celtic pottery, 279
Over low, 127
Ottcliffe knoll, 153
Ox, head of, 129

P.

Pavement, Roman, 251
Pins of bone, 75, 77, 83, 112, 143, 155, 156, 181
Pottery, Celtic, observations on, 279
Parcelly Hay barrow, C, 22
——— Vincent knoll, 42
Parwich, Shuttlestone, 34
——— Low moor, 49
——— Saints' low, 61
Poole's hole, Buxton, 246
Pilsbury, 81
Parwich, 183
Peak forest, 97
Pike low, 157
Pike hall, 183
Pickering, 204, 205, 209, 212, 221, 235, 237
Antiquities from 237
Patronymical names of places in Derbyshire, 296
Pin, 219

Q.

Querns, 99, 203, 100, 220, 231
Quoits, 220, 231

R.

Round low, 36, 114
Rusden low, 43
Rock grave, Longstone Edge, 42
——— Parcelly Hay, 23
——— Vincent knoll, 49
——— Smerrill, 103
Robin Hood's pricks, 247, 252
——— bay, 231
Robin Hood, 251
Repton, 93
Rushley, 162
Row tor, 252
Roman coins, 43, 54, 82, 122, 198, 201, 202
Romano-British village at Wetton, 193
Roman pavement, 251
Readon hill, 122
Ryestone grange, 61
Ringham low, 84, 94
Rowsley, barrows, 101
——— ancient chapel, 101

Ribden low, 127
Round knoll, 157
Ramshorn, 158
Ram's croft field, 158
Rillington, 231
Rocking stone, 253
Ring, silver, 189
——— jet, 233, 235

S.

Skeletons, skulls, &c., descriptive list of, 257
Sharp low, 26
Shuttlestone barrow, 34
Strynd's moor, 252
Saints' low, 61
Staffordshire barrows, opened by Mr. Carrington, 111, 128, 162, 174, 185, 189
——— list of, 289
Sheen, 62
Skulls, skeletons, &c., descriptive list of, 257
Staker hill, 67, 80
Stonesteads, 131
Sterndale, 67, 243
Steep low, 121, 125
Scrip low, 163
Smerrill, 102
Sword, Saxon, &c., from Brushfield, 69
Scampstone, 220
Slipper low, 71, 181
Sheen, 177, 179
Swinscoe, 133, 151
Stanton moor, 84
Stanton, 124, 127, 163
Stone circles, 84, 248, 255
Scambridge, 231
Stanshope, 142, 158, 173, 187
Smeet low, 154
Saltby heath barrows, 102
Spear of bone, 44
——— bronze, 219
——— iron, 50, 75, 79, 80, 99, 123, 126, 161, 195
Stag's horns, 22, 27, 52, 71, 73, 85, 161, 168, 187
Stone vessels, 173, 178, 213
Sword, bronze, 254, 255
Sepulchral urns, observations on, 279

T.

Tissington, Sharp low, 26
——— Crake low, 37
——— Newton grange, 178
Thorpe cloud, barrows near, 27
"Top o' the Hurst," 52
——— Saxon box, &c., 53
Top field low, 115
Top low barrows, 133
Taddington, 71
Throwley barrows, 112, 130, 154, 157, 162, 186
Thorncliffe, 118
Thors wood, 124, 165
Thors cave, 172

INDEX. 309

Three lows, 158, 161, 167, 178
Tweedale, 235
Tinker's inn, 245
Tideswell, 249
Tweezers, 169

U.

Upper Edge barrow, 68
Urns, culinary, 59, 62, 64, 77, 84, 141, 142, 143, 147, 150, 155, 169, 211, 219, 223, 225, 237, 240, 244
——————— observations on, 272

V.

Vincent knoll, 49, 68
Vegetable substances found in tumuli, 300
Vases, observations on, 279

W.

War paint, 169
Wormhill, 252
Wardlow, 74, 79

Warslow, 161, 162, 245
Waggon low, 34
Wilson's MSS., 246
Winster, 98
Whithy, 239
————— antiquities from, 239, 240, 241
Waterfall low, 114
Win hill, 255
Winkhill, 117, 165
Wolfscote hill, 177
Wetton, 121, 131, 144, 161, 167, 172, 178, 182
————— Near hill, 139
————— Romano-British village, 193
Waterhouses, 131, 245
Wyaston, 188
Waterings, 151
Windy harbour, 153
Woodlands, 254

Y.

Youlgreave, Conksbury, 44, 243
——————— Bee low, 71
Yorkshire barrows opened by Mr. Ruddock, 204

www.ingramcontent.com/pod-product-compliance
Lightning Source LLC
Chambersburg PA
CBHW030810230426
43667CB00008B/1154